ARISTOCRATS
OF THE
TREES

BY

ERNEST H. WILSON
M.A., V.M.H.

KEEPER OF THE ARNOLD ARBORETUM OF
HARVARD UNIVERSITY

SIXTY-SIX ILLUSTRATIONS

DOVER PUBLICATIONS, INC.
NEW YORK

Published in Canada by General Publishing Company, Ltd., 30 Lesmill Road, Don Mills, Toronto, Ontario.

Published in the United Kingdom by Constable and Company, Ltd., 10 Orange Street, London WC 2.

This Dover edition, first published in 1974, is an unabridged republication of the work originally published by The Stratford Company in 1930. The full-color frontispiece has been omitted from the present edition.

International Standard Book Number: 0-486-20038-8
Library of Congress Catalog Card Number: 73-86525

Manufactured in the United States of America
Dover Publications, Inc.
180 Varick Street
New York, N. Y. 10014

PREFACE

REES are the Aristocrats of the Vegetable Kingdom, the noblest expression of vegetable life. Take them from the landscape and its whole appearance changes completely—luxuriance gives place to barrenness. Herbs, shrubs and vines supply flowers of every hue, perfect in form, brilliant in color, exquisite of fragrance, rich in pleasing leafage and abundant of fruit, but they are lesser things and cannot take the place of trees—Monarchs of Woodland and Forest. The arresting characters of trees, their height, spread of crown, bulk of trunk and ruggedness of bark, are unique features without which this world would be largely bereft of its scenic grandeur. No, trees are virtuous citizens of the earth, rich in permanent qualities—indispensables.

Trees have always exercised a strong if unconscious influence over the human race. Sooner or later all who garden plant trees and where space permits more and more as the years pass. When first we dabble in the healthful pastime of gardening our interests may be in the lesser things; we may enthuse over tiny alpine plants, bulbs or tall herbs and toy with them for varying lengths of time. Later, we are attracted to shrubs, more permanent things. Finally we take to our heart trees, treasure them while life lasts, and hand them on, objects of lasting usefulness and beauty, an enduring legacy, to the generations that follow us.

All my life has been in close associationship with trees. It has been my privilege to make intimate friendships with the forest's monarchs near and far. I have found them excellent companions and have never felt lonesome in their company. Of the scenes I have witnessed the noble trees of a hundred lands remain most vivid in my memory. In America, Europe, Asia, Africa and Australasia they have bade me smiling welcome, nodding a friendly goodbye, and made me understand that the visit had been mutually enjoyable.

In the following pages is collected most of what I have thought and written about trees. Much of it has appeared scattered through ephemeral print. Several of the essays appeared in my *Romance of the Trees,* a work long since out of print; many are new. That on Autumn Colors was first published in my *Aristocrats of the Garden,* that on Street Trees in my *More Aristocrats of the Garden* and in corrected and slightly altered form are reproduced here for the sake of completeness. As thoughts on trees have come to me on my travels I jotted them down for elaboration later, and so these essays really are the thoughts and gleanings of a life interest in trees far and near. In sending them forth my earnest desire is to share knowledge and love with kindred spirits in the hope that it may increase the interest and the pleasure they derive from trees— Mother Nature's grandest expression of growth.

—E. H. W.

Arnold Arboretum,
February 15, 1930.

CONTENTS

ILLUSTRATIONS

ix

PROLOGUE

PROLOGUE

N MANY states April is the month in which Arbor Day falls. On this day, in response to proclamations and appeals issued by Governors of states, Mayors, educators, and others in authority, children and adults plant trees. The movement, originated by the late Hon. J. Sterling Morton of Nebraska City, Nebraska, in 1872, has spread throughout the length and breadth of the United States and Canada; and rightly so, for the benefits, both esthetic and economic, should be incalculable. From the dawn of history man has been busy destroying the forests of the world and the more he has advanced toward what we call civilization the more destructive he has become. A halt had to come sometime but it was not until the wise vision of race leaders saw catastrophe approaching that any check could be effectually called. It is only during the last fifty years that proper efforts have been made to place the nation's scenic wealth beyond the reach of those who would destroy whenever opportunity offers.

Arbor Day is now a great national movement toward, not merely preserving, but, rehabilitating scenic and forestal wealth. Thanks to the enthusiasm of a body of able men and women, the movement has made great progress. Indeed, it has gathered such momentum as to have firmly established itself in the popular mind, and to "plant a tree" has become a slogan approved by one and all. Enthusiasm is an essential factor in the success of any movement. It is much more infectious than cold reason and it will carry men and women through greater labor and suffering than any appeal to business instincts. However, enthusiasm may blaze a trail but if a cause is to be kept properly alive it must be guided by common sense and business acumen.

For many years now, I have watched with admiration the growth of the Arbor Day movement, but with much vexation have observed the actual outcome of its celebrations. There is nothing more laudable than to plant a tree, except to plant two trees, provided the right kind of tree be planted. This fact, as fundamental as it is simple, seems to be something that many Arbor Day enthusiasts completely lose sight of. It would appear that the time has come when the leaders of the movement should sit down and take stock of their accomplishments, audit the results to date and see how best the ideal can be fostered. This may sound paradoxical when in almost the same breath one has stated that the movement has swept the country. It has. Its popularity is assured; enthusiasm was never so great, but is it being properly directed? In other words, has the movement resulted not only in the planting of trees but in planting the right kind of trees—not in planting trees that will flourish for a week or a year—but trees that have every prospect of growing year by year into greater beauty over a century and more? The movement, great as it is, enormous as its efforts are and have been, is not a success if the output of its labors possess no lasting qualities. The actual labor of planting is no greater for the right and proper than for the indifferent and worthless. The effort required to find the right trees is greater, but if it is not made the whole movement suffers.

Very few American trees, and for that matter very few trees of any country, flourish under city conditions. In the eastern part of America two of the finest trees in all the world, two of the most common and two of the most planted are the American Elm and the Sugar Maple. For the highways and for non-manufacturing towns of this region they are unsurpassable, but for cities with their under-drainage and impure atmosphere these trees are worthless. Not long ago a great tree lover died, a man who did much honor to this country and one profoundly respected in his community. To his memory the Governor of the state dedicated and planted a memorial tree. The site chosen was in the heart of a city, and the tree, a native White Spruce, lover of pure air and of cool forest soils. I was invited to the ceremony but was tongue-tied. It was a beautiful tree and the Governor did his part well, but wasted effort will be the sole result. This White Spruce from the moment it was placed in the earth was doomed to a lingering death by suffocation and slow poison. In this case, if an evergreen was desired, a Japanese Yew should have been planted, since this best withstands city conditions in the climate where the tree-planting ceremony took place. Did they want a deciduous tree, then an English Elm, a European Beech or an Oriental Maidenhair-tree should have been planted, since one and all of these are well suited to city conditions and could be looked upon as promising to thrive for a hundred years or more.

Just for a moment let us look into the source of available tree supplies—the nurseries, either municipal, state, commercial or private—from which these are drawn. The trees raised in these nurseries are those of which seeds are most easily and cheaply procured. For ornamental purposes certain species and varieties are in demand and the supply is governed by the well-known law; but for movements such as that of Arbor Day, and to be frank, general forestry planting as ordinarily undertaken in America today, supply is governed by nothing except cost of production. Trees of suitable size are wanted by the thousand, by the tens of thousands, and cheapness in price is the only factor considered. Nurserymen, for the purpose of Arbor Day, raise the sorts of trees of which they can procure the seed in greatest quantity at the lowest rate. It is much easier to buy the tree seeds of Europe or Japan than to buy seeds of the trees native of this country. So far as the Arbor Day movement is concerned, no fault could be found with this did exotic trees all flourish in the places where Arbor Day enthusiasts plant them. Unfortunately, this is far from being the case. Certain exotics grow as well as, sometimes better than, native trees, but they are the exception, not the rule, and experience alone can teach just which these are.

In New England and in other cold parts of this country three of the commonest trees planted are the Norway Spruce, Scots Pine and English Oak. Now, each and several are quite unsuited to the climate and in consequence are valueless. The Norway Spruce grows well enough for twenty-five or thirty years, but so soon as its top comes under the influence of strong winds it starts to die. Scots Pine and English Oak as a rule grow freely for the first ten or twenty years, then stop suddenly and either die or linger.

In this same part of America the European Beech, the common Horsechestnut, the English Elm, the Norway Maple, the two European Lindens, the Austrian Pine and the European Larch do well. Contrariwise, the American Beech, the Sugar Maple, the American Elm, the American Lindens, the Red Pine and the White, Red, and Black Spruces either refuse to grow or are worthless in the British Isles. The Hemlock flourishes there; the Red and Scarlet Oaks do splendidly, but the White Oak refuses to grow. In Great Britain, Black Locust and White Pine, two eastern American trees, have in times past been planted by the million to the great loss and discomfiture of those who planted them.

If the very natural question of *why* be asked, no answer is forthcoming. Trees have their likes and dislikes which are none the less strong for being inarticulate. I cannot tell, no one can tell, why these trees behave in the manner stated. That it is fact, you have but to travel and look around. But the *why* is something that

WINTER LANDSCAPE, ROYAL GARDENS, KEW, ENGLAND

man has not yet wrung from his friend, the tree. For more than
fifty years the Arnold Arboretum has been raising and planting
trees. It is almost the only place in this country where records regard-
ing tree growth over more than fifty years can be found, or where
trees of this age can be seen and studied. Much disappointment has
been met with, but the experience of the Arboretum can help tree-
planting enthusiasts in this part of America.

Sentiment has a strong hold on the human race. It is, indeed,
a very laudable attribute if kept in proper bounds. We all have a
certain sentimental regard—love or affection, call it what you will
—for the lands from which our ancestors came. Some memento,
especially some living reminder of that land, gives pleasure and
this sentimental interest has had much to do with the introducing
and planting in this country of European trees, shrubs and herbs.
Nothing can be said against such work unless it be carried beyond
the bounds of reason and at the expense of the native flora. At the
conclusion of the World War the planting of memorial trees, either
as individuals, as groves or as avenues, was largely entered upon.
I was many times called upon to give advice as to the best sort of
tree to be planted, but it was on very rare occasions that my advice
was acted upon. Not because the inquirers took exception to it,
but because they could not obtain the trees suggested; and since the
urge to plant was strong, they willingly took substitutes.

As showing how far in the wrong direction sentiment can drive
man's effort, what I saw at Perth, Western Australia, will illustrate. In memory of the men sacrificed in the World War it was
decided to plant an avenue of trees and the tree decided upon was
the English Oak. No greater difference in climate and rainfall could
be found than in that of the district of Perth and the parts of Europe
where this particular Oak flourishes. Western Australia has many
magnificent native trees, including the wonderful Red-flowered Euca-

lyptus *(E. ficifolia)* which is the glory of many a cemetery, park and garden in California, but in Perth as elsewhere the native trees are despised. Sentiment lauds the exotic. Of course, nothing but utter failure can overtake the scheme and Perth will not have a memorial avenue until it decides to plant something other than English Oak. I have seen memorial trees planted in many lands but only here and there have I seen this most worthy cause regulated by common sense.

Buying a pig in a bag is out of fashion today, except when buying trees. Barnum had some wise sayings, one of which is familiar to all and need not be repeated, but gold bricks are not less numerous now than formerly. The superlative of liar is said to have something to do with one who makes holes in the ground. The very acme of foolishness is to plant trees blindly. Plant trees but plant the right kind of trees. Plant the tree that will be a thing of beauty year in and year out for a century and more. Plant for posterity.

It is a simple matter to urge the planting of the right kind of tree. It is by no means so easy to say just what that tree is since soil and climate vary so enormously in different parts of the country. What is good for New England is not suitable for the middle west, nor for the southwest, nor for California, and vice versa. For tree-less regions experiment alone can demonstrate what trees can be grown, but in regions where native trees are met with in meadows, woods or forests and where gardens and parks flourish a stroll of an hour or two will quickly tell the tree lover what thrives and what does not. One's eyes and common sense must be the guide.

Do not plant trees simply because they are cheap and easily obtainable. Inquire first, by looking around, whether the type of tree will grow or flourish in the district. If it will not, such a tree is dear at any price, but the pity of it is that often as not twenty years must elapse before a verdict can be had. Twenty years of wasted

effort is a heavy price to pay for ignorance even if begotten of enthusiasm. So far as New England is concerned, Norway Spruce,
English Oak and Scots Pine should not be planted, unless the passing
moment suffices to please the fancy. Plant native trees in preference to
exotics wherever possible. In selecting and buying trees use the
ordinary judgment that you would put into any everyday business
transaction.

> In the Garden of Eden, planted by God,
> There were goodly trees in the springing sod—
>
> Trees of beauty and height and grace,
> To stand in splendor before His face.
>
> Trees for fruitage and fire and shade,
> Trees for the cunning builder's trade;
>
> Wood for the bow, the spear, and the flail,
> The keel and the mast of the daring sail;
>
> He made them of every grain and girth
> For the use of man in the Garden of Earth.
>
> —BLISS CARMAN.

ARISTOCRATS OF THE TREES

TREES AND THE HEART OF MAN

*"No greater beauty can adorn
The hamlet, than a grove of ancient trees."*

REES have entwined the heart of man since he became a sentient being. They hold a prominent place in the legends and sacred writings of all ages and of all people, particularly in those of the old Hebrew race. In the Bible we are told that in the first garden God planted the "Tree of Knowledge of Good and Evil," and in the old Norse Sagas the Oak and Ash are frequently mentioned. Priest and poet in every land have sung their praises and down the ages a mighty literature on tree lore has been accumulated. From early times trees have afforded man shelter, food, and clothing, and have exercised a tremendous influence over his daily life. The more simple the people the greater their appreciation, at least so it would seem since as nations became civilized they one and all by fire and axe have destroyed the friendly trees and of these vandals the white man ranks head and shoulders above all others. From the early stages of his colonizing days down to within a few years of the present, wherever he has gone he has laid waste the tree wealth of the lands in an effort, often vain, to make a blade of corn grow where two trees grew before. A halt has been called to this ruthless waste and we are at least beginning to appreciate the danger done and cast about for means to amend the damage. Tree planting is now the vogue and ere long, maybe,

1

tree worship will yet again hold man enthralled. All tree lovers could wish that this lofty conception of Nature's grandest work could be widely inculcated. There is nothing statelier than a tree and no handiwork of man is one tithe so wonderful. In loftiness of stature, massiveness of trunk, architecture of branch and bark, shapeliness of crown and bud, and in beauty of foliage no living thing is comparable with a tree.

These United States are singularly blessed in their tree birthright. No other northern land is so richly dowered and no other land boasts such variety of useful and ornamental trees as does this country. From coast to coast and from border to the gulf except in the prairie states a rich assortment of trees are found. In all more than six hundred different species are recognized and these include the tallest and largest members of the tree world. The Mammoth-tree of California is mightiest of all living trees. Specimens more than 300 feet tall with trunks 100 feet in girth, clean, and without a branch for half their height, and clothed with bark often 2 feet thick, are numerous on the California Sierras. In the Redwood of California we have the tallest of living trees, although Australia with her lofty Eucalyptus stiffly challenges us. Redwoods measured at more than 350 feet in height are known; others have been reported as much as 400 feet. These giants with trunks 75 feet in girth, buttressed at the base, form natural groves scattered from the southern border of Oregon south to Monterey County in California. Not only is the Redwood the tallest of trees but it furnishes the most valuable timber of all the forests of the Pacific side of this great continent.

In the fertile bottomlands of the Mississippi Valley and of southern Illinois and Indiana grow Pecan and Black Walnut trees up to a height exceeding 150 feet with trunks 15 or 18 feet in girth. In the alluvial valleys of the Ohio River system and on the high

THE WRAITH

mountains of North Carolina and Tennessee the Tulip-tree exceeds in height 150 feet with its clean, bold trunk 18 feet in girth. In the south Atlantic and gulf states the Bald Cypress covers vast areas of the river swamps, attaining as much as 150 feet in height and 30 feet in girth of trunk.

New England, too, has its magnificent trees and none more so than the American White Elm, the most familiar wayside tree and commonly planted in front of old homesteads. In rich meadowlands individual trees 120 feet tall with trunks 25 feet in girth, often nobly buttressed at the base, are not infrequent. Oaks, dear to all white men, and among the most familiar of trees, are richer in species in this land than elsewhere in temperate regions, no fewer than one hundred and forty-five kinds being known. The tallest of all is the Burr Oak, which, in the lowlands of southern Indiana and Illinois, often towers 160 feet above the ground, its noble, broad-spreading head being supported on a trunk 20 feet in girth and unbranched for 70 to 80 feet. In the southeastern states the Live Oak is famous. A low tree, seldom more than 50 feet high with a comparatively small trunk, not more than 10 or 12 feet in girth but arising from a swollen and buttressed base, it supports a dense, wide-spread, round-topped crown often 150 feet through. In California the Valley Oak is the noblest representative of its tribe. Trees often 100 feet high with a short trunk 20 feet in girth give off massive, wide-spreading limbs, draped with graceful hanging branches that sweep the ground, the whole forming an umbrageous mass sometimes 200 feet in diameter. No land has a monopoly of tree growth, but these United States in their share are indeed well blessed.

In all countries where trees grow the noblest specimens ought to be preserved as national monuments since, when all is said and done, no nation can boast anything more magnificent than the forest giants Nature gave it. In the preservation of the Redwood and Mammoth trees of California a beginning has been made but it should be extended to include specimens of extreme size of no matter what species. These are more priceless than the arts of man and belong not to any person or group of persons but to the country at large, indeed, those who govern lands in which noble products of Nature's skill grow lustily ought to consider themselves as trustees of world treasures. Some day a country will awaken to the fact that its magnificent trees are truly national monuments. May this come while there are yet old giants to protect! Why should not the conscience of this great country lead in organizing a tree protective society and insure the preservation not only of the giant Redwood and Mammoth trees but the finest specimens of Oak and Ash, Elm and Maple, Tulip and Sweetgum, Cypress and Cedar, Pine and Fir, and, indeed, all other varieties of the rich and varied tree growth that North America boasts? It could be easily done in association with a newly awakened conscience in forestry matters. Forestry officers could report the subjects and then a simple law preserving them whether on public or private property would do the rest. No other land in this broad world boasts trees of greater bulk and height, of greater beauty, or greater usefulness, or in so great variety, as these United States and well would it be if as an example to the world at large we assumed the van in tree protection and preservation.

There is something friendly in a tree, friendly to man, to bird and to beast. From heat and cold alike it spreads a shielding crown of branch and leaf. To note at the approach of spring the melting snow around the base of a tree bole is to realize its warmth, and one has but to step beneath its shadow at mid-summer to appreciate its cooling shade. Man everywhere is fully alive to the value of trees and their products in the arts and crafts of human affairs.

Courtesy "House & Garden"

MONTEREY CYPRESS. CUPRESSUS MACROCARPA. 70 FEET TALL, TRUNK 15 FEET GIRTH. NR. MONTEREY, CALIFORNIA

MUDLARKS, TAXODIUM DISTICHUM, LOUISIANA

Courtesy "House & Garden

Would that a tithe of this appreciation could be aroused for the tree's esthetic charm.

Trees possess both character and personality as anyone may appreciate by contrasting, say, an Oak with a Birch. Each country and each nation has its favored trees but to the English no tree is so dear, so sacred as the Oak. Was it not beneath an ancient Oak that the Magna Charta of the English speaking people was signed at Runnymede? I like to marshal my tree acquaintances into groups and types and to compare them with similar members of the human family. To me the English Oak *(Quercus robur)* and the American White Oak *(Q. alba)* typify in one instance the Squire of Old England, and in the other a prosperous Plantation Owner of this country in days past. As tree lovers know, these Oaks thrive best in rich deep bottom lands and meadows where the soil is mellow and fat and where drought is never known and where good drainage always obtains. Under such conditions their short massive trunks give forth numerous stout wide-spreading branches, forming a broad flat-topped umbrageous crown. Under the shadow of one of these trees a herd of cattle or a flock of sheep can find shelter and in the branches a thousand birds can rest and gladden the ear with song. They may look smug and self-satisfied but such trees possess a tower of strength and unmoved have withstood storms of centuries. There is an air of prosperity about them, of good living, of contentment, exercising a soothing influence on the spectator. They may be greedy inasmuch as they will suffer no other tree to grow within their shadow; they may insist on enjoying to the full the good things of life but in return they show stability and give an air of prosperity to meadow or pastureland in which they flourish. And so, too, the Squire, the Country Gentleman, the Plantation Owner, or prosperous Farmer, exhibit all the characters enumerated, but who shall say when all is done that for centuries past they have not been the backbone of the country? Much has been written decrying the old English Squire but he has served his country well and so, too, has the lordly Oak, whose descendants are today pensioners in many an English park and meadow. The American White Oak is worthy of similar recognition.

If the White Oak be Lord of the Pasture, the American Elm is Lady and like her human analogue she is at times of masculine proportion and appearance. In rich soils magnificent specimens shaped like a wine glass, clean of bole or sometimes with feathered trunks, and pendent branches grace the countryside. These trees possess all the charm of femininity, and of wayside trees none is more lovely, but not uncommon are types with massive wide-spreading branches distinctively Oak-like in appearance and quite as masculine in character as any White Oak. Here in trees, as in the human family, we find types which would usurp their proper sphere and adopt the rôle of the opposite sex. In the Elm, at any rate, this is assumed at the expense of the charm of litheness and graceful beauty which all so much admire in the feminine.

The Coconut with slender trunk and long plume-like leaves fanning the breeze is queen of the tropic strand. She rules in equatorial regions. The mud larks of the tropics are Nipa Palms and Mangroves which people the muddy flats and estuaries of rivers, living in black, filthy ooze where malaria and other fevers are rampant. Their counterparts in the north are certain Alders and Willows which flourish in and about streams and lake shores. We have no envy or even admiration for such that prefer to live in regions so unhealthy and uninviting. A true amphibian is the Swamp Cypress *(Taxodium distichum)* which like a Marine is equally at home on land or on water. In the swamps of Louisiana and everglades of Florida this striking tree rules. Its trunk, fluted at the base, is a curious sight, especially when seen reflected in the water. Round about it are clustered gnarled knee-like growths, as to the function of which scientists dispute. This tree has a narrow crown clad with pure green feathery foliage which turns brown in the fall and its branches are usually hung with gray locks of Spanish Moss (*Tillandsia usneoides*).

The Monterey Cypress and other coastwise trees may be dubbed Coastguards, defenders of their rockbound homes. Wind is their great enemy and the feud between them is eternal. From youth to old age the struggle persists and marvelous is the fight the trees of the shore put up against their unrelenting, death-dealing enemy, wind. The struggle may go on through centuries yet sooner or later victory is with the wind, but nothing in the tree world commands admiration more than the magnificent fight an old Pine or Cypress puts up. In our illustration one giant Pine has succumbed but his neighbor still keeps up the fight. One can imagine the jaws firmly set, every fiber of the tree's existence stressed to hold its own and proudly floating from the treetop its flag inscribed *nil desperandum*. There is something sublime in the masterful struggle between the organic and inorganic forces and methinks old Mother Nature stands as umpire witnessing the noble game.

Forests, especially the coniferous forests of the northern hemisphere, boast a sheltered people, gregarious in habit like the denizens of towns and cities, a people fond of the soft things of life, happy enough when everything is going well but unable to bear adversity with impunity. Let wind or storm, axe or fire, isolate trees of the forests and they are doomed; they are as unable to adapt themselves to changing conditions as are the factory or shophands of our cities. So long as their normal life is not interfered with all is well but if brought face to face with changed conditions and adversities they have no reserve of adaptability and fall by the wayside. I have often noticed a Pine tree left on the edge of a clearing or a lake looking forlorn and miserable—a wraith shrieking for lost companions. In the picture of lake and lone Pine-tree one can almost hear the cries this wind-tossed survivor gives forth in loud appeal for the companionship of lost neighbors.

In deserts and arid regions no trees grow save in the vicinity of wells, as for example the Date Palm in the Sahara, but in certain dry regions where rain falls at infrequent intervals trees highly specialized to withstand drought find a home. These like the camel, "ship of the desert," are especially equipped to store and retain water over long periods. Most remarkable of these are the Bottle trees *(Brachychiton rupestris)* of Australia, whose flask-like trunks are reservoirs of water which in times of emergency have saved many a traveler's life.

Australia is, indeed, remarkably rich in trees and in her Eucalyptus boasts the loftiest types known outside the realm of Conifers. The species are very numerous—hundreds of them all told—but queen of all is the Karri *(Eucalyptus diversicolor)*. This is one of the tallest of the Eucalyptus and the polished white and gray trunks stand like marble columns in Nature's cathedral. Never shall I forget two glorious days in the wondrous Karri forests of Western Australia.

In the Sequoias western North America is blessed with the giants of the tree world which outstrip in size all other trees. Imagine trees nearly 400 feet high with trunks 100 feet in girth, the stupendous results of growth cell upon cell for two thousand years and more, the crowns, spare of branches, often broken by storms, yet resisting all adverse forces through century upon century—the oldest living thing extant.

The people of the Orient have a profound veneration for old trees and tree planting has been practised from time immemorial. The most wonderful deciduous-leaved trees planted by man that I have seen are the Oriental Planes *(Platanus orientalis)* in the

BATTLING TO THE LAST

KARRI, EUCALYPTUS DIVERSICOLOR, TRUNK 32 FEET GIRTH, NATIONAL PARK,
BIG BROOK, WESTERN AUSTRALIA

grounds of the old Mogul palace and temples at Srinagar, Kashmir. Avenues and groves of giants 100 feet high with trunks 20 feet in girth and wide-spreading crowns canopied in broad leaves afford most welcome shade to man and beast. Those who planted these trees knew how and did not stint them room to develop their full characters and they stand today majestic monuments to departed greatness.

In temple and palace grounds and sheltering shrines in southern India I saw a tree which in beauty of architecture ranks without a peer. It is a Fig-tree named *Ficus Benjamina,* a close relative of the famed Banyan-tree. Benjamin's Fig is evergreen with small lustrous dark green foliage, a monstrous trunk, short and fluted with a vast number of large ascending stems which give off myriad pendent branchlets that hang down to the ground. The crown is very shapely in form, being more or less rounded and so wide that it covers half an acre of ground. In the Lalbagh at Bangalore there is a tree that could easily shelter a company of soldiers.

In the tropic regions of Africa luxuriates the gigantic Baobab about which old travelers told many fabulous stories. At Mombasa it grows in quantity and in the dry season when the branches are naked of leaves there is no more ugly tree in all the world. The height is not great, seldom more than 80 feet, and the crown is of moderate size only, of no particular shape and made up of gnarled branches and stubby branchlets, suggesting a gigantic crow's nest. It is the bulky trunk that is so imposing, being often 100 feet in girth and clothed with a smooth bark. Thick as is the trunk a bullet from a rifle of high velocity will pass right through it for its tissues are soft and pulpy. The foliage is handsome and so, too, are the large white saucer-shaped flowers. The fruit is extraordinary, being as large as an ostrich's egg, pointed at both ends, and clothed with short yellowish brown hairs and hangs from a long stalk. Inside the fruit is a white powder which tastes like cream-of-tartar. On an island immediately above the Victoria Falls of the Zambesi River, the missionary explorer, David Livingstone, carved his name on a Baobab tree when he discovered this eighth wonder of the world.

The Horsechestnut of village blacksmith fame with its myriad white candles upthrust is a rather ostentatious member of the tree world. The Beech is the Adonis of the Forest, while the Silver Birch is Venus of the Woodlands. The Beech, like Adonis in Shakespeare's comedy, holds aloof, preferring his own company to that of Venus. She, too, strange to say, prefers the rôle of nurse and protector of the dark hued Pine, Spruce and Fir to the companionship of the more vigorous broad-limbed deciduous denizens of her own kin. Were squirrel and chipmunk consulted they would vote the Walnut, Hickory and Chestnut kings of the countryside. Indeed, their grief at the sickness which has overtaken the Chestnut cannot be assuaged although they find no reason for discontinuing their work as the greatest planters of nut trees in the northern world. Beavers acclaim the Aspen most useful of trees since with it they construct their homes. The gorgeous blossomed Flamboyant *(Poinciana regia)* of the tropics is, indeed, a living Prometheus still grasping in his hands and holding aloft the fire of Jove. Resplendent in autumn dress, the Red and Sugar Maples may be termed the Huntsmen of the Tree World, their brilliant autumnal tints outrivaling the colored jackets of those who follow fox and hound. Grief or love forlorn is well portrayed by the Weeping Willow, while no cleric is more upright in character than the Lombardy Poplar, and White Birch and trembling Aspen are the nursemaids of our northern forest trees.

The analogy of trees and the human family could be carried to extreme lengths with wholesome lessons to mankind. Indeed in the tree world may be found just as diverse groups, types and characters as in the human family—the strong, the self-willed, the reliant and masterful, the weak and clinging, those who only have strength when gathered into crowds, the beautiful, the ugly, the useful, the worthless, the fighter, the slacker, and so on *ad infinitum*.

MARCH OF AGES

ROM the earliest glimpses preserved to us of the development of the human race we find that trees have exercised a beneficent influence on man's character and uplift. They figure prominently in the records, written and oral, of all religious systems in all parts of the world. Indeed, the connection of trees with religion is as old as the conception of the Deity itself. North and south, east and west, we find the same idea. In the most universally prized of all the books, the Bible, trees are ofttimes mentioned. In Genesis, chapter II: v. 9, "And out of the ground made the Lord God to grow every tree that is pleasant to the sight, and good for food; the tree of life also in the midst of the garden, and the tree of knowledge of good and evil." All are familiar with the biblical story of man's fall and banishment from the Garden of Eden through disobeying God's commands in reference to these trees. Those who have studied the folk-lore of primitive man tell us that legends of good and evil trees are almost universal, and that they are intimately connected with man's own story of his development. As man congregated, built homes of mud, brick, and stone, his energies became more and more absorbed in gaining wealth, and this has repeatedly led to his own destruction and that of his kindred. The same thing obtains today. The happy and contented among us are those whose thoughts are not wholly engrossed in laying up treasure in gold, silver, and precious stones, but who take an intelligent interest in Nature's treasures, preserve them, and prize them at their true worth.

All who keep goldfish in a bowl or in an aquarium know that

green weeds of some sort must be kept in the water or the fish will die. Why? Because the fish inhale all the free oxygen in the water and poison themselves with carbon dioxide which they exhale unless plants are present to take up this gas and in exchange give back free oxygen and thus maintain the balance in nature. So on the grander scale. But for the presence of vegetation this earth would be uninhabitable for the animal kingdom in all its forms, man included.

The two kingdoms—vegetable and animal—are interdependent, but the vegetable kingdom is the more ancient of the two. Men of great minds, both of the past and of the present, who have studied deeply the problems concerning the origin of the world of life are of the opinion that the present state of development of the animal kingdom—the living types of today including man the complex—has been made possible by the steady change in the development of the vegetable kingdom. The fossil remains of plants and animals imbedded in the rocks of the different geological epochs of the world's history tell the story of the progressive changes that have taken place during the earth's history, from its youth and adolescence to its present age. Indeed this progressive development of organic life through successive geological periods is the theory on which the modern teaching of the science of natural history is based, and it must be confessed that it goes far toward rendering intelligible natural phenomena as they exist today.

Trees by no means represent the oldest type of life-forms in the history of the vegetable kingdom; on the contrary, they are fairly modern. Geologists tell us that in the earliest phases of the world's history of which organic remains exist, the vegetable kingdom was represented by simple, aquatic, or semi-aquatic plants, and the animal kingdom by sponges, worms, centipedes, and spiders. In succeeding ages land plants were developed. During the period represented by our coal measures (the Carboniferous period) and the lengthy epoch preceding it, the whole earth became more or less forest-clad with a low type of vegetation mostly allied to our Ferns, Horsetails, Lycopods and ancestral forms of the Cycad and Ginkgo families.

This earliest luxuriant land vegetation—that which formed the great coal-fields of the earth—was probably adapted to the physical environment alone and was almost uninfluenced by the scanty animal life of the period. Reptiles and mammals were then differentiated, but the former, being better fitted to live upon the vegetation and to survive in the heavily carbonated atmosphere, increased more rapidly. This increase continued through the next two geological epochs and culminated in the next, the Jurassic period, which has been fitly termed the "Age of Reptiles." Rocks of this age are prevalent in the states of Wyoming, the Dakotas, Kansas, and Texas, and from them have been excavated, and sent to museums for preservation, remains more or less complete of the largest, the ugliest, and the most extraordinary forms of animal life the world has known.

The development of vegetation reacting on the climate and on the animal kingdom, and each on the other, induced constant change. In due course reptiles gave place to mammals, birds were differentiated and likewise insects in variety; Cycads, Araucarias, Ginkgos, Yews, Cedars, and other Conifers came into being and, later, broad-leaved and coniferous trees similar to those of today. It is not my purpose to trace this progressive change in further detail, but the fact I do wish to emphasize is that isolated types of the archaic forms of trees have persisted down through remote ages to the present day. Of such may be instanced the Araucarias, now confined to South America and Australasia. A familiar example of these trees is the Norfolk Island Pine (*Araucaria excelsa*), so much in request for indoor decorative purposes in the colder parts of this country,

GRIZZLY GIANT, SEQUOIA GIGANTEA, MARIPOSA GROVE, CALIFORNIA

MAMMOTH-TREE, SEQUOIA GIGANTEA, MARIPOSA GROVE, CALIFORNIA.

and quite hardy in California. Other examples are the Cycads, which are found scattered through the southern hemisphere and northward to the Tropic of Cancer, the Cedars of Lebanon, of Cyprus, of the Atlas Mountains and of the western Himalayas; also the Ginkgo of China, Korea, and Japan.

Many persons take it for granted that the types of trees with which they are familiar are found all the world over; others more discerning know that every tree has but a limited distribution covering at most a few degrees of latitude and longitude. They know that the Oaks, Elms, Maples, Pines, and Firs are different on the east and west seaboards of this country; also that both differ from those of Europe on the one hand and of eastern Asia on the other. If one looks into the subject all sorts of curious facts are unearthed. For instance, the Tulip-tree and the Kentucky Coffee-tree are each represented by two species only, one of each in the eastern United States and another of each in central China. Of Douglas Firs, two species grow on the mountains of the Pacific Slope and three species in eastern Asia. The Honey-locusts grow in eastern North America, in eastern Asia, and in the Caucasus region. One species of Incense Cedar is native of the mountains of California, another of the mountains of Formosa and southern China, while several species are indigenous to South America, New Guinea, and New Zealand. Some groups of trees are represented by many species, others by one or two species. And so as study follows interest it is clearly seen that some groups are in the heyday of their youth, others in their prime, others on the wane—not as individuals but as groups. Reasoning on these facts the conclusion is naturally reached that in the progressive development of types of trees this is the natural sequence. It has been the same through the world's history. Types have arisen and disappeared, some completely, while others, altered and modified to meet the climatic and other changes, have persisted through very long periods of time, and are, as it were, living fossils.

With three of these ancient types of trees I shall deal at length in succeeding essays, but, as an explanatory introduction, it is necessary to enter a little into the subject of tree distribution in general. A popular book is hardly the place for a full discussion of these matters, yet they are of such interest and importance that a few salient points cannot fail to be of use in understanding present phenomena of tree distribution. Savants have written much to explain particular cases, and as knowledge increases the whole question becomes more simple. The geological records, even of the northern hemisphere, are notoriously imperfect but as investigations proceed many links are forged and abysmal chasms bridged. The human mind, collectively or individually, will never achieve the infinite but it may learn enough to explain much intelligently.

If we are in the least degree to understand the present-day distribution of plants, and especially the isolation of groups of trees like for instance the Honey-locust (Gleditsia), and Sweetgum (Liquidambar), which occur in Asia Minor, China, Japan, and eastern North America and each separated by thousands of miles of land and sea, it is necessary that we try and picture some of the changes time has wrought in the climate of the northern hemisphere. Geologists are pretty well agreed that the two great oceans, Atlantic and Pacific, have not changed much in the æons of time since this earth began to cool. Seas, plains, mountain ranges, and large areas of land have, however, changed vastly though probably the depressions and elevations have maintained a fairly stable equilibrium—a sort of compensation balance.

The Tertiary period, that is the geological era immediately preceding the present, was one of the great disturbances and the folding of the earth's crust, due to internal cooling and consequent

MONTEZUMA CYPRESS. TAXODIUM MUCRONATUM, MONTEZUMA, MEXICO

contraction, made vast changes in the earth's surface. Its close was marked by a period of great cold which wrought havoc among vegetation, and today much land that in Tertiary times was forested is hidden under enormous ice-fields. In Tertiary times most of the present Arctic Zone was probably free of ice, at any rate Spitzbergen, Greenland, Iceland, and the extreme north of the mainland of America and Asia enjoyed a climate at least as mild as New England does today. Vast forests circled the whole of today's Arctic regions, for the land connection was complete. In those times the types of tree vegetation were similar throughout the whole northern hemisphere. Doubtless, then as now, species had a limited distribution, but the genera then, much more so than today, were widespread. Tulip-trees, Magnolias, Sweet Gums, Ginkgos, Sassafras, Sequoias, and, indeed, countless others grew in Europe, in America, and in Asia.

As the period of great cold came on so the vegetation was forced to migrate down the mountains and southward to escape destruction. As the ice crept southward so it destroyed the vegetation. The trees of Greenland, Spitzbergen, Iceland, and of the regions separating North America and eastern Asia, were all destroyed. In this country they were forced south of Philadelphia (Lat. 40° N.) and where there was no continuous land connection they were obliterated. In Europe they were swept almost to the very fringe of the Mediterranean and virtually all destroyed. In Europe today only about three dozen genera of trees are found and even the species are very limited in number.

We are not concerned with the theories as to what particular astronomical change induced the Ice Age, but it is important to realize that the ice did not descend to equal latitudes all round the northern hemisphere. Japan and China escaped glaciation and, though the temperature must have been lowered, the vegetation suffered little harm. Of course there was a migration toward the south and a reverse one at the close of the glacial epoch. The net result is that the existing flora of the Chinese Empire and of central Japan southward, is really a miniature of the whole flora of the northern hemisphere in pre-glacial times. In China and in the parts of Japan indicated grow today many peculiar types, and all the principal genera of trees known from the other parts of the northern hemisphere except Robinia, Laburnum, Platanus, true Cedars (Cedrus), Sequoia and Taxodium; and of the latter two there are such very closely allied trees as Taiwania and Glyptostrobus. Fossils of many types which grow in the Orient today occur in Europe, and recent dredgings off the Dutch-English coast have added much to prove that the ancient flora of Europe was similar to that now flourishing in the Far East. I do not mean that they were specifically identical but that the generic types were similar. If we picture to ourselves the creeping inevitably southward of the ice we can easily understand how trees and other forms of vegetation were destroyed in its path, and only those which were able to reach places of sufficent warmth to maintain life survived. The greater the land extension toward the south the greater chances had the vegetation, and where the country was broken by mountain ranges advantageous regions were more easily found.

The ice on its path ground off the tops of mountains and scoured out valleys to a great depth, and when it retreated the face of much of the northern hemisphere was changed. It disappeared from sea-level valleys earlier than from mountain ranges and so isolated groups of vegetation. If we picture this, and remember that before the period of great cold set in the vegetation of the north was everywhere very similar, we can understand how today are found here and there groups of trees isolated by thousands of miles from their kindred. This explains the separation of the Cedars of Lebanon,

REDWOOD, SEQUOIA SEMPERVIRENS, SANTA CRUZ, CALIFORNIA

MAMMOTH-TREE, SEQUOIA GIGANTEA, MERCED GROVE, CALIFORNIA

of the Taurus, of Cyprus, of the Atlas Mountains and of the western Himalayas; also the isolation of the Nettle-trees, Honey-locusts, Sweet Gums, Walnuts, and others in the Caucasus region, in eastern North America and in the Orient. What were temperate regions in the north in Tertiary times are even now the frozen north, and the land of this region capable of growing forests is infinitely less than it was then. Deserts, seas, lakes, high plateaux, and mountain ranges influence climates, which strongly affect plant distribution. Birds, animals, air- and water-currents are all agencies in plant dispersal, and so to understand why this tree is here and not yonder involves the study of a number of cognate branches of natural history. Complex is the problem, but however little it is studied the marvels of the world we live in become more and more apparent.

Brief and fragmentary as this sketch is it would be more so did we omit mention of the influence of man. At what period in the world's history man first appeared is much disputed, but certain it is that, so soon as he became a sentient being, hunger caused him to investigate the vegetation and taught him to appreciate what was wholesome as food; providing himself with clothes, shelter, and weapons for protection followed. As he migrated so he carried with him plants that were of service to his needs, and, later, such as were a delight to his higher being. We know so little of the early peregrinations of the human race, or of where it had its cradle, that we can say nothing of that remote and most interesting period. In the mythology, folk-lore, and sacred writings of all races of which we have knowledge frequent mention of trees is made. Invading armies devastated countries and carried off useful plants, including fruit trees and the like, as spoils of war. Alexander the Great is but a name in history in spite of his great conquests, and of his work the only beneficial result to mankind remaining is the Orange-tree which his soldiers are said to have carried back from India to the shores of the Mediterranean.

Of the mighty migrations across Asia we know very little though it is certain that for centuries the great highways of commerce of the Old World were across central Asia. That the peach, orange, and certain of its relatives, were carried from China to Persia and that neighborhood is certain, and that the walnut and grape-vine were taken back is equally true. From the rich and famed China of old, plants useful and ornamental were also carried to Korea and Japan; even as the apple, the pear, the cherry, wheat, and barley were carried to America from Europe and later the peach, apricot, almond, date, vine, and the like. From this country the potato, tobacco, and maize were taken to Europe and to China. In later times ornamental trees, shrubs, and herbs have been carried far from their original homes.

In all this beneficent work man has been the organizing power, and could a thousand and one of the common plants around us tell their story it would fascinate the least attentive. This pen is indifferently equipped, but the purpose of this work is to show the intimate connection, the bond of companionship, as it were, between ourselves—mankind in general—and certain groups of plants. Animal life, in all its higher forms at any rate, is dependent for its very existence on the vegetable kingdom. Man draws much of his bodily sustenance from the products of plant life, and trees will yield, to all who heed their beauty and study them, mental enjoyment and healthful recreation.

ROOTS, SILENT AND INDEFATIGABLE

OOTS are bibulous things; in proof thereof may be cited a story told by a veracious Oxford Don. Years ago a mantle of Ivy was the pride of Magdalen College, Oxford, England, clothing the walls with dark green verdure throughout all seasons of the year. In the prime of life it was felled on the false assumption that it was harming the masonry of the Great Tower. At least this was the official charge alleged but the real reason was quite otherwise. In the vault of an adjoining wine cellar was stored in sawdust a goodly quantity of port and the roots of the Ivy, out of curiosity or on mischief bent, burglarized the vault and after branching and creeping about in the sawdust found a cork or two through which moisture was oozing. Entering through the corks, the roots drank up all the port and then filled the bottles entirely with a matted tangle of roots all growing in search of more of the ambrosial liquor but unable to get through the glass. They had trapped themselves but not until they had exhausted the supply. In high dudgeon the owners of the wine sought revenge and on the plea that the Ivy was defacing the masonry of the adjoining tower managed to get it destroyed. Yes, roots are great tipplers and so long as they have warmth for their bodies and air to breath they drink unceasingly. It is well they do since the water they lap and the food-salts in solution therein form the very life blood of every living tree, bush, herb, and vine.

This is an age of publicity, an age of the slogan, "it pays to advertise," an age when everything is shouted from the housetops, and he who bawls the loudest receives the most attention. It is no age in which to hide a light under a bushel, for in the glamour of things seen and heard there is no place for silent, shy and retiring natures. In an age like this it is no wonder that roots, which are unseen things, are passed over in silence and suffer utter neglect. At least this would seem to be their position in the world of things. Books, extolling the beauty of leaf and flower, of bud and bark, innumerable there be, but none that I know of tell the virtues of roots. Even in botanical text books roots are dismissed in a few paragraphs after their structure and functions are cited.

Now, gardeners, at any rate, ought to be appreciative of roots for without a healthy mass of these no plant is worth a sixpence. It is all very well to buy a good-looking plant. It may be shapely in form, beautiful of flower and of the highest breeding, but if it lacks a good rootsystem the chances of its living and flourishing are remote. Indeed, in buying a tree or bush the gardener should first assure himself that a good rootsystem is present. Too much attention is often paid to externals which are not so essential as things least obvious. In the erection of a building the foundation, even to the greatest ignoramus in engineering, is of first importance. The foundation of any plant is its rootsystem and unless this be well and truly founded the plant cannot persist. In the erection of a tower, a factory, or a hotel, which is to be, say a couple of hundred feet high, great care is taken that its foundations are sufficiently broad and deep to support the structure. Many a tree grows 200 feet tall so think of the foundation system necessary to hold it strong and erect against the maddest gales and the wildest tempests Dame Nature can let loose. Watch a tree during a heavy wind storm and the enormous stress and strain on its rootsystem is apparent. It is no small thing for a mass of tentacles to grip the earth in such a manner as to hold erect a tree trunk crowned with a broad, branching head weighing many tons against the impetuous rush of a sixty to a hundred mile gale. Talk of clinging for grim life, that must be the condition of roots often during any one season and, as if this in itself were not enough, be it remembered that to the roots fall the vital function of supplying the leaves and plant tissues with every drop of water with food salts in solution necessary to maintain them in living condition. The collecting system of any water-shed or of any river-system is simple compared with that of a tree. A thousand tiny rills and rivulets may converge to form a river or a lake but a billion tiny root hairs are necessary to absorb the water needed daily by every living tree.

Man is proud, and rightly so, of his organizing abilities such as serve a bank, a railway, a mercantile marine or naval system, but these are simple when compared with the collecting system that serves any and every living tree. If scoffers there be, think for a moment of the Mammoth trees of California, which have borne themselves aloft for some two or three thousand years, have withstood many a cataclysm, and earthquakes, storms and fires unnumbered. These throughout their long life have been served by one continuous collecting system. Think of the billions of gallons of water that have been sucked up by the roots of these ancient giants and transported through the stem to the leaves. Nothing that man has conceived or erected has remained in continuous service a tithe of the time that the collecting system of the Mammoth trees has performed, and performed perfectly, the service for which they were developed.

Now, the function of roots are two-fold. First, to anchor the tree, bush, vine or herb firmly in the soil. Second, to absorb from the surrounding medium water with food-salts in solution and carry them to the trunk where they pass upwards into the leaves, the chemical laboratories of the plant, where they are manufactured into food capable of supporting and developing the life of the plant. If we consider a plant as composed of ascending and descending axis, the former develops into trunk and branch, bearing leaves, buds and flowers. The latter dives and delves into the earth, giving off branches and sometimes bearing buds but is always destitute of leaves. In the germination of any and every seed, the first organ to be pushed forth is the primary root, which turns towards the earth, penetrates and becomes the tap-root or roots, giving off rootlets which immediately absorb water to help in the development of the young stem and its first leaves.

Large roots in their efforts to anchor the tree in position and to evade obstructions are often forced to assume grotesque forms and shapes. In our northern forests and meadows, where deep soil obtains, a few stout roots are launched from the base of the trunk in several directions and spread far under the ground to effect their purpose. Often in the space between them cozy nooks tempting animals to burrow and tired travelers to rest upon or between are formed. If rock be present near the surface, many of the larger roots nakedly display their efforts to get a firm grip of Mother Earth. They twist and squirm in many directions always in search of a penetrable substratum. Sometimes, as in one of our pictures, they suggest several alligators stretched full length on their stomachs with legs outthrust. On a sloping bank or on the face of a cliff the roots must give of their utmost power to hold the tree aloft. They dive and sprawl in every direction, gripping everything within reach in fierce determination. Their contortions are almost painful to observe but their tenacity of purpose is enviable. In tropic lands where abundant rains and a rich deep humus keeps the soil moist, roots spread themselves to great distances and in some trees, like certain Figs, the Silk-Cotton trees, and many others assume grotesque appearances.

The roots, especially those developed from near the base of

ELEPHANTINE ROOTS OF SILK-COTTON TREE, ERIODENDRON ANFRACTUOSUM, HAVANA, CUBA

the tree, ramify in all directions and twist and curl round and about obstructions in one mighty effort to do their part of holding the trunk and limbs firmly erect and at the same time developing millions of rootlets that carry on the drinking business of the whole system. The slender, fibrous roots and rootlets pursue their functions doggedly and unceasingly ever increasing the area from which they draw liquid supplies. When they strike a rich pasture, so to speak, they pause for a while but their absorbing properties are pressed to the utmost and so soon as the source of supply dwindles they travel onward. The tip of every little rootlet is armed with scaly tissue known as a root-cap which is constantly renewed and serves the purpose of a drill. The rootlet winds its way through the soil, abandons as it proceeds the older wasted scaling tissue of the root-cap and as this is flung aside young rootlets develop to increase the suction powers of the whole system.

In a normal, well-behaved plant that arises from a seed or from a cutting the root or roots are the first things that develop. These penetrate the soil, increase and multiply, and carry out the function for which their being is ordered. There are certain trees, however, which start life other than in the prosaic manner of the majority. Take the great family of Figs, of which there are more than two hundred species. A great many of these prefer to start life in a manner of their own—a bird or some furry animal carry their fleshy fruits into the upper forks or crotches of tall trees where the seeds are deposited, maybe in a bunch of collected humus, in a hole in the trunk, or even in a niche in the bark itself. The seed germinates, the root starts downward, branches and gives rise to others, continues to grow down and down until it reaches the earth, embracing in the passage and exercising a strangle-hold on the host plant in such manner that in a few years the Fig's roots completely enclose the the trunk of its host and squeezes it, as it were, to death, its rotting tissues forming food for the epiphytic and now semi-parasitic upstart Fig. In tropical countries many plants other than Figs start life this way. Figs are typical rapid growing and cosmopolitan members of the tropics remarkable for many extraordinary methods of root development, and, if one may coin the phrase, root fashions. The fruit in all the species is filled with tiny seeds embedded in a sweet fleshy pulp of which birds and the lesser animals are inordinately fond. The fruits are eaten and the seeds, undigested by bird and animal, are deposited in all sorts of queer places, not on other trees only but on walls and roofs of temple, castle and hovel, and, indeed, on any and every place where birds alight or animals tread. In India, where many Figs luxuriate, they may be seen growing in and upon nearly all the older and more massive buildings, in many instances completely hiding the masonry and usually ruining it. The roots hang down over the walls like pythons and not infrequently among them nestle cobras and other deadly snakes.

Of these Figs the most famous is the Banyan, which has the curious property of sending down slender roots from the branches to the ground, forming stilt-like structures with which to support branch and branches. By a rapid development of these stilt-like roots and corresponding increase in the branching of the tree the original single plant becomes a vast grove. The natives improve upon Nature by placing hollow bamboos beneath these growing lots to protect them. By this means they quickly become stout supporting buttresses. A Banyan thus treated and famous throughout the length and breadth of India is to be seen in the Botanic Garden at Calcutta, where it covers nearly two acres of ground.

The major roots of our northern forest trees spread over the ground and clothed with moss and lichens are objects of quiet beauty and typical of strength in repose. On rock and steep bank, where they are exposed to the weather and where the struggle is keen, their tenacious gripping qualities call forth admiration. In the tropics the roots of epiphytic types exercise an inexorable strangle hold on everything within reach and cause one to think furiously of the grim determination of Mother Nature's forest children.

In the tidal waters and littoral swamps of the tropics and the subtropics another type of root is found. Uncanny, unclean, resembling myriad serpents coiled in swarming masses, slimy, untouchable is the suggestive rootsystem of a Mangrove swamp. The deadly fevers which inhabit these swamps are well known to all who read books of travel as well as to those who sojourn in the tropics. Indeed, of all types of vegetation the Mangrove swamp excites the greatest horror. Even the parched aridity of the desert and the desert flora does not chill the human spirit as does the dank, dark, steaming fastnesses of a Mangrove swamp. These trees start life in a curious manner; the seed germinates on the tree itself, the root, a stout structure, in some species as thick as a pencil, grows downward until its sheer weight dislodges the plantlet from its parent. It plunges vertically downward into the mud, where it anchors itself and develops a tree.

When one thinks for a moment of the seashore, how each tide, in its flow and ebb, brings and takes away mud, sand, and stones of all sizes one realizes that to withstand such conditions a very intricate rootsystem is necessary and so the tides have fashioned that of the Mangrove. At high water when the rootsystem is hidden Mangroves look like other trees supported by a perfectly respectable rootsystem, but at low tide the system is displayed in all its abominations—serpent-like, inextricably coiled with crawling horrors of all sorts caught in its meshes. Its very sight is repellent and to traverse the mazes of a Mangrove swamp is impossible for its rootsystem alone renders it impenetrable.

One other type of rootsystem may be sketched ere this essay

closes. We have mentioned earlier that roots drink so long as they have air to breath. The uninitiated perhaps think that since roots delve in dark earth and slimy places the fresh air of heaven is not necessary for their well-being. However, in the interstices, below the surface of the ground, but not deep down, air is present and it is only when the soil becomes sodden with water that oxygen necessary for root development is unobtainable. This can easily be tested by planting a tree too deeply or by keeping the surroundings flooded when the trees will become sickly and in due course die. Our friends, the Mangroves and other trees, whose homes are tidal flats and swamps of the tropics, have developed a remarkable system of root aeration. From the roots colorless structures are upthrust and the theory is that these serve as breathing tubes. They are known technically as pneumatophores. Often thousands of these are upthrust a few inches to a foot or more above the surface level and at low tide resemble nothing so much as a myriad of porcupine quills dotting the sandy or muddy flat. They look their part—uncanny, leprous, fitting offspring of the unclean serpent-like rootsystem that thrusts them forth.

RUGGED BARK

N THE summer time, when clothed with leafage, all deciduous trees may look very much alike to a casual observer. In the fall, when the change of color in the leaves takes place, variety becomes apparent, but it is in the winter when the trees are naked that they best display their peculiar characteristics. A very brief study will enable anyone in winter to pick out the Elm, Oak, Sugar Maple, Beech, Hickory, and Silver Birch. The general aspect, position of main branches, thickness of shoots, character of the bark, and often of the buds, each or several, afford easy clues to identity. Those who are born and live in the country readily recognize by intuition their neighboring trees. Townsfolk have not the same opportunities and must learn by study what countryfolk acquire through association.

Of the many attractive features of trees not the least is their bark, and in winter this feature is not only very pronounced but is often characteristic. The various organs of a tree, like those of the human body, have each their function, and that of the bark is protection. It protects the vital tissues, which lie near the periphery, from the heat of the sun's direct rays and from the intense cold of winter. We are not concerned with a scientific treatise on the origin of bark but a few simple facts are instructive since they enable us to understand how the various forms of the bark arise. When transplanting trees it is well known that care must be taken not to injure the bark, especially when it is smooth, and that in certain trees, the Holly for example, even moderate injury is fatal. In the Holly (Ilex), in *Acer pennsylvanicum* and other striped-barked Maples, and in a few other trees, the original cells of the outer surface keep pace by growth with the formation of new tissue in the interior. In this case no proper bark is formed, and any considerable injury to the skin, as it may be termed, of the trunk is fatal, since it cannot heal over. Such trees grow naturally in the shade of others and are thereby much protected. Most commonly, however, it is the layer of cells immediately within the outer surface which becomes active and forms bark and continues to do so during the life of the individual. In some trees, like the Birch, as new layers are formed the older ones are partially or completely thrown off. In others, like the Beech, the growth is continuously on the outside. In the Oak, Elm, and Chestnut successive formations are amassed and the bark, though firmly coherent, becomes fissured and with age deeply and ruggedly so. In some trees the bark-forming cells, after a time, cease to function and fresh layers arise successively deeper and deeper within the tissues. When this happens, as in Sequoia, the bark is made up of different tissues and is known as fibrous. In most cases the bark is either thin and papery, firm and smooth, or fissured, but in some —Cork Oak, Cork Elm, and other trees—it is thick and corky.

Without entering further into the origin of bark, our purpose is served if it be remembered that the character of the bark depends largely upon its seat of origin and the nature of the tissues of which it is composed; that its appearance depends mainly upon degrees of coherence and upon the stress and strain it is submitted to as growth continues year after year. It is the tree itself that fashions the bark in all its varied forms and not external elements, though wind, heat, and cold assist in the removal of loosely coherent barks.

In different groups of trees the bark varies enormously in thickness. We have stated that in the Holly no true bark is formed; in the Beech it is firm and smooth, and on trees several hundreds of years old it is scarcely more than half an inch thick; in the Chestnut

Burley Oak, Quercus alba, trunk 18 feet girth, Oak Hill, Danvers, Massachusetts

it is thicker, but in none of our common trees is the bark of any great thickness. In the Mammoth-tree of California it attains its maximum development, being in adult trees often as much as 30 inches thick.

But mere thickness has no bearing on the ornamental character of bark. The White or Paper Birch, often felicitously called "My Lady of the Woods," is known to all by its smooth white bark which peels off in thin layers. No other tree has such pure white bark though many Poplars have pale, yellowish gray bark, smooth except on the lower and older parts. In the River Birch the papery gray-brown bark clings in loose masses of irregular shape. The Beech has smooth, grayish white bark and in the American species in particular the effect from a distance is like white mist. The Hornbeam also has a pale gray bark like the Beech, but rather darker, and on old trees it becomes shallowly fissured. The Red, Silver, and Sugar Maples have smooth, pale gray bark which becomes darker and on old trees fissured.

The deciduous Oaks according to their bark fall into two groups. Many of the White Oaks *(Quercus alba, Q. macrocarpa, Q. bicolor, Q. stellata)* have light gray bark which becomes fissured with age. Others like the European Oak *(Quercus robur)*, and the Red, Black, and Chestnut Oaks of America have dark gray bark, varying from nearly smooth to deeply fissured according to the species. The Chestnut also has dark gray, deeply fissured bark. In the Sweet Birch the bark is smooth and almost black, in the Cherries it is lustrous, chestnut-brown, and peeling. In the Plane and certain Hickories the bark flakes off in plates or strips leaving smooth white or pale brown scars; in Stewartia and the Crepe Myrtle (Lagerstroemia) this is carried to the extreme and the trunks become smooth and polished. The Robinia has a dark, grayish, deeply fissured, fibrous bark, and that of the Elm, Linden, and many other common trees, is dark and irregularly fissured. In the American Honey-locust *(Gleditsia tria-canthos)* the bark is almost black, cracked and fissured, whereas that of its Chinese relative *(G. macracantha)* is quite smooth and pale gray. A similar difference obtains between the Kentucky Coffee-tree and its Chinese congener. In the former the bark is dark, fissured, and rugged, in the latter perfectly smooth and gray-green. Many are familiar with the dark, fissured bark of the valuable Black Walnut but fewer, perhaps, with that of the American Persimmon *(Dios-pyros virginiana)*. In this tree the bark is almost black and is deeply fissured, both longitudinally and transversely, in such manner that the trunk is studded with close-set rectangular knobs which form a perfect mosaic. Among trees I know of only one other, the Korean Cornel *(Cornus coreana)*, that has this peculiar and striking kind of bark. In conclusion it may be said that nearly every kind of tree has its own peculiar form of bark, differing slightly or conspicuously from that of its neighbors. Quite often the bark is remarkable for its color or form, and in winter it is especially attractive and beautiful.

AUTUMN GLORY

N SEPTEMBER, when the beauty of the Aster displaces that of the Goldenrod, when blue and purple transcend the yellow in field and border, the deep green mantle of foliage draping hill and dale, mountain and ravine, streamside and roadside commences to show portentious signs of change. The Pines, Hemlocks and their kin look even darker as the contrast with their deciduous-leaved neighbors becomes stronger. In the swamps, about the last week of August and at the first whiff of autumn in the air, the Red Maple begins to assume a purplish tint and its example is soon followed by other kinds of trees. To all of us the season of the year becomes apparent, warning signs of stern winter's approach increase rapidly, and soon the whole country puts on its gayest mantle of color. The people of the tropics, where monsoon rains are followed by burning heat and where the young unfolding leaves of many forest trees are brightly colored, never enjoy the wonderful feast of color displayed in the forests and countrysides of this and other northern continental areas. They have other things which we may envy them but the autumn tints of leaves are peculiarly our own. The brightly colored Codiaeums of the tropics and of our hothouses, beautiful as they are, do not equal the Red Maple, Sugar Maple, Sassafras, and Tuliptree in the fall. No scene in nature is more delightful than the woods of eastern North America in the fullness of their autumn splendor.

It is a weakness of humans to crave most those things beyond their immediate reach, but the wise among us are content to enjoy those which fall within the scope of every-day life. To revel in the splendid riot of autumn color no long journey has to be undertaken. It is at our very door. From the St. Lawrence Valley and the Canadian lakes southward to the Alleghany Mountains there is displayed each autumn a scene of entrancing beauty not surpassed the world over. Central Europe, Japan, China, and other parts of eastern Asia have their own season of autumn color and each area has an individuality of its own but, if they rival, they cannot surpass the forest scenes of eastern North America.

But wherefore and why all this gay autumnal apparel? Is it the handiwork of the charming fairies and wood-nymphs of our childhood beliefs and nursery days? Surely some guiding hand, some beneficent agency, some lover of mankind must have prepared the scene as the final tableau of the seasons! Of a truth the talent of the Master Artist is unveiled, and the picture surpasses the dreams of those who live in less-favored areas of the world.

Those skilled in the mysteries of organic chemistry and plant physiology tell us that autumn tints are due to chemical changes associated with the storing away of food material and the discharge of certain waste products. This explanation, though matter of fact and disturbing to our youthful belief in fairies and wood-nymphs, opens up a field of inquiry which must tend to enlarge our viewpoint and increase our appreciation of Nature's wonderful methods. We find that all is governed by laws which act and react in such manner as to insure the end and object desired.

Briefly the autumn metamorphosis is effected as follows:

At the approach of winter leaves which cannot withstand frost cease to function as food factories and the residue food substances are conveyed from the leaf-blade into the woody branches or subterranean rootstock and there stored, chiefly in the form of starch, until the season of growth recommences the following spring. The leaves from which everything useful has been transported form

BENJAMIN FIG, FICUS BENJAMINA, 100 FEET TALL, TRUNK 27 FEET GIRTH, SPREAD 140 FEET, LAL-BAGH, BANGALORE, INDIA

nothing more than a mere framework of cell-chambers containing merely waste products, such as crystals of calcium-oxalate, which are thrown off with the leaves and help to enrich the soil. But while the process of food evacuation is going on other changes take place. In many plants a chemical substance, known technically as anthocyanin, is produced in the leaves and often to such an extent as to become plainly visible on the exterior. It appears red in the presence of free acids in the cell-sap, blue when no acids are present, and violet when the quantity of acids is small. In a great many leaves the bodies which contain the green coloring matter become changed to yellow granules while the evacuation of food substances is in process. Sometimes these granules are very few and anthocyanin is absent, then the leaf exhibits little outward change except losing its freshness before it falls. In others the yellow granules are abundantly developed, and if anthocyanin is absent or nearly so the whole leaf assumes a clear yellow hue. If there is an abundance of yellow granules together with free acids and anthocyanin the leaf assumes an orange color. Thus the leaf at the period of autumnal change by the presence of these substances in a greater or lesser degree loses its green hue and becomes brown or yellow, crimson or orange, purple or red. The play of color is greater according to the number of species and individuals associated together in a particular spot. But the greatest display of color is seen when the neighborhood is sprinkled with trees having evergreen foliage, when it often happens that a relatively small area of woodland appears decked in all the colors of the rainbow.

The most casual observer knows that all trees do not assume tinted foliage in autumn. Some, like the Alder, the Black Locust (Robinia), the Elder, and most Willows exhibit little or no change save, perhaps, a number of yellow leaves scattered through the green before the fall. But this group is relatively small and only adds additional contrast to the landscape. Again, plants whose leaves are covered with silky or woolly hairs or with a felted mat of hairs never present any autumn coloring, and in those in which the green color disappears the change is to pale gray and white.

In a rather large group of trees which includes the Walnut, Butternut, Catalpa, Elm, Hickory, Chestnut, Horsechestnut, Linden, Button-tree, Gray Birch, and others, the tints are a general mixture of rusty green and yellow and, occasionally, pure yellow under favorable circumstances. In the Poplar, Tulip-tree, Honey-locust (Gleditsia), Mulberry, Maidenhair-tree or Ginkgo, Beech, and most of the Birches, the leaves change to pure yellow of different shades. In none of the above-mentioned groups is purple or red of any shade developed.

In favorable years the American or White Ash *(Fraxinus americana)* is unique in its tints passing through all shades from a dark chocolate to violet, clear brown, and salmon but it has no reds.

The Peach, Plum, Pear, Apple, Quince, Cherry, Mountain Ash, Hawthorn, and the Silver Maple, have a predominance of green with a slight or considerable admixture of purple, red, and yellow, and individuals are frequently strikingly brilliant. In another group purple, crimson, and scarlet, with only a slight admixture of yellow if any, obtain. Here are the Tupelo, Scarlet Oak, White Oak, Sumach, Viburnum, Sorrel-tree, Cornel, and many other trees. A final group—to which belong the Red, Sugar, Striped, and Mountain Maples, the Smoke-tree (Cotinus), Poison Dogwood, Sassafras and the Shadbush or Snowy Mespilus—has variegated tints comprising all shades of purple, crimson, scarlet, orange, and yellow on the same or different individuals of the same species. Often the leaves are tinted and sometimes figured like the wings of a butterfly.

Careful observers will note that the gradations of autumn tints in all cases are in order of those of sunrise; from darker to lighter hues, and never the reverse. The brown leaves which long persist on some trees (Beech, Chestnut, Hornbeam and certain Oaks), though darker than the yellow or orange from which they often turn, are no exception, since these leaves are dead and the brown color is only assumed after vitality has vanished.

Some species are perfectly uniform in their colors; others, on the contrary, display a very wide range of color. For example, the Maidenhair-tree, the Tulip-tree, and Birch are invariably yellow; the Tupelo, Sumach, and White Oak chiefly red, while Maples are of as many colors as if they were of different species. But each individual tree shows nearly the same tints every year even as an Apple-tree bears fruit of the same tints from year to year.

The Red Maple *(Acer rubrum)*, so abundant in swamp and wood, roadside, and on dry hilltop, is the crowning glory of a New England autumn. By the last week of August it commences to assume a purplish hue; sometimes a solitary branch is tinted, frequently the coloring process begins at the top of the tree and the purple crown of autumn is placed on the green brow of summer. Trees growing side by side are seldom alike, and in a group may be seen almost as many shades of color as there are trees. Some are entirely yellow, others scarlet, some crimson, purple, or orange, others variegated with several of these colors. Indeed, on different individuals in the Red Maple may be seen all the hues that are ever displayed in the autumn woods. The Sugar Maple *(Acer saccharum)*, though more brilliant, has a narrower range of color and is more uniform in its tints, which range from yellow and orange to scarlet.

The common Tupelo *(Nyssa sylvatica)* more invariably shows a mass of unmixed crimson than any other New England tree. The foliage first assumes shades of purple which change into crimson or scarlet before it falls.

The Oaks, the noblest group of trees in eastern North America, assume their autumn tints very late and are not at their zenith until after those of the Maples have past. In the Scarlet, Red and White Oaks the tints are ruddy, varying from reddish purple and crimson to pale red, and when at their best, after the middle of October, these trees are the most beautiful of the forests and pastures. The Black and Swamp Oaks develop imperfect shades of orange to leather-colored tints.

In the White Oak, the Beech, the Chestnut, and the Red Oak when young, the leaves as they die become russet-brown, and, remaining on the trees through the winter, give a sensation of warmth to the woods and landscape in the coldest days of winter. The period of retention varies greatly in different individuals; often the leaves are retained on the lower branches when the upper parts of the tree are bare.

In Great Britain the native trees, with few exceptions, such as the wild Cherries and Beech, assume no autumn tints comparable with those of their American relatives. Indeed, in England the most varied and brightly colored tints are found not on the indigenous trees but on the Brambles (Rubus). Long ago many English trees were planted in eastern North America and some, like the Elm, Linden, and Oak, have grown to a large or moderately large size. In autumn such trees stand out very clearly with their mantle of green foliage when the native trees around are of all tints or have shed their leaves. These English colonists preserve their green hues until late into October when finally the leaves become mottled, yellowish or brownish, and fall.

The Asiatic trees in cultivation assume their wonted tints, and

BAOBAB, ADANSONIA DIGITATA, 100 FEET TALL, TRUNK 40 FEET GIRTH.
VICTORIA FALLS, RHODESIA, SOUTH AFRICA

so also do those of central Europe. The trees of Japan and China color with us rather later than the native trees and lengthen the season of color fully two weeks.

In Japan, where an intense love of nature is innate among all classes, there prevails a custom which might well be adopted in other lands. The beauty spots in that country are many and are justly celebrated in poetry and song; august Fuji-san with its perfect cone and snowy mantle; the Pine-clad islets of Matsushima; the Inland Sea with its hundreds of islands clad with verdure to the water's edge; the Nikko region with its mountains and lakes, its waterfalls and woods, and hundreds of other places more or less famous. In October, when the woods assume their autumn splendor, children from primary and secondary schools, high schools, and colleges with their teachers and professors make excursions of three or four days' duration to noted places and revel in the feast of color. The railways offer cheap fares and from all the large towns and cities children, youths, and maidens journey to the mountain woods. In the autumn in the Nikko region I have seen thousands of scholars, boys and girls varying from eight to twenty years of age (and a happy, orderly throng they were), enjoying to the full the scenery, breathing in the freshest of mountain air, and building up healthy minds and bodies. Their joyousness was wholesomely infectious and it was good to mingle with them. As I look back on the many pleasant experiences I have enjoyed in that pleasing land none gives me greater pleasure than the memories of those throngs of happy scholars in the woods and woodland paths of Nikko, Chuzenji, and Yumoto.

Autumn tints is a subject that belongs more to the sphere of the artist than to that of the scientist; the poet can sing their song more easily than a writer of prose can describe their beauty; yet, equally with all, ordinary folk can enjoy their splendor. Let us then in autumn time lay aside for a brief moment the cares of life; let us break away from engrossing tasks of every kind and linger for a while among the trees and shrubs of the roadside and woodland, drink in cool draughts of fresh air, and revel in the galaxy of color beneficent Nature so lavishly displays on every side.

PATRIARCHAL GINKGO

HE oldest existing type of tree, a veritable living fossil, is the Ginkgo or Maidenhair-tree. It is the sole survivor of a family, rich in species, which was distributed over the temperate regions of both the northern and southern hemispheres when the Terrible Lizards (Dinosauria and Iguanodon), the Winged Lizards (Pterodactylus, possible ancestors of our birds) and the Paddle-bearing Lizards (Plesiosaurus) roamed the earth, and whose fossil remains, so plentiful in the rocks of Wyoming, North and South Dakota, Kansas, Texas, and elsewhere, alone remain to tell of their existence. The fossil evidence is insufficient to prove the existence of the Ginkgo in the age of the coal measures (Carboniferous period), but as fossils from Virginia show there is a strong suspicion of its presence in the next (Permian). From the Triassic rocks (the oldest group of Secondary period) several species of Ginkgo have been described from Australia, and it seems fairly certain that during this epoch the tree flourished in the southern hemisphere. In the strata of the Jurassic or Reptile Age the Ginkgo is abundantly present in America, Asia, and Europe. From rocks of this age in Canada, China, Japan, Germany, and Great Britain northward to Greenland, Siberia, and Franz-Josef-Land many fossil species have been described. In some the leaves are quite indistinguishable from those of the existing species and from the rocks of the Chalk Age of North America, Greenland, and Vancouver Island, fossil species have been named which are probably identical with that living today. From the Tertiary period, fossils of several species have been described from widely separated parts

41

of the northern hemisphere, and it may be concluded with approximate certainty that the living *Ginkgo biloba* flourished at that period; also that it was a common tree in the present temperate and circumpolar regions of the whole northern hemisphere.

The close of the Tertiary period was marked by a glacial epoch which, in Europe and North America in particular, destroyed much of the vegetation. In eastern North America the ice-cap extended as far south as Philadelphia (Lat. 40° N.) as the scarred rocks, erratic boulders, and detritus amply testify. This ice-cap did not reach any part of China, Korea, or Japan, though, of course, the climate there was very considerably modified by its influence. The glaciation of North America, Greenland, Europe and western Siberia probably caused the extinction of the Ginkgo in those lands, whereas in the Orient, thanks to the milder climate that obtained, it survived. But be the explanation what it may, the record of the rocks demonstrates both the antiquity and wide geographical range of the Ginkgo-tree down to the Tertiary glacial epoch. Today, the Ginkgo, statements to the contrary notwithstanding, no longer exists in a wild state, and there is no authentic record of its ever having been seen growing spontaneously. Travelers of repute of many nationalities have searched for it far and wide in the Orient but none has succeeded in solving the secret of its home. Once or twice the statement has been made that it "was seen wild" in northern Japan, in western or eastern China, or in Korea, but subsequent visits by those competent to judge have proved the authors of such statements at fault in their identification of the tree, or misled and hasty in their judgments. In Japan, Korea, southern Manchuria, and in China proper it is known as a planted tree only, and usually in association with religious buildings, palaces, tombs, and old historic or geomantic sites. While excessive cold may reasonably explain its disappearance from much of the northern hemisphere, it does not account for its absence in a wild state in the Orient, where fossil evidence proves its presence in epochs coeval with those of America and Europe. Having successfully withstood varying conditions throughout an inconceivable period of time, as the geological record demonstrates, it seems strange that this tree should so comparatively recently have disappeared. What caused its disappearance we shall never know, but the same has happened to billions upon billions of organic forms since first progressive organic development began.

The earliest known mention of the Ginkgo in books is in a Chinese work on agriculture which dates from the Eighth Century of our era. At the beginning of 1000 A.D. the fruit was taken as tribute by the newly established Sung dynasty. In the great Chinese Herbal, issued in 1578, the author calls it the Ya-chio-tzu, which signifies "the tree with leaves like a duck's foot" and is quite descriptive. This old name may be in use in parts of China today, but I never heard it; those in general use in those parts of the Flowery Land I traveled are Yin-kuo-tsu (Silver nut-tree) and Pai-kuo-tzu (White nut-tree). In Korea it is known as Eun Haing-namou which is simply the Korean rendering of the Chinese name. In Japan the tree is known as the I-cho, and the fruit as Gin-nan, which again is a translation of its Chinese name. The tree reached Japan with Buddhism in the Sixth Century of the Christian era and Ginkgo is simply the Japanese rendering of the Chinese name Yin-kou. In this connection it must be remembered that the Chinese ideograph and Chinese literature were adopted by the Japanese long, long ago. The best authorities claim that the first Chinese books were brought to Japan in 285 A.D., that Buddhism was introduced from China via Korea in 552, and that the Chinese calendar was introduced in 602. It is, of course, possible that the Ginkgo in those early days existed as a wild tree in the forests of Japan, but it may be assumed with almost absolute certainty that in any case it was brought to Japan by Korean and Chinese Buddhist monks and planted by them in the earliest days of their proselytizing. Many of the magnificent old Ginkgo trees in Japan are claimed to be more than a thousand years old and there is no valid reason for disputing the statement.

We of the West owe our first knowledge of the Ginkgo-tree to Engelbert Kaempfer, who, as a surgeon in the service of the old Dutch East-India Company, visited Japan in 1682 and made an overland journey from Nagasaki to Tokyo. He returned to Europe in 1694 and published a book in 1712 in which he gives a good figure of the Ginkgo. In 1771, an Englishman named Gordon, sent a living plant of it to the great Linnaeus who adopted Kaempfer's name for the generic title of the tree, calling it *Ginkgo biloba*. In 1796 an English botanist, one Smith, renamed it *Salisburia adiantifolia* on the grounds that Linnaeus' name was "equally uncouth and barbarous." This act of pedantry was very properly objected to and Smith's name was abandoned for the older and legitimate one given by Linnaeus.

The Ginkgo tree was first introduced into Europe by the Dutch, some time between 1727 and 1737, and planted in the Botanic Garden at Utrecht, but the date is uncertain. It came to England between 1752 and 1754, presumably by seeds brought direct from Japan and the first tree to flower in Europe was in Kew Gardens in 1795. This proved to be a male. The famous Jacquin planted a tree in Vienna about 1768, and this when it flowered, proved to be a male also. Of its first introduction to France the following interesting story is on record as related by Mons. Andre Thouin, when delivering his annual Cours d' Agriculture Pratique in the Jardin des Plantes, Paris. In 1780 a Parisian amateur named Mons. Petigny voyaged to London in order to see the principal gardens there. Among those he visited was that of a nurseryman who possessed five young Ginkgo

MAIDENHAIR-TREE, GINKGO BILOBA, 90 FEET TALL, TRUNK 24 FEET GIRTH, KIATING FU, W. CHINA

SPLIT TRUNK OF GINKGO BILOBA WITH KEAKI-TREE, ZELKOVA SERRATA, IN CLEFT,
TRUNK 15 FEET GIRTH, NARA, JAPAN

plants, all in one pot, raised from seeds received from Japan. The plants were very rare and the nurseryman valued them highly, but after abundant hospitality, in which wine was not omitted, he parted with them for twenty-five guineas which the Frenchman promptly paid, and lost no time in taking away his valuable acquisition. Next morning the Englishman's generosity of spirit induced by the wine was replaced by a keen sense of business acumen and he bewailed his loss of the five Ginkgo plants. He sought out Mons. Petigny and tried to buy them back, finally offering for a single one the twenty-five guineas he had received for the five. The Frenchman refused and carried the plants to France. His story of outwitting a native of perfidious Albion was much enjoyed in Paris, and, as each plant had cost him about 120 francs or 40 crowns, the tree was christened "Arbre aux quarante ecus."

Most of the older trees in France are said to have been derived from the above five, but Sir Joseph Banks, in 1788, gave to Broussonet a Ginkgo plant which he sent to Professor Gouan of the Montpellier Botanic Garden where it was planted. In 1790, an English amateur named Blake, sent a Ginkgo plant to Mons. Gaussen de Chapeau-rouge who had a garden at Bourdigny, a village two leagues from Geneva, Switzerland, where he cultivated many rare trees. This tree is historical. It proved to be a female, the discovery being made by August Pyramus de Candolle in 1814, and scions from it were distributed over Europe by its discoverer and grafted on the male trees, including those at Vienna and Montpellier. In fact, all the fruiting trees in Europe up to 1882 are believed to have originated by grafting from the tree near Geneva. As one result the tree at Montpellier produced perfect fruit for the first time in Europe in 1835. The original female tree at Bourdigny was cut down before 1866 by order of a new proprietor who cared nothing for trees.

The introduction of the Maidenhair-tree to America is said to be due to William Hamilton who obtained it from England in 1784 and planted it in his garden at Woodlands, near Philadelphia, where it grows today though the garden itself has become a cemetery. In the first years of the Nineteenth Century it was planted by Doctor Hosack at Hyde Park on the banks of the Hudson River. On the north side of Boston Common grows a historic Ginkgo which probably came direct from China. It is said to have been a tree of "full size when Mr. Gardiner Greene purchased the garden in 1798." The site of the garden is now occupied by the Court House in Pemberton Square. After Mr. Greene's death in 1832, the grounds were sold and the tree moved to its present position in 1835. The city paid a portion of the cost and each of Mr. Greene's children contributed one hundred dollars. The tree when moved was 40 feet tall and 4 feet in girth of trunk. Those were times of great financial stringency, and there was some opposition to the spending of public money on moving a tree. The talk was considerable and the famous physician, Dr. Jacob Bigelow, a friend of Gardiner Greene, and himself mainly responsible for saving the tree, wrote a lengthy and amusing poem on the incident, beginning:

> Thou queer, outlandish, fan-leaved tree,
> Whose grandfather came o'er the sea
>   A pilgrim of the ocean,
> Didst thou expect to gather gear
> By selling out thy chopsticks here!

In China the Ginkgo as a planted tree is associated with Chinese civilization almost throughout the length and breadth of the kingdom, but where I have seen it most plentiful is in the western province of Szechuan. There I saw the most perfect specimen of a Ginkgo-tree imaginable. It was growing a few miles above the city of Kiating on the left bank of the Min River, and in 1908 was about 100 feet tall, had a symmetrical, narrow-oval crown with branches almost sweeping the ground, and a trunk 24 feet in girth.

I have seen other trees with larger trunks but never one quite so tall or so lovely in form. In the grounds of the Yellow Dragon Temple at Kuling, a summer resort in the Lushan Mountains behind Kiukiang on the Yangtsze River, grows a famous old Ginkgo not especially tall (about 70 feet) but with a trunk 25 feet in girth. A little to the west of Shanghai in a district unfrequented by foreigners the late Frank N. Meyer, plant explorer in China for the United States Department of Agriculture, found the Ginkgo to be common and used for fuel, and he suggested that it might be truly wild there. Meyer's opinion is more worthy of respect than those of many other travelers who have made similar assertions but I am an unconvinced sceptic. A Russian botanist, Dr. Alexander von Bunge, who accompanied the eleventh Ecclesiastical Mission sent by the Russian Government to Peking in 1830, tells of seeing a Ginkgo-tree near Peking "of prodigious height and 40 feet in circumference."

In Korea, especially in Keijyo, the capital city, grow fine specimens of the Ginkgo trees from 80 to 90 feet tall and from 18 to 20 feet in girth of trunk being fairly common. In the courtyard of Choanji Temple in the Diamond Mountains, a Buddhist sanctuary and one of the loveliest spots on earth, there is a fine old specimen some 80 feet tall and 14 feet in girth of trunk and with abundant sprouts. The most northerly place in which I saw the Ginkgo growing in Korea was about 40 miles east of Gensan. The Koreans claim that one may sit on the ground beneath the shade of a Ginkgo tree and not be pestered with ants, but my experience does not support this claim.

It is in Japan and in the city of Tokyo, however, that I have seen the finest average trees and the greatest in size of trunk. Every park, temple ground, and palace yard has its Ginkgo-tree which is usually of great size. There are handsome specimens in Hibya and Shiba parks, but the best I saw grows in Koyenji temple grounds and is about 85 feet tall and 28 feet in girth of trunk. In the grounds of the Zanpukuji Temple in Azabu, Tokyo, there is a grand old tree with a trunk 30 feet in girth but the top has been broken off by a storm. In the Imperial Botanic Gardens in Koishikawa, Tokyo, grows the Ginkgo-tree on which Professor S. Hirase in 1896 carried out the experiments which led to his remarkable discovery of the motile male sperms. At the Hachiman shrine in Kamakura there is a Ginkgo, said to be more than a thousand years old, about 20 feet in girth of trunk. In the old capital of Kyoto the tree is common, and in the courtyard of the Nishi-Hongwanji there is an old tree, much broken by storms and some 15 feet in girth of trunk, which is supposed to protect the temple against fire by discharging showers of water whenever a conflagration in the vicinity threatens danger. In the old Eighth Century capital Nara, and quite near the hotel, there is an extraordinary Ginkgo out of which is growing a Keaki-tree (*Zelkova serrata*) with a trunk 8 feet in girth. It evidently originated from a seed planted in a fissure of the Ginkgo-tree by the wind or by a bird. The trees are about equal height (75 feet) and the composite trunk is 15 feet in girth. It is entitled to rank among the marvels of Japan for it looks as if two trees had been grafted together. Of course, no organic union between two trees representing almost the poles of the vegetable kingdom is possible, but they thrive together harmoniously.

On the massive lower branches of old Ginkgo trees thick, peg-like structures develop which grow downward and on reaching the ground develop true roots from their apex and give off branches above. The growths are often very numerous and are sometimes as much as from 12 to 16 feet long and one foot in diameter. This phenomenon is rare in China and Korea, but it is common in Japan where the growths are styled chi-chi; that is, teats or nipples. Their true character is not properly understood but evidently they serve to prolong the life of the tree by developing new stems and branches.

From the trunks of old trees many sprouts develop which sometimes form a veritable thicket of ascending stems. If the top of the tree be broken, as frequently happens in the long life of the tree, new shoots arise, grow upward, and make a new crown. The vitality of the tree is marvelous and Mother Nature seems to have endowed it with a thousand and one means of maintaining its existence. I never saw a dead Ginkgo during the twenty years I traveled in the Far East.

Japanese gardeners raise many seedlings in a pot or pan and use them for table decorations, but as a dwarf tree the Ginkgo is not much in request in Japan.

As far as authentic records go the oldest Ginkgo trees in this country are the two in Woodlands Cemetery, Philadelphia, which were planted by William Hamilton in 1784. The largest, a male, measures 7 feet 7 inches in girth of trunk; the other is female and measures 6 feet 6 inches in girth. Both are fully 75 feet tall and in vigorous health. The late Professor Harsberger, to whom I am indebted for the above measurements, thought the Ginkgo in the old Bartram Garden in West Philadelphia the oldest and the first planted in America, basing his opinion on the facts that this garden is older than that founded by Hamilton and that the tree is larger, being 9 feet 3 inches in girth. I have told of the old tree on Boston Common and in the Public Gardens of Boston there are a number of fine trees, the best being 60 feet tall and 7 feet in girth of trunk. In Mount Auburn Cemetery, Cambridge, Massachusetts, there is a handsome specimen, probably planted under the direction of Dr. Jacob Bigelow soon after the cemetery was started, which the Superintendent, Mr. John Peterson, kindly informs me is about 88 feet high and 7 feet 11 inches in girth at five feet from the ground.

Unfortunately, the symmetry of the tree was spoiled some years ago by a storm which broke off one of the principal branches. In the Missouri Botanic Garden, St. Louis, grows a fine Ginkgo-tree, which is about 65 feet tall and 7 feet in girth. Probably the largest and best Ginkgo in this country is at Hyde Park, on the Hudson, New York, which as before stated was planted very early in the Nineteenth Century by Doctor Hosack. In a letter, the present owner, F. W. Vanderbilt, Esq., courteously informed me "that it measures 11 feet 2 inches around the trunk two feet from the ground just where the branches begin to spread, 11 feet 1 inch at six inches from the ground, 70 feet spread from tips of branches, and the height from 80 feet to 85 feet. This tree is in splendid condition and vigorously healthy. It is always perfectly clean and has never had a dead branch on it of even the smallest size and the tree has never required spraying during the twenty-four years I have been here."

Perhaps the best known Maidenhair trees in America are those forming the avenue in the Department of Agriculture grounds, Washington, D. C. There are some ninety trees in the avenue and on the curves of the drive which lead into the avenue. The trees were all planted at the same time but vary greatly in size. The tallest is about 52 feet and a good many of them are about 48 feet in height, the average being about 40 feet tall; in girth they vary from 2½ feet to 7½ feet. In the parks of Minneapolis, Minnesota, the Superintendent, Mr. Theodore Wirth, tells me that the Ginkgo is hardy but that so far they have not found a satisfactory place for it. As to its behavior in Canada, Mr. W. T. Macoun, Dominion Horticulturist, obligingly informs me that he has "seen very few specimens of this tree in Canada, but we have been growing it here for twenty-five years and there are a few specimens on the grounds of about that age. They are from 25 to 30 feet high, and, although rather slow in growth may be considered, I think, perfectly hardy although occasionally the tips kill back. So far as I know they are not grown in any colder part of Canada. The winter of 1917-18 was the most trying on both fruit trees and ornamental trees that we have experienced in thirty years, but the Ginkgo was not injured. During that winter it was below zero on fifty-seven days, the lowest temperature being thirty-one below zero, Fahrenheit. We have tested the Ginkgo in our prairie provinces but it has not proved hardy there." On the Pacific seaboard I do not remember any remarkable trees, and a friend in Oregon to whom I wrote tells me that they do not seem happy in the neighborhood of Portland.

The first tree to fruit in this country was probably one in the grounds of the Kentucky Military Institution, in 1878, and seeds from this tree were sent to the Arnold Arboretum. Trees in Central Park, New York City, have fruited for a number of years past. So, too, have those in Washington, D. C., and others in various parts of the country.

In England, the tallest Maidenhair-tree is said to grow at Melbury, Dorchester, which in 1904 was more than 80 feet tall, but the best known example is that in Kew Gardens, a male tree, 64 feet 9 inches tall and 10 feet 7 inches in girth of trunk. At Frogmore, one of the gardens belonging to England's King, there is a Ginkgo-tree which in 1904 measured 74 feet in height and 9 feet 3 inches in girth of trunk. At Blaize Castle, near Bristol, there is a tree 68 feet tall and 9 feet 3 inches in girth of trunk. It is graceful in habit and said to have come from Japan on the same ship with the one at Kew and another in the Bishop's garden at Wells, Somersetshire. In Wales the finest example known is at Morgan Park, Glamorganshire, which in 1904 was about 70 feet tall and 6 feet in girth of trunk.

On the continent of Europe, where the climate is apparently

more to the tree's liking„ many magnificent Ginkgos may be seen.
In the Botanic Garden at Milan there are handsome specimens; growing in the old botanical garden at Geneva is a male and a female
tree planted in 1815; in 1905 the male measured 86 feet high and
4 feet 10 inches in girth of trunk and is straight and upright in
habit; the female, which bears good seed, is much smaller.

It is hardy in New England as far north as Hanover, New Hampshire, is unaffected by summer drought, and thrives under city conditions as well as in the pure air of the country; it is not known to
be attacked by any pest, insect or fungoid, and lives to a great age.
It transplants readily when of large size, as the tree on Boston
Common testifies. The Japanese think nothing of moving trees 40
feet tall and more than a foot in diameter of trunk. An avenue of
Ginkgo trees of this size was planted in 1914 on the boulevard leading from the terminal station in Tokyo and not one died. However,
in this connection it must be remembered that Japan enjoys a more
generous summer rainfall than North America does.

It is claimed that in Europe the Ginkgo will live outdoors as
far north as Viborg in Finland (Lat. 60° 45′ N.) and that
it thrives in Riga (Lat. 56° 57′ N.). In Norway, in the Botanic
Gardens at Christiania, it has grown outdoors on a wall facing
east since 1839. In southern Sweden, in Skaone, and on Gothland,
it grows well, and in Denmark it thrives in many gardens.

Apart from the typical tree there is a form *(pendula)* with
pendent branchlets; another *(fastigiata)* with upright growing
branches; a third *(variegata)* has leaves blotched and streaked with
pale yellow, and a fourth *(macrophylla)* is characterized by its
larger, more deeply cut leaves. The pendulous and upright forms
are worth cultivating, but the other two have nothing to recommend
them except that they are curious.

This sole survivor of an extensive family in prehistoric ages of the earth's history is quite unique among existing trees. It boasts a whole catalogue of peculiarities and is not closely related to any living family or group in the whole vegetable kingdom. Its leaves resemble the pinnae of the common Maidenhair Fern; its plum-like fruit is not a fruit in the true botanical sense of the term but is a naked seed somewhat resembling that of the California Nutmeg *(Torreya californica)* or that of the Cycads; it is fertilized by a motile sperm like the Cycads, Ferns, and Club Mosses; its shoots are of two forms like those of the larches and like them it loses its leaves in autumn. But whilst it possesses these points of similarity it is closely related to none and constitutes a family of its own which forms an obscure connecting link between the Yew family, the Cycads, the Ferns and their allies.

At maturity the Ginkgo is a stately tree 100 feet or more tall with a cylindric, slightly tapering trunk sometimes 30 feet in girth at breast height above the ground. Young free-growing trees commonly have their primary branches radiating in clusters (false whorls) from the stem, tier above tier, and the outline of the tree is distinctly spire-like. Very rarely does this habit obtain at ripe old age. Most usually the crown is made up of several massive, ascending and ascending-spreading branches and innumerable irregularly disposed, but more or less horizontally-spreading, often semi-pendent, branchlets. In such trees the habit is from loosely pyramidal to more or less conical. Round-headed trees are not uncommon but a flat-headed one I have never seen. The branches are rigid and when clothed with leaves decidedly plumose in appearance. The bark on the trunk is from pale to dark gray, somewhat corky, and fissured into ridges of irregular shape. The wood is white or yellowish white and is not differentiated into heartwood and sapwood; it is finely grained, something like that of a Maple, is easily worked, but is of no great value. In Japan it is used as a ground work for lacquer-ware and for making chess-boards and chessmen.

The leaves are quite unlike those of any other tree or shrub and are unique in their fan-like shape; they are stalked, have no midrib but many forked veins and no cross veinlets; the apex is irregularly crenate and usually cleft, more or less deeply, into two or more lobes. In bud the leaves are folded together not rolled up crozier-like as in the Ferns; they are scattered on the long free-shoots and crowded at the apex of the short, spur-like branches. In size they vary from 2 to 3 inches in width on the spurs, but on the free-shoots, and especially those which freely develop from the base of the trunks of old trees, they are sometimes from 6 to 8 inches broad, and are bright, grass-green when young, and dull green at maturity. They are leathery in texture, and in the autumn assume an unvarying tint of clear yellow before they fall. In China the leaves are sometimes placed in books as a preservative against insects. In the Orient the lovely yellow autumn foliage renders the trees most conspicuous, and after the fall of the leaf they are easily recognized by their rather stiff and decidedly stately appearance.

The trees bear either male or female flowers but the two sexes are never found on one and the same individual unless deliberately grafted together. In some books it is claimed that the "male trees are pyramidal and upright in habit, the ascending branches of free and vigorous growth"; that the "female trees are more compact in habit, more richly branched below and the branches sometimes becoming even pendent." Personally I have not found it possible to determine the sex of the tree by its habit and the many Japanese, Koreans, and Chinese whom I have questioned on this point assert that it is utterly impossible to do so. Could some reliable means of distinguishing the male from the female trees be found it would be of considerable value, for as an avenue tree the female, on account of the evil smell of its ripe seed, is not desirable, as the people of Washington, D. C., will testify. The flowers are developed from among the leaves at the end of April or beginning of May; the males in arching catkins, superficially not unlike those of the Oak but rather stouter and less pendent; the females in pairs on the apex of slender footstalks, each flower consisting of a minute, globuse little body tipped by a short point and subtended at the base by a cup-shaped swelling. Indeed, they are very like the flowers of some Oaks *(Quercus glauca,* a Japanese species, for example). The pollen is scattered by the wind and settles on the tip of the female flower, after which the cup grows up and encloses the globose body. Fecundation takes place early in September, being preceded by many changes within the growing nut-like body which culminate in the development of a motile male sperm from the pollen and an egg cell in the female flower. Their union consummates fecundation. The development of the embryo takes place early in November when the seed is full grown, yellow in color, and ready to fall. Often, indeed, the development of the embryo does not take place until the seed has actually fallen to the ground. If one asks *why* this essential is so long delayed no answer is forthcoming. Two or three embryos are sometimes developed in one seed. The seeds germinate in the following spring and the manner is very like that of the Oak, the thick fleshy cotyledons (seed leaves) with their food stores for the developing young plant remain under or on the ground; the primary leaf-scales are 3-seriate.

But we are getting ahead of our story for we have omitted to describe the plum-like fruit which, as stated before, is not a true fruit but is a naked seed. It is a round, bright orange-yellow, about an inch in diameter, and consists of a thin, outer fleshy layer, like a plum, covering a pointed oval nut from one-half to three-quarters of an inch long, keeled lengthwise on both sides, with a smooth, fragile white shell enclosing a soft kernel. On or soon after falling to the ground the fleshy covering splits and emits a most offensive, nay, abominable odor. If the ripe seeds are handled or touch one's clothing the odor is not eradicated for a day or more. This penetrating offensive smell is due to a peculiar crystallizable, fatty acid, akin to butric acid, which was first extracted about 1830 and named ginkgoic acid. When extracted it forms tufts of acicular crystals, brownish yellow in color. It is easily soluble in alcohol or ether and in either case exhibits a strong acid reaction; when heated with a solution of potash it forms a soap-like compound. I do not know if any attempt to use this ginkgoic acid in the arts and sciences has been made.

The nuts, denuded of their offensive pulp and washed, are pure white, and are on sale in most of the market towns in China and Japan, and in a lesser degree in those of Manchuria and Korea. They are known in China as "Pai-kuo" or "Yin-kuo" (white or silver nuts) and after roasting are eaten at banquets, weddings, and convivial gatherings generally, being supposed to promote digestion and to diminish the effects of wine. There is told a story of their being introduced, on one occasion at least, by Chinese to a mining camp in north Australia, rubbed with some bad scent to imitate Tonquin beans and sold as such. Their avowed virtue was to destroy moths but for such purpose they and also the true Tonquin Bean (the seed of *Dipteryx odorata,* a tree native of Guiana and belonging to the Pea family) are equally worthless. In the Orient these ginkgo nuts are still an important commodity, but formerly they were even more so. Pallas, a famous Russian botanist, visited the market town of Mai-mai-chang, opposite Kiakhta in Mongolia, in 1772 and saw there the nuts on sale. They had been brought from Peking.

That the Ginkgo has been closely identified with Buddhist

institutions from early times, and by adherents and missionaries of this religion planted wherever they have obtained a stronghold in the Orient, is beyond question. It may not be too much to say that its very existence today is due to the adherents of this faith. Very probably they found it in some way associated with Taoism and other forms of nature worship which were current in China when first they established their faith there and with the tolerant catholicism which characterized the early fathers of this religion, adopted it as their own. But whatever the actual motive which induced the Buddhists and other religious sects to protect and preserve by wide planting the Ginkgo-tree it may safely be inferred that its edible nuts played no important part. In fact, the Ginkgo is the oldest cultivated nut tree.

JEHOVAH'S TREE, THE CEDAR
OF LEBANON

HE Holy Land has undergone many vicissitudes from early biblical times down to its deliverance from the Turks by General Allenby in October, 1918. The very aspect of the country has changed enormously in the few thousand years of its record as set forth in Holy Scripture. It is true that the physiognomy of every country is based primarily on its geological structure, that is, on the character and arrangement of its rock masses, but the clothing of its stony skeleton and its numberless modifications of external form and color are due to its vegetable life. More than skies and clouds, more than villages or hills, more than sentient creatures of high or low degree, the trees, shrubs, and herbs of a land give character to its scenery, impressing the mind by their grandeur, or charming it by their beauty. Denuded of its vegetable growth the very skeleton of a country changes and decays; even the skies and clouds are altered. How great the changes that have taken place in Palestine we can but faintly imagine, but many of the trees mentioned in the Bible still grow there if in much reduced numbers. On Lebanon grow the Cedars in all their pristine majesty, but vastly fewer in number than in the days when Baalam compared the far-stretching encampments of the Israelite tribes in the Jordan valley to "cedar trees beside the waters."

Whether the word "cedar" in the Old Testament connotes one or many kinds of trees may be left to the biblical critics and Hebraists, but there is ample and unmistakable proof that the Cedar of

58

LEBANON CEDAR, CEDRUS LIBANI, LEBANON MOUNTAINS, SYRIA

ATLAS CEDAR, CEDRUS ATLANTICA, TENIET-EL-HAAD, ALGERIA

Lebanon was well known to the Prophets and other teachers of the old Hebrews. By their poets, as every Bible reader knows, the Cedar forests of Lebanon were regarded with sacred awe. They were the type of power and majesty, of grandeur and beauty, of strength and permanence; as "trees of Jehovah planted by His right hand crowning the great mountains"; masterpieces in lofty stature, wide-spreading shade, perpetual verdure, refreshing perfume, and unfailing fruitfulness. Some of the finest imagery in Old Testament song is drawn from this oft-frequented source. The mighty conquerors of olden days, the despots of Assyria, the Pharaohs of Egypt, the proud and idolatrous monarchs of Judah, the Hebrew Commonwealth itself, the warlike Amorites of patriarchal times, and the moral majesty of the Messianic Age, are all compared to the towering Cedar in its regal loftiness and supremacy. Its huge trunk, massive branches, great height, wide-spreading, tabular, densely umbrageous crown, dark green at all seasons, are so well known that they have been condensed into the phrase "cedar-like," in common use today by writers who wish to portray the general aspect of certain trees. Further, the color, character, and peculiar fragrance of the wood frequently mentioned by Old Testament writers lead, both in ancient and modern times, to the name "cedar" being given wide application. Today it is applied to a variety of trees, some closely and others very remotely related to the true Cedars. In fact, nowadays its use is far too ambiguous and connotes little besides character of wood and perhaps fragrance. It is, however, an unconscious tribute to the reputation of the Cedar of Lebanon so deeply established in the minds of mankind and, perhaps, the most venerated natural monument in the world.

In modern times many distinguished travelers and men of science have visited the Cedar of Lebanon in its home and their story, old yet ever new, has been written over and over again. A Frenchman, Pierre Belon, author of *De Arboribus Coniferis,* published in 1553, and the first treatise on Conifers ever written, ascended Mount Lebanon in 1550 and visited the Monastery of the Virgin Mary, situated in a valley below a grove of Cedar trees where the festival of the Transfiguration was held. Then as now this and other groves belonged to the Patriarch of the Maronites—a Christian sect inhabiting Mount Lebanon. Belon states that after celebrating High Mass upon an altar erected under one of the largest trees, said to have been planted by King Solomon, the Patriarch threatened with ecclesiastical censure those who presumed to hurt or diminish the Cedars then remaining. Since Belon's time many travelers have visited the Cedars on Mount Lebanon the most experienced of all being the late Sir Joseph Hooker, the eminent English botanist, who was there in the autumn of 1860. Sir Joseph's visit was for the special purpose of examining the Cedar groves, and in the *Natural History Review,* January, 1862, he published a most interesting account of them.

The elevation of Mount Lebanon was found to be 10,200 feet and that of the Kedisha Valley where the trees are growing 6200 feet. The whole of this area is, to quote the article, "a confused mass of ancient moraines which have been deposited by glaciers that, under very different conditions of climate, once filled the basin above them and communicated with perpetual snow which then covered the whole summit. The rills from the surrounding heights collect to form one stream and the Cedars grow on that portion of the moraine which immediately borders the stream, and nowhere else. They form one group about four hundred yards in diameter with an outstanding tree or two not far from the rest, and appear as a black speck in the great area of the corry and its moraines which contain no other arboreous vegetation. The number of trees is about four hundred, and they are disposed in nine groups, corresponding with as many hummocks of the range of moraines. The trees are of various sizes, from about 18 inches to upward of 40 feet in girth; but the most remarkable and significant fact connected with their size and consequently with the age of the grove is that there is no tree of less than 18 inches in girth, and we found no young growth." Sir Joseph Hooker found only fifteen trees above 15 feet in girth and these all grew in two of the nine clumps. He estimated the age of the youngest at about one hundred years and the oldest at twenty-five hundred years, but with no degree of certainty.

Today some five groves of *Cedrus libani* are known on Lebanon, the one containing the oldest trees being on the northern slopes above Bsharri. The largest tree, but not one of the very oldest, is 48 feet in girth, in full growth and vigorous health. In one grove, that of Baruk and the largest, are many young trees in all stages of growth. Several travelers have noted that seedlings spring up readily but are browsed off by goats. With proper protection against these animals, and the forbidding of the people cutting them, these Cedar groves would increase in size and in time become forests, as in the days of King Solomon.

The Cedar of Lebanon is not confined to the mountain of that name but grows also on the Taurus and Anti-Taurus ranges in Asia Minor, from the province of Caria in the west to near the frontier of Armenia in the east. On these mountains it forms a considerable portion of the coniferous forest between 4000 and 7000 feet but appears to attain its maximum development on the Cilician Taurus, where the climate is severe, the snow lying several feet deep on the ground for fully five months of the year. At least such is the statement of Walter Siehe.

The late Director of the Arnold Arboretum heard of this discovery on the Cilician Taurus and commissioned Siehe to secure seeds of the Cedar of Lebanon from this cold region. On February

4, 1902, ripe cones were received at the Arnold Arboretum and the seeds sown. They germinated freely and many plants were raised. These Cedars have grown more rapidly in the Arnold Arboretum than any other Conifer. In fourteen years the tallest was 22 feet high. They passed the winters unscathed until the dreadful seasons of 1917-18 and 1919-20 which badly scorched the leaves. This retarded their growth though none died, and they are now well-furnished with foliage and are growing well. The leaders of many have suffered from the Pine-needle borer but new ones take their place. The experiment is most promising, and certain it is that if the gardens of New England ever enjoy Cedars of Lebanon as hardy trees it will be through the far-sightedness of the late Professor C. S. Sargent. Under cultivation several varieties of the Cedar of Lebanon have appeared, and the more important are distinguished by such names as *argentea nana, pendula, stricta, tortuosa* and *viridis*.

The grandest of all forms of vegetation known to the Hebrews, the Cedar of Lebanon has rightly found favor in many lands. It loves a warm, deep, well-drained soil, and it thrives in southern California. In England no other exotic tree has been more generally planted for ornamental purposes during the past two and three-quarter centuries. Thousands of noble old specimens are scattered from one end of the country to the other, and they are among the most impressive objects in many a stately park and pleasure ground. Visitors from this and other lands are familiar with the majestic Cedars on estates in England. Many specimens have been written about, measured, and photographed, and we can do no more than incidentally mention one or two. Just when the Lebanon Cedar was introduced into England is not clearly known and probably never will be. The evidence available points to that at Childrey Rectory, near Wantage, as the oldest in England. It is claimed that it was planted by Dr. Edward Pocock, who was chaplain to the Turkey

Company at Aleppo in 1629 and afterward to the Embassy at Constantinople. Returning home in 1641, Pocock was appointed to the living of Childrey in 1642. In 1903 his Cedar was a handsome tree still growing vigorously, and measured 25 feet in girth, five feet from the ground and its spread of branches covered an area of 1,600 square yards.

Wilton House near Salisbury is famed for its Cedars. In 1874 a specimen 36 feet in girth was cut down and its annual rings, carefully counted, numbered 236. According to this the tree must have been a seedling in 1638, and very probably it is of the same origin as the one at Childrey Rectory. Loudon thought the Cedars in the old Physic Garden at Chelsea, planted in 1683, but now dead, and those at Chiswick House, which was still flourishing, were the oldest in England. One at Enfield is known to have been planted by Dr. Robert Uvedale, Master of Enfield Grammar School, between 1662 and 1670; another, also still living, at Bretby Park, Derbyshire, was planted in 1676.

Among the many noble specimens in England it is difficult to state which is the largest but that at Pain's Hill, near Cobham, figured by Elwes and Henry in their great work *The Trees of Great Britain and Ireland* and by them measured in 1904 and found to be from 115 to 120 feet tall and 26 feet 5 inches in girth of trunk with a wide-spreading crown and in perfect health, must be counted among them. Another in Goodwood Park, the seat of the Duke of Richmond, was measured in 1906 and found to be about 96 feet tall and 26½ feet in girth of trunk. Goodwood is probably more celebrated for its Cedar trees than any other place in England. There is a record of Peter Collinson in 1761 supervising the planting of a thousand Cedars for the then Duke of Richmond. The tallest tree in England is perhaps that on the grounds of Petworth Park which was measured in 1905 and found to be about 125 feet tall and 49 feet in girth of trunk. Another in the Royal domain at Windsor is fully 115 feet tall. The finest avenue of Cedars is that at Dropmore, planted in 1844, but there is some question as to whether they are Lebanon or Atlas Cedars.

In Scotland there are many fine Cedars of Lebanon and some are scarcely inferior to the best in England. Perhaps the finest is that at Hopetown, the seat of the Marquis of Linlithgow, which in 1904 measured 80 feet in height and 23 feet 8 inches in girth of trunk. In Wales and Ireland the Cedar of Lebanon has not been so much planted and there are very few notable specimens. One at Maesleugh Castle in Wales is said to be about 100 feet tall, 16½ feet in girth, and one at Carton, Ireland, in 1903 was 93 feet high and 14 feet 9 inches in girth and is said to have been the first planted in the country.

On the continent of Europe the Cedar of Lebanon is much less plentiful than in England owing largely to a less congenial climate. The tallest is said to be on the grounds of Madame Chauvet at Beaulieu, near Geneva. It is about 102 feet by 16 feet with a spread of 102 feet. Many incorrect statements have been made as to the date of the Cedar's introduction to France but it is now pretty well accepted that it was in 1735, by seed carried from England by Bernard de Jussieu, and that the historic tree in the Jardin des Plantes, Paris, is of this origin and was planted in 1736. From this seed was also derived the tree at Beaulieu, and another at Montigny which is considered to be the finest in all France and about 26½ feet in girth of trunk 6 feet from the ground.

In this country, except in California, the Cedar of Lebanon is rarely seen, and no specimens exist comparable with those in England. In the New England states the typical form is not hardy and the winter of 1917-18 played havoc with the odd trees which have existed with a struggle for a number of years. For that matter it did the same with the Atlas Cedar which is the hardier of the two. In the most interesting *Memorials of John Bartram and Humphry Marshall* by William Darlington, published in 1849, on page 67 is printed a letter to John Bartram from Peter Collinson, dated from London on February 12, 1735, in which the following statement occurs: "The Lebanon cone, with a knife carefully pick out the seeds; sow in a box, put large holes in the bottom and cover with shells, in sandy light mould. Let it only have the morning sun." Whether Bartram succeeded in raising plants and if so what became of them is not ascertainable. In reports of his historic garden no mention is made of the Cedar of Lebanon.

Some 1400 miles from the Cedar forests of Asia Minor and separated by the whole breadth of the Mediterranean Sea grows the Atlas Cedar *(Cedrus atlantica)*. This forms the prevalent arboreous vegetation throughout the eastern province of Constantine which borders on Tunis. It also abounds on the eastern Atlas ranges according to Hooker. Augustine Henry, a more recent visitor, states that "In Algeria this Cedar forms a considerable number of isolated forests, none of them of great extent, at altitudes between 4,000 and 6,900 feet." Likewise it grows on the mountains in Morocco, but its distribution there is still not properly known though it was in this country that this Atlas Cedar was first discovered. Philip Barker Webb visited Tangiers and Tetuan in the spring of 1827, and from a native obtained branches of a Cedar which had been collected on the impenetrable mountains of the province of El Rif where there were said to be vast forests. Webb's specimens are preserved in the museum of the city of Florence, Italy.

The Atlas Cedar differs from that of Lebanon in having a perfectly erect, rigid leader, straight stiff ends to the branches, all of which in the Lebanon Cedar droop more or less, shorter leaves and a smaller cone. It is also more easy to transplant, and endures exposure and bad soil better than the Lebanon. In this country it is generally considered to be the hardiest of the true Cedars. The Atlas Cedar also grows faster than the Lebanon. The date of its introduction into England is not precisely known, but the oldest recorded tree is one at Eastnor Castle and was raised in 1845 from cones gathered by Lord Somers at Teniet-el-Haad. In 1906 this tree was 77 feet tall and 8 feet 1 inch in girth of trunk. At Linton Park, Kent, there is a tree 80 feet tall (in 1902) and very glaucous. In Ireland are even taller trees; one at Fota, also of the glaucous variety and planted in 1850, was 83 feet tall and 7 feet 7 inches in girth in 1904. At Carton, the seat of the Duke of Lienster, is a reputed Atlas Cedar which in 1903 was 80 feet high by 9 feet in girth of trunk. In the south of France and northern Italy the Atlas Cedar grows faster than in England. In the public garden at Aix au Savoie there is a grove, planted in 1862, with trees from 90 to 95 feet tall. There are varieties such as *glauca, pyramidalis, columnaris,* and *fastigiata* which are sufficiently described by the names they bear.

On the principal watershed of the southern ranges in the island of Cyprus grows a third species of Cedar *(C. brevifolia)*. This was discovered in 1879, by Sir Samuel Baker. Since then it has been found by other travelers and, today, it is known to occupy about five hundred acres of forest mixed with Pines and broad-leaf evergreen trees. All the Cyprus Cedars discovered are comparatively young and small, the largest measured being about 60 feet tall and 11 feet 6 inches in girth of trunk. This Cedar has a slightly drooping leading-shoot and the ends of the branches are pendent as in the Cedar of Lebanon but the leaves are quite short and the cones are smaller than those of the Atlas Cedar. Seeds were sent to Kew from Cyprus in 1881, but the trees have grown slowly.

It is unknown in this country but in all probability would thrive in parts of California.

Eastward from Mount Lebanon some 1400 miles are the Deodar Cedar forests of Afghanistan which extend continuously eastward on the Himalayas almost to the confines of Nepal. This Cedar (C. deodara) is in India exclusively a western tree; it begins where the influence of the monsoon is much diminished, that is where the climate begins to approximate that of the Levant. Its altitudinal range is between 3500 and 10,000 feet and from 6000 to 8000 feet, and though it grows gregariously it never forms pure forests. The leading shoots and the ends of the branches are more pendulous and the leaves longer than those of the Cedar of Lebanon; the cones are the same size, but the cone-scales and seeds are of the same form as those of the Atlas Cedar.

Seeds of the Deodar were first sent to Great Britain by the Hon. Leslie Melville in 1831, and sown at Melville in Fifeshire, at Dropmore, and elsewhere. In 1841 it was introduced in quantity. The finest trees recorded are at Bicton where one in 1902 measured 80 feet tall and 11 feet 8 inches in girth and another 90 feet tall and 9 feet 1 inch in girth of trunk. There are many others in England more than 80 feet tall. In Ireland are specimens approximately as fine; but in Scotland, where it is hardy in the warmer parts of the country only, the tallest recorded are less than 60 feet. There are varieties known by such descriptive names as *albo-spica, crassifolia, fastigiata, nivea, robusta, verticillata* and *viridis.*

These four Cedars, differing but slightly one from another yet occupying five distinct geographical areas, present a most interesting problem in plant distribution. Northern Syria and Asia Minor form one botanical province so that the Lebanon groves, though so widely disconnected from the Taurus forests, can be regarded in no other light than as outlying members of the latter. Sir Joseph Hooker in the paper already referred to suggests that in pre-historic times the Cedar forests occupied much lower levels and were continuous. He adduces geological evidence to prove that vast changes took place in the Mediterranean basin during Tertiary times, and shows that in the warm period which followed the glacial epoch the vegetation of the lower levels was forced to seek colder situations and so migrated northward and up the mountains. This would bring about the geographical isolations of the Cedar and the differences now apparent between the four species are mere variations fixed and accentuated through time.

The Cedars though not so ancient as the Ginkgo are an old type of tree-life. Fossil remains of the ancestors of the present race have been found in the Lower Greensand of England around Maidstone and Folkestone in Kent, and at Shanklin in the Isle of Wight. This Lower Greensand underlies Chalk and belongs to the Cretaceous or Chalk Age, a geological era remarkably prolific in animal life. In this period birds very probably first appeared, the Terrible Lizards of the Reptilian Age disappeared, but a race of extraordinary, serpent-like Reptiles (Mosasaurus) flourished. These were long, snake-like animals with pointed teeth, and were furnished with swimming paddles and a long powerful tail. One species of these astonishing creatures of which fossil remains have been unearthed in this country is estimated to have been from 75 to 80 feet in length. The mammals of this epoch were apparently marsupials like those of Australia today. But the important fact from the viewpoint of the Cedars is that Cretaceous rocks agreeing in their lithological and palaeontological facies occur in all the Alpine ranges from Provence to Dalmatia, in the Atlas Mountains, in Syria, Palestine, Arabia, Persia, the Caucasus, and the western Himalayas. The Libyan Desert of northern Africa is also floored by Cretaceous rocks though of a different lithological character but apparently of the same age.

In the Tertiary period which succeeded the Cretaceous epoch, Cedar forests composed of one species were doubtless more or less continuous on the mountain ranges throughout the Mediterranean basin and Asia Minor to the western Himalayas. Owing to the tremendous depressions and elevations for which this epoch is remarkable the continuity was broken. During the era of glaciation which ushered in the close of the Tertiary Age the Cedars and all other vegetation were forced to lower levels. When perpetual snows covered the great axis of Lebanon and fed glaciers which rolled 4000 feet down its valleys the climate of Syria must have been many degrees colder than now; the position of the Cedars fully 4000 feet lower, and the atmosphere much more humid. At the close of the Glacial period the increased temperatures forced the Cedars and other cool-temperate vegetation to seek colder localities and so they migrated up the mountain slopes and northward. Those that failed to do so would be killed, and this would lead to their present-day occupation of isolated sites. On the mountains of Cyprus and on Lebanon, and to a less extent also on the Atlas mountains of northern Africa and on the Taurus ranges of Asia Minor, the Cedar groves and forests are merely surviving remnants of prehistoric forests of enormous magnitude.

In closing this sketch of the Cedars, their history and geographical distribution, a few brief remarks on the character and usefulness of their wood seem appropriate. It is fragrant, easily worked, and of lasting quality. That of the Deodar is the most important of any timber in northwestern India. It is used in quantity for railway-ties, for bridge-building, for general construction work; also for roofing shingles. That of the Atlas Cedar also is valuable and especially in the ground. The Cedar of Lebanon in

England grows rapidly and its wood is of poor quality, but that of the trees on Lebanon is excellent. The subject has been much debated, but the consensus of opinion now is that the wood used in building Solomon's temple and by Nebuchadnezzar was in all probability that of the Cedar of Lebanon. It is a known fact that the character and quality of timber are strangely influenced by soil and climate. The Old Testament references afford some idea of the enormous consumption of these noble forest trees. If to these, and the like demands by the Tyrians and others, we add the wanton destruction by invading armies we need not wonder at the diminished glories of Lebanon but rather be surprised that any Cedar trees remain.

KINGLY OAK

ONARCH of the woodland is the Oak, of all trees most dear to us who live in northern lands. It is celebrated in literature from the earliest times, indeed, of no tree has more been written than of the Oak. The genus to which it belongs is widely distributed through North America, Europe, and Asia where it reaches the Equator, but the species with deciduous foliage, those that we know best as Oaks, are all northern. Many of these are unsurpassed in beauty, size and stateliness among the trees of the whole world. Notwithstanding our admiration, indeed reverence, we have paid very little attention to the Oak in ornamental planting. Possibly because of the dignity and majesty of old giants scattered through this country and the parks of the Old World, where age and strength stand forth so prominently, the tree lover has assumed that Oaks grow too slowly for practical ornamental purposes. Whatever its origin this fallacy is deeply rooted yet it is a fallacy none the less. It is the experience of the Arnold Arboretum, which goes back for fifty-six years, that Oaks are the most rapid growing of all the deciduous-leaved trees. The oldest planted Oaks in the Arnold Arboretum were placed out some fifty-four years ago when they were seedlings only a few inches high and are now 60 feet tall. They are taller with thicker trunks than other hardwood trees, like Hickory, Walnut, Elm and Maple, planted at about the same time. The tallest of these are Pin Oaks *(Quercus palustris)* and the tree with the thickest trunk is a hybrid between the White and the Burr Oak called *Q. Bebbiana.*

71

Some fifty years ago and less it was very difficult to obtain American Oaks in American nurseries, for being native trees they were neglected. If one wanted a Scarlet or Red Oak it had to be imported from Europe. Nowadays, fortunately, our nurserymen are somewhat more enterprising and a limited number of American Oaks can be obtained. However, something can be said for nurserymen since Oaks in general are by no means easy to handle. Unless transplanted with great regularity they are difficult subjects to move successfully. In the Arnold Arboretum, where many thousands of Oaks have been planted, the method pursued has been to sow the acorns in flats and when the seedlings are from 4 to 6 inches high plant them out in permanent sites. An even better plan is to sow the acorns *in situ*. The Red and Black Oaks transplant fairly easily but the White Oaks, most lordly of the clan, are exceedingly difficult to move. Still, with the modern appliances used by those who make a business of moving large trees the difficulty, once formidable, is now virtually overcome. The experts in big tree-moving now move Oak trees, within certain limitations of size, as successfully as they do Elm trees. If anyone interested in roadside planting or in planting of parkways in suburban areas wishes to see the value of the Red Oak *(Q. borealis)*, for this purpose he has but to visit Boston, Massachusetts, where double and in some parts triple avenues of these trees extend for several miles along the main parkway. The Pin and Scarlet Oaks are equally good for this purpose.

In the Arnold Arboretum a complete collection of the Oaks hardy in Massachusetts may be seen but we are too far north to make possible the growing of a very varied collection. Of the one hundred and forty-five species and hybrids which are trees and grow naturally in the United States, some fifty-five are established in the Arnold Arboretum. Among the Oaks which are shrubs and not trees only *Q. prinoides,* the Chinquapin

ENGLISH OAK, QUERCUS ROBUR, BURNHAM BEECHES, SLOUGH, ENGLAND

ANCIENT WHITE OAK, QUERCUS ALBA, TRUNK 18 FEET GIRTH, WAYSIDE INN, SUDBURY, MASSACHUSETTS

Oak, is properly at home. A few of the Rocky Mountain shrubby species just manage to exist but none give promise of success. No evergreen Oak can withstand this climate and the deciduous Oaks of Europe, except the Hungarian Oak *(Q. conferta)* are not free-growing and do not promise to be long-lived. The deciduous Oaks of northeastern Asia, however, grow well and trees of half a dozen species are well established, the largest of which are *Q. variabilis* and *Q. dentata*.

The natural woods assiduously preserved in the Arnold Arboretum are rich in Oak trees and some of them are now among its finest possessions. But when the Arboretum was started these trees were in an exhausted state of health, which necessitated severe pruning of the crown. For many years afterward they were unsightly in appearance but gradually they improved and now and for years past the rejuvenescence of a majority is complete. The White Oaks best respond to this treatment and many of them have not only taken on a new lease of life but are among the most vigorously healthy and shapely trees in the Arboretum.

Sometimes I think that I like the Oaks best in the springtime when their leaves are unfolding in soft grays, pinks and varying shades of red. At this season the northern Oaks can be studied to advantage for the color of the very young leaves and the amount and character of their hairy covering is different on every species. These vernal characters are constant from year to year and it is easier to distinguish, for example, a Black Oak from a Scarlet Oak, by the unfolding leaves than it is by the mature foliage.

Anyone, and an American especially, who happens to be in England during May will note the yellow-green of the unfolding foliage of the English Oak in meadow, park and woodland. So striking is this that the tree is almost as showy in its expanding foliage as the Norway Maple is in blossom.

To speak of the autumn glories of the Oaks is like trying to paint the Lily. In late October and November they claim the stage and the whole countryside is brilliantly lit with their autumnal foliage. The leaves of Oak trees turn later than those of other deciduous-leaved trees; the color, however, is assumed irregularly on different individuals of the same species and on some of them they are green while on others they are red or yellow. In late October when the leaves of most trees have fallen, the most gorgeous tree is the Scarlet Oak *(Q. coccinea)* which has no rival among northern trees in the bright scarlet of its lustrous deeply-cut leaves. The leaves of some trees of the Pin Oak *(Q. palustris)* turn scarlet or crimson when other individuals of the same Oak are still green and often green and scarlet leaves may be seen on the same branches at the same time. This is also true of the Red Oak *(Q. borealis)*, the autumn leaves of which on different individuals vary from yellow to dark red, red and yellow, and brown. On the trees of the White Oak group the handsomest autumn foliage is found on the White Oak *(Q. alba)* itself. The leaves of this Oak turn later than those of most Oaks and when in perfection are a deep rich vinous red. The leaves of the Burr Oak, Swamp White Oak, Post Oak, Chestnut Oak and others turn yellow and leather-brown and from most of them the leaves fall earlier than those of the White Oak.

Those interested in matters trivial, but often of great importance, will note that the Red and Black Oak groups, which are peculiar to this country, take two years in which to ripen their acorns, whereas all the White Oaks of this country, as well as of Europe and elsewhere, mature their acorns in one season. As a matter of fact, except for two oriental species, named *Q. serrata* and *Q. variabilis,* all the deciduous-leaved Oaks of the Old World ripen their fruit in one season. Another interesting fact is that auricled leaves, a feature of the European and certain eastern Asiatic

Oaks, are unknown among American Oaks. One other point, on the Black and Red Oaks the curious will observe a hair-like thread projecting from the marginal lobes of the leaves. This is absent entirely among the White Oak group.

In the north the climate is such that the growing of evergreen Oaks is utterly impossible, but from Virginia south to Florida and west to Mexico there is no more splendidly umbrageous tree and none of larger size than the Live Oak *(Q. virginiana)*. Easily transplanted and of rapid growth, it is frequently used as a street tree in the southeastern states and no tree is better fitted for such purpose. In California one of the dominant trees is the evergreen *Q. agrifolia* with, at least when young, holly-like leaves. There are in different parts of the world quite a number of evergreen Oaks that have spiny, polished, holly-like foliage.

The most famous in history is the Ilex or Holm Oak *(Q. Ilex)* of southern Europe. Pliny, writing in the First Century of the Christian era, has a great deal to say about the Holm Oak in the grounds of the Vatican. He tells us that there was a Holm Oak older than the city of Rome bearing a brazen plant inscribed with Etruscan characters, showing that it had been sacred of old. He also states that at Tivoli there were flourishing three Holm Oaks, which were growing there when Tibur was founded, centuries before Rome. The Holm Oak is native of the Mediterranean region but is perfectly hardy in southern England and should thrive in California and in the warmer states. It develops a stately domed mass of foliage quite distinct in character from that of other evergreen trees. It grows 80 to 90 feet tall and the spread of its crown is 100 and more feet. The general effect is sombre yet the leaves glitter delightfully in the sunlight and in cloudy weather when the winds sweep up their white undersides and set them a-twinkle the effect is singularly pleasing.

Very near akin to the Holm Oak is the Cork Oak *(Q. suber)*, which, from its extreme usefulness, is entitled to rank among the most important of the world's trees. A small tree, it is common throughout the Spanish peninsula and in much of the Mediterranean region where limestone is absent. Of all the Oak family this comparatively humble member is of most importance to civilized man since it furnishes him with cork, the annual consumption of which is enormous. The bark is carefully stripped from the trees and in the course of time new layers grow. Yet, in spite of this it is wonderful, very wonderful, how the supply is maintained. In China, especially western China, a number of evergreen Oaks are found, one of the most beautiful of which is *Q. spinosa*. This is a relatively small tree with an oval crown and long pendent branchlets. In winter the contrast between this and its deciduous-leaved neighbors is striking.

Trees are singularly like humans in some respects. Not all of them acclimate and make themselves at home in foreign lands. Some of the members of the Oak tribe are good illustrations of this. The Red, Scarlet, Pin and Black Oaks grow quite well in England, but the White Oak clan are much more fastidious and, except in one or two rare instances, refuse absolutely to grow in the British Isles. As if to show its independence the so-called English Oak *(Q. robur)*, the noblest tree native of the British Isles, is equally obstinate in the matter of flourishing in eastern North America. When young it grows fairly well but when about twenty years old it ceases activities in this direction and becomes stunted and merely exists. In fact, of the European species the Hungarian Oak *(Q. conferta)* does best in New England. This has handsome, deeply sinuate leaves.

From the books one would gather that the Oaks of England grow to a much larger size than those of this country. It is from the timbers of this Oak that the famous "wooden walls" of England were constructed. But England is not the only country in which Oak timber has been used for ship building. If all the stately White Oaks which were built into the sturdy frame of "Old Ironsides" could be accounted for we would have had a list of historical trees whose adventures would fill a volume. The Avery Oak at Dedham, Massachusetts, was once selected as suitable material for this celebrated and much honored frigate. The amount offered was seventy dollars but fortunately, thanks to the intervention of the owner's wife, Mrs. William Avery, her husband refused to sell the tree. This took place in the Eighteenth Century and the Avery Oak is today gnarled but vigorous and in splendid health, being about 70 feet tall and some 23½ feet in girth. The tree is older than the town of Dedham and has the distinction of being adopted as the model for the town seal.

Youth denies these United States such ancient, historical trees that are famous throughout the British Isles, yet there are in New England alone a great many trees connected with important events in the history of the New World. Among them Oaks play an important part, and foremost must be mentioned the famed Charter Oak, which stood across the river from Hartford, Connecticut. In the bowels of this tree was secreted by Captain Wadsworth the charter of the Connecticut Colony. In 1687 it had been demanded by the Royal Governor in the name of King James 2nd of England, and after a heated discussion in which the lights were summarily extinguished the charter was rushed away and hidden. In 1689 it was recovered and free government restored to the Connecticut Colony. This famous old Oak was destroyed by a gale in 1856.

In Massachusetts and elsewhere there are a number of historical Oak trees. Many of them, alas! dying. At the Wayside Inn at Sudbury, where Longfellow wrote his *Tales*, the ancient Oaks still stand but are doomed to pass in a year or two. The Eliot Oak at

South Natick, under which John Eliot is supposed to have preached to the Indians in the Seventeenth Century, died four years ago. The Grafton Oak, not far from the town square, under which the sons of the soil assembled at the outbreak of the Revolution, still flourishes and so, fortunately, do many others. The above are White Oaks, but near the town of Lancaster there is an enormous Red Oak which has a girth of 20 feet, a height of 75 feet and a spread of branches about 90. This is accounted the largest Red Oak in the state of Massachusetts.

The Greeks and Romans believed that the Oak was the first tree that grew upon the earth and was the tree of Zeus or Jupiter, the King of Gods. In the Roman period the civic crown was of oak, and a chaplet of oak leaves was the greatest honor it was possible to bestow upon a soldier. In Anglo-Saxon mythology, legend and literature the Oak is enshrined. In the economic life of many nations the Oak has played a wondrous part. The wood has ever been famous for its strength and durability. The bark and cupules of certain species have for centuries had a great reputation as tanning agents. The acorns of certain species have served mankind as food. Steel has ousted it from its premier position in ship building and constructional work, but it remains the emblem of strength and durability. That a tree so intimately associated with our race has not yet been given its proper position in ornamental planting, is not to our credit. Let us begin and at once. The needs of the Oak are simple. It flourishes best on a deep and heavy loam, depth being of more consequence than quality, since the tree sends its roots deeper into the soil than do most trees. As Virgil says:

> "Jove's own tree,
> That holds the woods in awful sovereignty,
> Requires a depth of loding in the ground,
> And next the lower skies a bed profound:
> High as his topmost boughs to heaven ascend,

So low his roots to hell's dominions tend.
Therefore nor winds nor winter's rage o'erthrows
His bulky body, but unmoved he grows.
For length of ages lasts his happy reign,
And lines of mortal men contend in vain.
Full in the midst of his own strength he stands,
Stretching his brawny arms and leafy hands;
His shade protects the plains; his head the hills commands."

QUEENLY ELM

HE American or White Elm *(Ulmus americana)* is the largest and most graceful tree of the northeastern states and Canada and one of the most beautiful trees of the northern hemisphere. Found wild from southern Newfoundland westward to the eastern base of the Rocky Mountains and southward to the Gulf, it attains its greatest size and majesty in the colder and moister parts of this area. Of all the trees of New England it is the most prized, and many magnificent specimens adorn the countryside, either as isolated specimens, fine rows by the wayside or as grand avenues in country towns.

A good deal of America's history had its beginnings 'neath the shade of these fine trees. History recalls that William Penn made his famous treaty with the Indians beneath the shade of an Elm tree; at Cambridge, Massachusetts, under the shadow of an Elm, alas! no longer living, Washington took command of the Continental Army on July 3, 1775. Other Elm trees in widely separated places were rallying points for the early settlers to defend their homes and families against enemies of all kinds. At Kennebunk, Maine, a magnificent specimen is the Lafayette Elm named in memory of General Lafayette, who once visited the house in whose grounds the tree stands. This tree, now deeded to the town, has a trunk 17 feet 3 inches in girth and its spread of branches is 131 feet. Nearby the grim penitentiary at Wethersfield, Connecticut, stands an Elm with a trunk 28 feet in girth and considered to be the largest Elm in the United States. At Milton, Massachusetts, quite near the Academy, stands the Gulliver Elm, so-called because it was deeded in

1833 by the First Congregational Parish in Milton to Isaac Gulliver, who gave a bond for its perpetual exemption from molestation. Many readers will call to mind other Elm trees which, if they could speak could set forth the history of stirring events and tell many tales of quiet country life. No other tree was so intimately bound up with the life of the first settlers and their immediate descendants. In early times it was a pleasing custom to plant in front of the homestead of a couple just setting up housekeeping a pair of Elms and many of the finest of these trees living today had their origin in this sentiment. This custom recalls and may well have had its origin in the legend of Baucis and Philemon, who prayed that since they had passed their lives in love and concord their wish was that one and the same hour should take both from life that neither might see the other laid in the grave. The prayer was granted by the two being transformed into leafy trees and as the bark closed over their bodies they bade each other farewell.

Its attractive beauty and plentifulness, and the ease with which saplings can be transplanted, no doubt assisted in the general planting of this tree. Economical reasons caused the general planting of the Sugar Maple tree but it was its esthetic appeal that brought the Elm into such prominence. Many of the finest Elms have passed or are passing but the present generation has every reason to bless its forebears for the legacy of the grand old Elms left facing homesteads or bordering the roads, or streets of country towns.

In general appearance no other American tree exhibits so much variation as the White Elm. At least three distinct types are commonly seen. Perhaps the most frequent is that with a crown made up of a number of stout, ascending stems which give off spreading branches and pendent branchlets, the whole forming a round-topped, shapely mass, lithe and graceful in consequence of its hanging branchlets. Another type, of which the Lafayette Elm at Kennebunk is a noteworthy example, has many massive, wide-spreading branches shading an enormous area of ground. Such trees form an umbrageous mass in summer and in winter their gaunt, widespreading limbs are exceedingly picturesque. Another common type has comparatively few ascending stems but slightly diverging from the straight trunk giving off spreading and hanging branchlets, the habit of the whole tree strongly suggesting an old-fashioned wine glass. In this form the trunk and main stems are often covered with short, somewhat pendent branchlets, giving them a feathered appearance. Between these three extremes every intermediate condition may, of course, be found. The main types themselves have their own particular use in landscape work. The first is best for avenue planting, the wine-glass type for lawns, and the wide-spreading form for park or meadow where space is ample.

The American Elm is beautiful at all seasons of the year; when its minute flowers, harbingers of spring, cover the branches; when in summer it rises like a great fountain of dark and brilliant green above its humbler companions of the valleys, or sweeps with long and graceful boughs the placid waters of some stream flowing through verdant meadows; when autumn delicately tints its leaves, and when winter brings out every detail of the great arching limbs and slender pendulous branchlets standing out in clear relief against the sky.

This American Elm may be the most beautiful of its clan but it is by no means the only member. As a matter of fact, Elms of different species are found in the northern forests of Europe and Asia as well as in those of North America. A number of the species grow to a great size and have been known in the parks and gardens of civilized lands from immemorial time. The early settlers in this country brought or caused to be brought over quite a number of European plants and among them the so-called English Elm, a tree

PL. XXIII.

LAFAYETTE ELM, ULMUS AMERICANA, 80 FEET TALL, TRUNK 17 FEET GIRTH, SPREAD 131 FEET, KENNEBUNK, MAINE

common in the hedge rows of the British Isles whose ancestry has given rise to much speculation. At one time tree lovers accepted without question the name of *Ulmus campestris* for this old Elm but in recent times pedants have decided that it has no right to this name and that it should be called *Ulmus procera*. However, the old name sticks with most of us.

During the Eighteenth Century, a period when tree-planting was much in vogue, many of these English Elms were brought to Massachusetts, planted in the streets of Boston and in those of suburban towns, like Milton, Dedham and others. Some were planted in front of the old Granary Building on Tremont Street and on Boston Common. The oldest inhabitant on Boston Common today is one of these Elm trees. It is on record that on October 26, 1780, a day after the infant sovereign Commonwealth of Massachusetts was started on its career by the inauguration of John Hancock as Governor, the selectmen made application to break ground on the Common and plant trees. The request was granted and, facing John Hancock's residence, an English Elm was planted. For one hundred and fifty years this tree has withstood the vicissitudes of wind and weather and though somewhat broken is today a grand old specimen. If it had voice, what a story it could tell of scenes witnessed and history made. It has been the subject of a delightful book published in 1910 entitled *Life of The Campestris Ulm*. Its author, Joseph Henry Curtis, has a fascinating style and his pages are rich with humor as well as historical facts. For instance on page 29 we get an intimate picture of what the Sabbath day was like in Puritan New England. "From midnight Saturday to sunset Sunday was weekly a day of rest for Campestris. He hardly dared to stir a leaf; even the cows abstained in large measure from chewing their cuds and the Common was deserted. One Sunday, however, he was astonished and shocked to observe the Governor taking a turn in the mall on his way home from church. He was glad to learn the next day that the Governor was fined, and, much as he respected his sponsor, felt that it served him right."

When one remembers the events that were taking place at the end of the Eighteenth Century and the opinions John Hancock and his fellow Bostonians held of England the irony of planting an English tree is evident although the humor of it never appears to have dawned upon them. However, this accident or lack of thought was really fortunate. Had they realized that this tree was native of hated England they might possibly have crushed out its life in the same spirit as they wrested the country from British dominion. It is fortunate, and for this reason, the English Elm is of all trees the one that best withstands smoke and toxic gases which our modern cities are ever vomiting into the air. Its American cousin resents most strongly the deleterious atmosphere of the cities and pines for the pure air of the country. It so happens that the young sapling set out in 1780 has seen the decline and death of, not only the older American Elms on Boston Common, but also of many that were planted since the day it was placed where it still stands. On Commonwealth Avenue, Boston, Massachusetts, a number of English Elms are mixed with the American Elms and the day is not far distant when they will rule that noted thoroughfare. By the Art Museum and around the reservoir at Chestnut Hill many fine English Elms may be seen. To those who have charge of street planting in our cities I would emphasize the value of the Campestris Elm for cities, and to the nurserymen who make a business of growing street trees I would urge them to get busy and raise a stock of this most indispensable tree. It lacks the grace and beauty of its American sister but has much character of its own. It never develops a very wide crown but has numerous ascending, spreading stout branches. Until past middle life its crown is more or less

pyramidal in outline but with age it becomes dome-shaped, somewhat sparse and distinctly characteristic.

The Ainus, the aboriginal people of Japan, consider the native
Elm *(Ulmus japonica)* the most important of all trees. Many of
them considered it was the first created tree, being sent already grown
direct from heaven. Its roots dried served as tinder to generate fire
by friction; the inner layers of the barks after maceration in water
are woven into cloth and were formerly the chief source of material
used for making wearing appearel. The outer bark is employed in
roofing and covering the sides of their huts. Naturally such an
important tree figures largely in Ainu mythology. At its best it is
a handsome tree comparable with the European Wych Elm in
general appearance.

Since the dawn of this century a species of Elm has been brought
to us from northern China, which promises to be of immense value
in the Middle West and useful throughout the northern portion
of this country and lower Canada. It has proved very fast-
growing, good-natured and adaptable. A tree in the Arnold Arboretum raised from seeds which I collected in the grounds of the
Temple of Heaven at Pekin in May, 1910, is now 35 feet tall—this
in the poor soil and climate of Massachusetts. In the state of Washington I understand the growth is twice as rapid. It would appear
to have first reached this country in 1905 through Mr. J. G. Jack
who sent plants from Pekin to the Arnold Arboretum. Through
lack of information and possibly misled by its relatively small leaves
the great Linnaeus named this Elm *Ulmus pumila,* an egregious
misnomer. To add insult to injury *Standardized Plant Names* by
a literal translation of this name dubs it Dwarf Asiatic Elm. In
Korea, Manchuria and in many parts of northern China this tree
is comparable in size and bulk to the English Elm. In water
courses and elsewhere in Korea I have seen trees exceeding 80 feet

in height and 11 feet in girth of trunk. When young the branches are slender, lithe and arranged to form a narrow, pyramidal crown. In adult trees the crown is made up of few massive, wide-spreading branches which form an irregular mass. The bark on old trees is particularly striking, being very deeply fissured and roughly corrugated. It flowers at the first blush of spring and its fruits are ripe in May. This tree would appear to be destined to enjoy a bright future in this country and the confusion which exists with it and another Elm is unfortunate. The other Elm, by *Standardized Plant Names* called the Chinese Elm, is a totally different tree. It rejoices in the name of *Ulmus parvifolia* and is found wild in parts of Japan, Korea and China. It is always a slender tree; I never saw one with a trunk more than 6 feet in girth, and has thin scaling bark, small, more or less oval and rather thickish leaves which in warm districts are retained far into the winter, and it produces its blossoms in the autumn. As a matter of fact, no two Elms are more widely dissimilar in habit of growth, general appearance and time of flowering than *U. pumila* and *U. parvifolia*. I fear, however, that many years will elapse before the confusion existing between them is straightened out.

There are many other kinds of Elms including curious sports and freaks. Some, like the Camperdown Elm, have an umbrella-like crown with stiff hanging branches; others, like the Wheatley Elm, have ascending-spreading branches forming a narrow spire-like head, but space forbids a review of the whole Elm family. It would not be fair, however, to omit the Wych Elm, one of the famous trees of Europe, which, formerly known as *U. montana*, now goes by the name of *U. glabra*. At its best this is a tree as much as 120 feet tall with a trunk 20 feet in girth supporting a massive, wide-spreading, more or less dome-shaped or flattened crown made up of hundreds of stout branches and branchlets. It is one of the stateliest trees to be found in the lordly parks of England. In this country it has been planted although it is only found here and there. More common in America as a planted tree is the Huntington Elm *(U. vegeta)* which as usually seen has a relatively short trunk, sometimes 12 feet or more in girth, and many ascending branches which spread to form a broad, rounded crown. In the autumn these European Elms are easily detected by their lateness in assuming autumn tints. Usually the American Elms are naked whilst the European brethren are still a mass of green. Yellow is the autumn tint of all the Elms except individual trees of the small-leaved *U. parvifolia* which I brought from the heart of China. These, in autumn, assume reddish, even crimson, tones.

LORDLY YEW

THE discovery of gunpowder with the resultant development of arms of precision may at first sight appear to have little to do with the planting of trees in general or with the Yew in particular. As a matter of fact the connection is close. For centuries long prior to the introduction and general use of gunpowder the people of the world used bows and arrows. and in temperate regions where grows the Yew the best bows were made of the wood of this tree. Certain simple people like the Ainos of Hokkaido and Saghalien still use the bow in the chase but in general archery is now regarded as a pastime. It is beloved by the Japanese, Koreans, and Chinese; in the West associations and clubs have been founded to preserve this ancient sport and in Great Britain it is a favorite with women.

But if archery be now regarded as merely a healthy pastime its rôle in the grim affairs of human history has been among the greatest. With the story of William Tell every schoolboy of the West is familiar; and the appreciation of the skill of this Swiss archer has lost nothing through lapse of time, for, whether fact or fiction, William Tell typifies sturdy patriotism's stand against tyranny and aggression. The long-bow and the cross-bow are famous in history. Were not the battles of Crecy, Poictiers, and Agincourt won by the English mainly with the long-bow in the hands of archers of wondrous skill? Three English kings met their deaths from the yew-bow, and it was the most popular weapon through the internecine wars of the Roses.

Indeed, in both warfare and the chase the bow was held in

exalted estimation long after the invention of gunpowder had paved the way to a complete change in the arms of warfare. In the early days of English history there were in force special enactments for the planting and protection of the Yew trees. As far back as the Thirteenth Century every person not having a greater revenue than one hundred pence was obligated to have in his possession a bow and arrows, and all such as had not possessions but could afford to purchase arms were commanded to have a bow with sharp arrows if they dwelt without the royal forests. Since bows were of so great value in warfare it is not strange that English kings should have made strenuous efforts to plant and protect Yew trees, and to encourage the use of bows by various edicts, and Acts of Parliament which also regulated their price, making provision for their importation and forbidding their exportation. From the time of Edward IV to quite a late period in the reign of Elizabeth, these Acts continued in force, being renewed by each successive sovereign, and it was not until the latter reign, when firearms came into more general use, that less consideration was paid to the long-bows. A petition from the Commons to Edward IV states that "such bowstaffes as be brought within this Realm, be set now to outrageous prices," and prays that "every tun-tight of merchandise as shall be conveyed in every Carik, Calec, or shipp, iii bowestaffes be bought, upon pain of forfeiture to your Highness, for lacke of bringing every such bowestaff vi-s. viii-d." The last statute issued with regard to the use of bows is the 13th Elizabeth (cap. XIV) which orders that bow-staves shall be imported into England from the Hanse towns and other places. Through Saxon-Norman-Plantagenet to late Tudor times the yew-bow played a famous part in the national history of England, and no English tree has gathered around itself so much historic, poetic, and legendary lore as the Yew.

The association of the Yew-tree with early English history is varied and important. Venerable trees still mark the spots where great events have taken place, and many are associated with the names of historic personages. The Ankerwyke Yew at Staines witnessed the conference between King John and the English Barons in 1215, and in sight of this tree the Magna Charta was signed. This Yew is 30¾ feet in girth at three feet from the ground and is probably more than a thousand years old. Under the Loudon Yew in Ayreshire it is said that Bruce bestowed the ancient castle and estate on the Loudon family, and on the same spot some centuries afterward John, Earl of Loudon, signed the Act of Union between England and Scotland.

Up and down the length of England are ancient churchyards famed for their magnificent old Yew trees. The reason for the association of the Yew with churchyards has been much debated; in all probability it is several-fold. It is by no means confined to England but is a custom common in Ireland, and also in Normandy, Germany, and elsewhere on the continent of Europe. That it is a very old one is proved by a statement of Giraldus Cambrensis, who visited Ireland in 1184 and observed the tree in cemeteries and holy places. It has been stated that the Yew was a funeral tree, the companion of the grave, among the Celtic tribes, but there is no reliable evidence of the aboriginal tribes or the Druids holding the Yew in any esteem. On the other hand, it has been surmised, and with some show of truth, that it was used by the early Roman invaders of Britain in their funeral rites in lieu of their accustomed Cypress and Pine, and it was thus associated with the passage of the soul to its new abode. Certain it is that from very early times it has been used at funerals for the practice is mentioned by many early English writers. Evelyn in his *Sylva* says: "The best reason that can be given why the Yew was planted in churchyards is that branches of it were often carried in procession on Palm Sunday instead of

ANCIENT ENGLISH YEW, TAXUS BACCATA, 45 FEET TALL, TRUNK 35 FEET GIRTH, TISBURY, ENGLAND

IRISH YEW, TAXUS BACCATA FASTIGIATA, 38 FEET TALL, TRUNK 9 FEET GIRTH,
CIRCUMFERENCE 91 FEET, SEAFORDE, CO. DOWN, IRELAND

Palms." As a confirmation of this it is said that the Yew trees in the churchyard of Kent are to this day called Palms, as also in Ireland, where it is still the custom for the peasantry to wear in their hats or buttonholes from Palm Sunday until Easter-day sprigs of Yew, and where the branches are carried over the dead by mourners and thrown beneath the coffin into the grave. The Yew being evergreen was in olden times considered typical of the immortality of man. Having in mind primitive man's reverence for trees there is good reason to believe that the Yew tree had a part in the pagan religion of our remote ancestors and that Christian monks later engrafted it on Christianity. While admitting this and other probable causes, a more cogent reason for planting Yew trees in churchyards was the necessity for providing a supply of bow-staves for bow-men.

In English history we find many enactments both for planting and protecting Yew trees. Thus there was ordered in the reign of Richard III, 1483, a general planting of these trees for the use of archers. And in the reign of Queen Elizabeth it was enjoined that Yew trees should be planted to insure their cultivation and protection and partly to secure their leaves from doing injury to cattle. With all the efforts the supply was not equal to the wants of the villagers, and there was an enactment put in force providing for a certain number of bow-staves to be imported with every butt of wine from Venice and elsewhere. In Italy, Normandy, and Picardy and other parts of Europe similar laws were in force. Without pursuing this further, certain it is that, no matter what caused their planting, venerable Yew trees are the pride and glory of many old churchyards in western Europe.

In ornamental gardening the English Yew was employed as early as the Tudor times to form hedges, and was placed and clipped into the forms of grotesque beasts, birds, cones, pyramids, and

other fantastic shapes. During the Seventeenth Century the taste
for this kind of art increased and in the time of William and Mary
reached its highest point. Even today in Europe there are many old
places and in this country at least one, the Hunnewell garden,
Wellesley, Massachusetts, famous for this topiary art, but in general
it has rightly fallen into disrepute. Evelyn claims the credit of introducing the Yew into fashion for this work. Quite early topiary had
its opponents. Lord Bacon in the Seventeenth Century condemned
the practice. "I for my part," he says in his *Essays*, "do not like
images cut out in Junipers and other garden stuff; they be for
children." But it was mainly due to the ridicule thrown upon the
practice by Addison and Pope in the Eighteenth Century that it fell
into disuse. Pope, deriding the fashion, says, "An eminent town
gardener has arrived at such perfection that he cuts family pieces
of men, women, or children in trees. Adam and Eve in Yew; Adam
a little shattered by the fall of the Tree of Knowledge in the great
storm; Eve and the serpent very flourishing. St. George in Box, his
arm scarce long enough but will be in a condition to stick the dragon
by next April; a green dragon of the same with a tail of Ground-ivy
for the present. (N. B.—These two not to be sold separately).
Divers eminently modern poets in Bays somewhat blighted to be
disposed of at a pennyworth. A quickset hog, shot up into a porcupine by its being forgot a week in rainy weather."

Very many Yew hedges and clipped trees were swept away in
the middle of the Eighteenth Century by the celebrated landscape
gardener, "Capability" Brown, who dealt ruthlessly with all clipped
hedges and topiary work. But there appears to have been a natural
rebound in the public mind with regard to Yew hedges after the
attacks of Addison and Pope and the wholesale manner in which
they were swept away to make room for Brown's new style of
landscape gardening. The Yew is indeed one of the very best hedge

plants in temperate lands. It has been much used for this purpose in England where famous Yew hedges from 10 to 20 feet high and 9 to 12 feet through may be seen. A Yew hedge is indeed an ornamental adjunct to the flower garden and pleasure grounds for which it not only forms an efficient screen but always produces a pleasing effect.

Although its geological antiquity does not compare with that of the Ginkgo it is probably as ancient as the Cedars. In early Tertiary times, when the elephant and rhinoceros roamed through Britain, Greenland and the now Arctic regions of this continent, the Yew formed a common ingredient of the forests of those lands. Today the Yew is found widespread in the temperate regions of the northern hemisphere. The family likeness everywhere is very strong, so strong in fact that many botanists consider all to belong to one species. Under cultivation, however, they behave differently, especially in degrees of hardiness, and there are other and more subtle points of difference which merit recognition. The Arnold Arboretum recognizes eight species with many varieties and forms and, from the garden viewpoint at any rate, this classification is satisfactory.

In this continent are found four species—the Canadian Yew *(Taxus canadensis)* which is common in swampy woods and thickets from Newfoundland and Nova Scotia, through Canada to the northern shores of Lake Superior and Lake Winnipeg, and southward to Minnesota in the west and to New Jersey in the east; the Western Yew *(T. brevifolia)* is wide-spread, but not common from the Rocky Mountains in Montana to the Pacific, from Queen Charlotte's Island in the north to the Bay of Monterey in California, but is abundant on the Selkirk Mountains in British Columbia up to 4000 feet altitude, and on the western slopes of the Sierra Nevada up to 8000 feet altitude; the Mexican Yew *(T. globosa),* a little-known species which grows on the mountains of southern Mexico; and the Florida Yew *(T. floridana)*, native of a restricted area extending some thirty miles along the eastern bank of the Apalachicola River in western Florida. In Asia grow four species— the Japan Yew *(T. cuspidata)*, which is found from Japanese Saghalien southward through Hokkaido, Hondo, and Shikoku of Japan proper, and on the mainland from the Amur Valley south to the extreme limit of Korea; the Chinese Yew *(T. chinensis)* is scattered through central and western China and also on the mountains of Formosa; the Himalayan Yew *(T. Wallichiana)*, which is found between 6000 and 11,000 feet on the Himalayas from Afghanistan and Kashmir to Assam, on the Khasia Hills and through Upper Burmah and Malaya to Sumatra and the Philippine Islands; the European Yew *(T. baccata)*, which grows on the Cilician Taurus in Asia Minor, in Armenia, the Caucasus, and northern Persia. In Europe this species is more or less common in all mountainous and hilly districts from Lat. 63° 10′ N. in Sweden and Norway, in Esthonia, and through Great Britain from Aberdeen in Scotland south, and from Donegal in Ireland south to the Mediterranean; also it grows in northern Africa and on the Atlas Mountains in Algeria.

The Mexican and Florida Yews have never been introduced into cultivation, and so far as I can discover this is also true of the Himalayan Yew. The Canadian Yew is grown to some extent in New England gardens but, in the open, browns badly in winter, and except as a ground cover in shady, moist places has little value. It is said to have been introduced into England in 1800, but has never obtained a place in English gardens. Quite recently a low-growing erect form of the Canadian Yew has been put on the market under the name of *T. canadensis stricta*. This is a very pleasing evergreen suitable for low edgings where Boxwood is not hardy.

It has black-green foliage and if this be retained throughout the winter the plant will speedily become a warm favorite.

The Western Yew is not cultivated in eastern North America and I do not know that it is on the Pacific Slope. It was sent to England by William Lobb in 1854, but is still a very rare plant in gardens. The Chinese Yew was introduced by myself to the Arnold Arboretum in 1908, and has been distributed, but in New England it is tender and of little value. In California it will probably thrive and be a useful, ornamental tree. The same remark holds good for favored areas in the British Isles. At its best it is a fine tree 50 feet tall and 15 feet in girth of trunk, with large spreading branches.

In Great Britain and Ireland only the Common Yew and its numerous varieties are grown but in this country both these and the Japanese Yew are available, and for gardens north of Washington, D. C., the latter is the Yew *par excellence*. At Haddonfield, New Jersey, grow two famous trees of the Common Yew which were planted in 1713 by Elizabeth Haddon Estaugh, a Quakeress, whose history is partly given in Longfellow's poem *Elizabeth*. The circumference of each tree-trunk is about 12½ feet. These have several times suffered from winter storms. It is true that around New York, Philadelphia, and Baltimore, on Long Island, and along the Hudson River, there are large old specimens of the English Yew, but in severe winters they brown badly. In New England this happens nearly every winter and this Yew—except a variety of which mention will be made later—cannot be recommended for gardens. In Virginia there are fine old trees which must have been introduced in the Eighteenth Century, if not earlier; in California, in the neighborhood of San Francisco, the English Yew is a success.

The principal varieties of the English Yew are about a dozen in number, and of these the Irish or Florence-court Yew *(fastigiata)* is, perhaps, the most strikingly distinct and best known. A detailed account of this Yew will be found in our essay on upright trees. The Dovaston Yew *(Dovastonii)* is another well-known form, and a fine specimen of this grows on the old Dana estate, Dorosis, Long Island. This is a tree or wide-spreading shrub with branches arising in whorls and becoming very pendulous at their extremities. The original tree was planted as a seedling about 1777 at Westfelton near Shrewsbury, England, and is a female. There is a form of this Yew *(aureo-variegata)* in which the leaves are variegated with yellow. There is another weeping Yew *(pendula)* which is a low, dense shrub with no definite leader. There are several forms of Golden Yew and one is known to have been growing in Staffordshire in 1686. The best known *(aurea)* is a male, a dense shrub or low tree with narrow sickle-shaped leaves which are variegated with yellow. Another good sort is *Washingtonii*, a low dense shrub in which the leaves on the young shoots are golden yellow. Of low-growing forms there are several, including *horizontalis, recurvata,* and *procumbens,* sufficiently distinguished by their names. But another dwarf form which is grown in the Arnold Arboretum under the name of *T. baccata repandens* is worthy of fuller mention. Its origin is unknown and it is remarkable as being the only form of the English Yew which is properly hardy although it, too, suffered slightly during the winter of 1917-18; it has wide-spreading, semi-prostrate branches and broad black-green leaves.

There are many other forms of the European Yew differing more or less from one another. These include the Glaucous Yew *(glauca),* the Yellow-fruited Yew *(fructu-luteo),* and several small-leaved Yews of which *adpressa* is very distinct. This variety is a large, spreading bush with densely crowded branchlets having remarkably small, broad leaves each not more than one-quarter to one-half inch long. It is a female, and originated as a chance seedling in the nurseries of Messrs. Dickson at Chester, England, about 1826,

JAPANESE YEW, TAXUS CUSPIDATA, TRUNK 8 FEET GIRTH, DIAMOND MOUNTAINS, KOREA

and is sold under the erroneous name of *T. tardiva*. Of this pleasing Yew there are varieties *aurea* and *variegata*. Altogether fifty or more varieties of the European Yew have received names, and they exhibit the widest possible range of variation in form and general appearance. I forbear mention of more in detail, but I do wish to emphasize the fact that the most distinct forms are of seedling origin, mostly chance finds during a long period of cultivation.

The Japanese Yew was introduced into America in 1862 by Dr. George R. Hall who gave it to Parsons and Company, nurserymen, Flushing, New York. It appears to have made slow headway for many years, but is now becoming well known and its merits as the hardiest of all Yews properly appreciated. It came through the winters of 1917-18 and 1919-20 unscathed in the Arnold Arboretum and is known to be hardy as far north as central New Hampshire, and also in Minneapolis, Minnesota. On Long Island there are a number of fine specimens, so also are there in the Hunnewell Pinetum, Wellesley, Massachusetts, and in the Arnold Arboretum. But, undoubtedly, the largest in America is on the estate of the late Dr. George R. Hall, Bristol, Rhode Island, which is 22 feet high and 120 feet around, but, unfortunately, in poor health.

In Japan *T. cuspidata* is found scattered through woods and over the countryside from the south to the extreme north, but is nowhere common. I saw more of it in Hokkaido than anywhere else but even there it is now rare. Its wood is useful for a variety of purposes and lasts especially well underground. Of late it has been used in Japan as pencil-wood. On the central slopes of the Diamond Mountains in central Korea grow more trees and finer specimens than I have seen elsewhere. Scattered through woods of Spruce, Fir, Oak, Birch, and other broad-leaf trees are hundreds of specimens—trees from 40 to 60 feet tall, and from 6 to 10 feet in girth, with large, spreading branches forming handsome crowns.

On the Korean island of Quelpaert, in pure woods of Hornbeam, I found the Japanese Yew in bush form to be a common undergrowth. In Japanese gardens it is a favorite, being kept as a low, clipped bush, and it is also used as a hedge plant, but not extensively. It was one of those garden forms *(nana)* that was first introduced into this country and this has been propagated largely by cuttings. It is a wide-spreading shrub with short leaves. There is also another form *(densa)* which is a low, compact shrub. When seedlings from these dwarf forms are raised they usually revert to the tree type. The first tree forms of this Yew raised in this country were from seeds collected in Japan by Professor Sargent in 1892, and the tallest of these in the Arnold Arboretum is now 15 feet high. If the Japaness Yew is largely raised from seeds other forms will appear and there is little doubt that it will ultimately produce as great a variety as the English Yew has done. This is a matter nurserymen should pay attention to.

Until just recently American gardens knew only the three species mentioned but now races of hybrids have appeared. Yew plants as a rule bear flowers of one sex only but they seem to court companionship and the result is chance hybrids. The first of these to be recognized originated in a batch of seedlings raised in the nursery of Isaac Hicks & Son, Westbury, Long Island, and is presumably the offspring of the Japanese and Irish Yews. It is columnar in habit with perfectly erect branches, radially arranged leaves but with the dark foliage and cold resistant qualities of its Japanese parent. It is a fast-growing, very hardy and useful plant for which a great future is assured. *T. media Hicksii* is its name. The type of this hybrid race was raised in the famous Hunnewell Pinetum at Wellesley, Massachusetts, by its competent superintendent, the late Mr. T. D. Hatfield. In this pinetum is a collection of all the varieties of Yews which can be grown in the climate. For more than twenty years Mr. Hatfield gathered the seeds and raised plants. As a result of his labors a whole series of new forms have originated. The typical *T. media* is intermediate between the Japanese and European species and forms a broad pyramidal bush with spreading branches. Another variety with erect branches and dense habit is *Hatfieldii*. A form of compact, conical habit with ascending branches and radially arranged leaves has been named *Brownii* by the raiser. At the Centennial Fall Flower Show of the Massachusetts Horticultural Society, Wyman's Framingham Nurseries exhibited in their group eight other forms of *T. media* all raised by Mr. Hatfield of which the judges thought so well as to give each an award of merit. In all its forms this Yew is perfectly hardy in northern Massachusetts and promises to rank among the most valuable plants ever raised.

PRINCELY MAPLE

F THE Oak be King of northern meadows and woodlands, the Maple is entitled to rank as Prince. In size of
trunk and limb and crown the Maple does not approach
the majesty of the Oak, but in shapeliness of growth, in
beauty of bark and brilliancy of autumn foliage it excels. And
Maples are no mean trees in themselves for several species exceed in
height 100 feet and in girth of trunk measure fully 20 feet. The
timber lacks the strength and durability of Oak but its usefulness
in furniture making, in cabinet and construction work is well
known. Once it was the vogue, and even today Birdseye Maple
is highly appreciated. Maples are multitudinous in species and very
variable in habit of growth, character of bark, leaf and inflorescence.
They possess many all-round ornamental qualities and some are
of great economic value. The autumn tints of the Red and Sugar
Maples are one of the most wondrous spectacles that the forests
of North America boast, and in the winter the green and white
striped stems of *A. pennsylvanicum* and the steel-gray bark of the
Red Maple attract the attention of even the least observant. The
flowers are usually greenish yellow but in some they are red, in
others purplish and the fruit in all cases is a two-winged samara,
known familiarly as Maple keys. A sweet sap characterizes many
species, reaching its greatest development in the Sugar Maple *(Acer
saccharum)*, beloved by the people of the northern states and lower
Canada. Much history has been made beneath the shade of this
most useful tree and if it had speech what stirring tales of love
and fight it could tell and of the festive gatherings it has witnessed

SYCAMORE MAPLE, ACER PSEUDOPLATANUS, TRUNK 20 FEET GIRTH, BIRNAM, PERTHSHIRE, SCOTLAND

RED MAPLE, ACER RUBRUM, 75 FEET TALL, TRUNK 9 FEET GIRTH, ARNOLD ARBORETUM,
JAMAICA PLAIN, MASSACHUSETTS

at the season of sugaring off. Sargent in his *Silva of North America* states that about four million pounds of maple sugar and some two million gallons of maple syrup are made annually in this country, chiefly in Vermont, New York and Michigan. Today, thanks to the cheaper sugar derived from Beet and Sugar-cane, maple sugar is no longer of great economic importance, yet few there be in the Maple lands of America who will admit that any other sugar approaches in quality that of the Maple-tree. To many Americans and Canadians maple sugar is as dear as the Heather and the Shamrock are to the hearts of the Scotch and Irish. The sugar producing qualities of this Maple were well known and utilized by the Indians, and according to the books it was from them that the French learned the method of sugar making and handed it on to later colonists.

Much is made of the Sugar Maple as a shade and avenue tree in villages and country towns. It is, however, a lover of pure air and is quite unsuited for manufacturing districts or thickly populated cities. At its best in the colder districts it is a noble tree 100 to 120 feet tall with a trunk 10 to 12 feet in girth and ascending-spreading branches forming a bell-shaped crown. In the early spring every branchlet puts forth tassels of pendent primrose-yellow blossoms slightly in advance of the leaves and the light green of the latter and the pale greenish yellow of the flowers blend well. In the autumn the foliage assumes the most brilliant polychromatic tints, varying from yellow through orange to deep red and scarlet. Indeed, much of the autumn splendor of our northern forests is due to the abundance of Sugar Maples which are unsurpassed in color effects by any upland tree, as all who traverse the northern parts of this country or the St. Lawrence Valley of lower Canada in the fall will agree. Curiously enough, this tree, so abundant, so lusty and vigorous, and one that is so readily raised from seeds, will not flourish in the British Isles. This peculiarity also obtains in a number of other eastern American trees, the mystery of which is beyond our ken. Though not much cultivated outside of eastern North America two or three distinct forms are known, among them the variety *monumentale,* a narrow tree with perfectly upright branches, rather gaunt in appearance but decidedly picturesque and quite unlike any other known maple. Closely related to the Sugar Maple is *A. grandidentatum,* found from Wyoming south to New Mexico. This is a small tree, seldom 40 feet tall, of bushy habit and small, deeply divided leaves. It colors early and assumes all the wondrous tints of its kinsman, the Sugar Maple. Given a sloping bank, where it can enjoy good drainage and full sunshine, there is no more brilliantly hued tree in the fall than this.

Very common and very beautiful is the Red Maple *(A. rubrum),* abundant from New Brunswick south to Florida, being particularly plentiful in swamps and meadows. It is the first of trees to assume autumn tints in Massachusetts; usually about the third week in August signs of color change are apparent. Often it is just a branch or maybe it is the top of the tree which displays a ruddy tone; the rest may at the moment be deep green. Sooner or later the whole of the foliage becomes orange, scarlet or yellow. In the winter the steel-gray bark on the branches and upper trunk of the Red Maple make it singularly attractive, and in the early spring every branch and branchlet is clustered with masses of orange-red to crimson flowers of two sexes. In the male flower yellow anthers like bright eyes stand prominently forth. The female flower is of an even deeper hue and as the young fruit swells whole branches are garlands of vivid crimson. The Red Maple equals the Sugar Maple in size but has a more open and less regular crown, giving it a picturesque appearance. Its wood is less valued, its sap only slightly sweet, but it is less exacting in its tastes and is one of the few trees of eastern North America that flourishes in the British Isles. There are several varieties of this Maple known. One of them *(columnare)* is a truly delightful tree with short, horizontally disposed branches, forming, as its name indicates, a columnar mass. Another, known as *globosum,* is of low, compact habit and has its place where dwarf trees are in request.

The third great Maple of eastern North America is the Silver or Soft Maple, widely known as *A. dasycarpum,* but correctly as *A. saccharinum.* It is fond of rich soil and grows to its greatest size in the alluvial bottom-lands of the Mississippi Valley, but in Connecticut fine trees are common. At its best it is 120 feet tall with a trunk some 15 feet in girth which divides up into a number of ascending stems. The leaves are sharp-pointed, silvery gray on the under surface but assume no pleasing autumn color. It is the first of all trees to unfold its blossoms which are borne along the naked branches and push forth at the first flush of spring. In the vicinity of Boston they have been known to blossom in January. March, however, is their proper month, preceding by about two weeks the appearance of flowers on the Red Maple. Authorities consider that there are in the world about one hundred and fifteen species of Maple, and of all that are known the Silver Maple and the Red Maple together with one rare species in Japan *(A. pycnanthum)* are the only sorts that bear their flowerbuds naked on the branches. It is a handsome tree but, unfortunately, its wood is brittle and although it has been much used in ornamental planting it is of much less value than many other species. Unlike the Red and Sugar Maples the Silver Maple assumes no brilliant autumn tints. It does very well in Europe, where it has been long cultivated and several varieties are known; the most useful of these is *Wieri,* with pendulous branches, and deeply cleft leaves, dissected into narrow lobes. Like the type, owing to the brittleness of its wood, this often suffers from strong winds.

In America about twelve species of Maples are recognized, two of them being confined to the Pacific Slope. One of these is *A. macrophyllum*, the Broad-leaf or Oregon Maple which in size vies with its eastern congeners. Unfortunately, this noble tree is not hardy in New England; it does well as far north as eastern Pennsylvania and from British Columbia to middle California it is most useful. It has a tail-like inflorescence and broad leaves, deeply divided and sharp-pointed, which in autumn become bright orange-colored. The branches are arranged to form a compact dome-shaped crown and the bark is reddish brown, deeply furrowed and broken on the surface into plate-like scales.

Similar in many respects to the Oregon Maple is the Sycamore Maple of Europe *(A. pseudoplatanus)* which agrees closely in character of bark and habit of growth but in the autumn assumes no conspicuous tints. It is easily the largest of all the Old World species of Maple. Trees 100 feet tall with a trunk 20 feet in girth and massive branches, forming a wide-spreading, round-topped crown are not uncommon. It does very well in eastern North America and is especially valuable for planting near the coast. Indeed, I know of no tree that better withstands salt spray and the murderous onslaught of winter gales than the Sycamore Maple. Under such conditions it is stunted and its head ragged and torn but it resists the worst of storms and as a nurse for other things is invaluable. Long cultivated in Europe, a great many varieties have arisen, several of them with variegated and spotted foliage but of little beauty. One form, *purpureum* or *atropurpureum*, which has leaves purple on the underside has been known for more than a century and is one of the best of all purple-leaved trees.

Widely planted in this country is the Norway Maple *(A. platanoides)*, a good-natured and beautiful tree which in spring bears erect, flattened clusters of bright greenish yellow blossoms above unfolding green foliage. In the autumn the leaves assume clear yellow tints. In Europe specimens 90 feet tall and 15 feet in girth are known. Normally the crown is dome-shaped but in old trees it becomes open and irregular. This tree has been planted in enormous quantities in this country and for suburban districts it is recommended for street work, but in manufacturing towns, where one often sees it, it is no more suited than any other species of Maple. Of the many varieties of this tree *columnare* and *globosum*, both sufficiently described by their names, are small but useful trees. The favorite variety, however, is *Schwedleri*, whose leaves when young are bright red changing with age to a very dark green.

Although a majority of species of Acer are natives of the Orient few of these are trees of notable size. The only one that is worthy of mention on this account is *A. pictum* which is often met with in gardens. This species is abundant throughout China, Korea and Japan, and at its best is a tree 80 feet tall with a rough, gray-barked trunk 10 feet in girth. It has yellow flowers in hanging clusters and palmately lobed bright green leaves which in the autumn change to yellow. It is a feature of the northern forests of Japan, where its timber is valued for furniture making.

Maples are an important constituent of the forest flora of Japan, where they color in the autumn as brilliantly as in this country. The Japanese are particularly fond of autumn coloring and places where Maples are abundant are famed resorts. Three species (*A. japonicum, A. palmatum* and *A. Sieboldianum*) have been cultivated from immemorial time by the Japanese and scores of varieties have resulted. Whole gardens are devoted to their culture, and viewing the multifarious forms of Maple and their wondrous autumn tints is a pastime dear to the hearts of the nature-loving Japanese. In this country and in Europe when Japanese Maples are spoken of forms with wine-colored or finely divided leaves are immediately envisaged.

They form a very attractive group; indeed, among no group of shrubs and small trees is greater variety or greater beauty of foliage to be found than in these Maples. Less popular today, perhaps, than formerly these varied foliaged forms of the Japanese Maples have been known in American gardens for three-quarters of a century and still command their place. Among all the trees and shrubs we cultivate none have more exquisitely dissected or more beautifully colored foliage. They are principally the product of *A. palmatum*, a small tree very abundant on the mountains of Japan. The typical form has a 5-lobed leaf which in the autumn becomes yellow, salmon or crimson. Under cultivation there is a form with yellow leaves *(aureum)*, one with very narrow green leaves *(linearilobum)* and one with leaves rose-pink along the edges *(roseo-marginatum)*. Another group has 7-lobed leaves, larger than the type, suffused with red when young, afterwards green and finally brilliant red in the autumn. Among these the most popular forms are *atropurpureum* with wine-purple foliage, and *bicolor* with leaves of two colors, carmine and red; sometimes the carmine is laid on in blotches, sometimes one-half the lobe or one-half the leaf is of that color. In yet another group of this species the number of lobes vary from seven to eleven in number and reaching to the leaf-stalk are again finely cut to the mid-rib, the effect being web or lace-like. Of these the variety *multifidum* or *dissectum* is best known; *ornatum* another form, is similar with deep red leaves. A few of the forms of Japanese Maples are referable to *A. japonicum*, also a bushy tree with from 7 to 11-lobed leaves and purplish red flowers. There are a number of varieties of this of which the most popular are *aureum* in which the leaf is wholly of a pale golden yellow and *Parsonsii* or *filicifolium* in which the leaves are cut and divided after the manner of a fern frond. One other species also comes under this Japanese group, that is, *A. Sieboldianum*, which has 7 to 9-lobed leaves and yellow flowers. There are many other named varieties of these Japanese Maples, although the list available today is much less than formerly. Grouped near the house or where they can be seen from the windows they have a decided use in landscape planting. The Japanese grow them in pots, training them into all sorts of curious shapes and among no group of trees is their ingenuity and taste better displayed than in the fashioning of Maples in a Maple garden.

Very beautiful is *A. crataegifolium,* whose small, oblong-ovate, pointed leaves change from yellow to crimson or black-purple in the autumn. No other Maple assumes such dark tones as this Japanese species. It is a bush or small tree, seldom more than 20 feet tall, with smooth purplish branches, very slender and spreading. Among the lesser trees of Japan this is one of the most lovely.

Quite unlike any other Maple and strangely mimicking the Hornbeam is the Japanese *A. carpinifolium* with narrow, ovate, sharply pointed, serrated and many veined leaves. This is a bush or small tree with slender, spreading branches clothed with gray bark. Unless in flower or fruit this tree is difficult to recognize as a Maple.

One of the hardiest and most attractive of all Maples in the autumn is *A. ginnala,* a large bush or small bushy tree with abundant ovate, pointed and coarsely toothed leaves. No Maple is more umbrageous during the height of summer and in the early autumn it assumes blazing fire-like tints and might well be called the Burning Bush. Those who want a feast of brilliant orange and crimson in the fall should plant *A. ginnala.*

The Moosewood or Striped-bark Maple *(A. pennsylvanicum)* is typical of a small group of species characterized by their thin, perfectly smooth bark striped alternately with white and olive-green, the white being particularly prominent in the winter. All are slender trees or large bushes and confined to moist woodlands. The Moosewood is the only species known from this country and it is characterized by its palmate, 3-lobed leaves on long petioles which change to clear yellow in the fall. There is a variety *(erythrocladum)* with salmon-red twigs, particularly brilliant in the winter. A very similar species wide-spread in the forest of Japan is *A. rufinerve*. More graceful with reddish veined leaves and petiole is *A. capillipes*, one of the most charming of all Maples. Similar in character of bark but with a more or less ovate, long-pointed leaf is *A. Davidii*, a very common Maple in the forests of central and western China.

In Maples the variety in form and shape of leaf is not confined to mere cutting of lobing but it goes a step further and the leaf becomes pinnate like that of the Ash tree. There is a group of these of which the American Box Elder *(A. negundo)* is a well-known example. At its best this is a tree 60 feet tall with a trunk 10 feet in girth supporting a round-topped crown. In its different forms it is found wide-spread throughout the United States, being represented in California by a distinct geographical form. In Texas and other states it is commonly used as a street tree for which purpose it has been widely carried about the world and is in request in South Africa, Australia and elsewhere. In cultivation a number of forms with variegated foliage have arisen, none being better than the typical *variegatum*, in which the leaflets have a broad white margin. There is a form *(aureum)* in which the leaves are wholly yellow and another in which they are margined with yellow *(aureo-marginatum)*. The Box Elder and its varieties are quick growing trees, easily accommodated in ordinary soil. Their wood, however, is brittle and on this account they are often damaged by storms. In a small garden they can be kept into round-topped affairs by close pruning.

NOBLE BEECH

MONG the familiar trees of the northern forests none is more stately or beautiful than the Common Beech *(Fagus sylvatica)*. A clean looking tree, the very personification of vigor, the Beech has been aptly termed the Hercules and Adonis of European forests. There is something peculiarly attractive about this Beech at all seasons. In winter the pale gray, smooth bark and the delicate tracery of the myriad branches suggest a light white mist hovering in and about the trees; in spring, the clear green mantle of foliage is exquisitely delicate but soon assumes a darker hue and forms a dense and cooling shade in the summer heat, and in autumn the warm yellow to russet-brown tints, and the long persistence of the dead leaves on the branches all have peculiar charms. Further, the ground beneath Beech trees is generally dry and free from weeds and is inviting to sit upon and rest.

The crown of the Beech tree is broad and far-spreading; the middle and upper branches are sharply ascending, the lower spread horizontally often downward to midway in their length but are upturned at their extremities. There are famous trees, like the New-battle Beech near Dalkeith, some eight miles from Edinburgh, in which the lower branches lying on the ground have taken root and developed into independent trees. The branches of the Beech are very numerous and crowded and, having a smooth bark, are particularly liable to cross and grow into each other and, as it were, inosculate. Hence, according to some old authorities, it was this tree that first gave the idea of grafting. At its best the Common

Beech is a magnificent tree 100 feet or more tall with a trunk fully 20 feet in girth. When growing thickly together the trunk is straight and free of branches for from 30 to 50 feet or even more, but usually the unbranched trunk is not more than 20 feet high. On old trees, and especially on those pollarded, as in Epping Forest or the famous Burnham Beeches, huge gnarled burrs develop on the trunk and arrest attention. It is gregarious, and its branches so numerous and dense that few plants will grow beneath its shade. The firm, close, smooth pale gray bark, "its glossy rind," from early times seems to have proved an irresistible attraction to love-sick swains, sentimental adolescents, and other irresponsibles. Everywhere one sees lovely Beech trunks disfigured by letters and symbols cut into the bark. No other tree suffers to the same extent from this peculiar form of egotistical vandalism.

Geologically, the Beech is not ancient, having apparently first appeared in Tertiary times. It is in fact an aggressive modern type of tree. Lyell in his *Antiquity of Man* speaks of it as follows: "In the time of the Romans the Danish Isles were covered as now with magnificent Beech forests. Nowhere in the world does this tree flourish more luxuriously than in Denmark, and eighteen centuries seem to have done little or nothing toward modifying the character of the forest vegetation. Yet in the antecedent bronze period there were no Beech trees, or at most but a few stragglers, the country being then covered with Oak. The Scots Pine buried in the oldest peat in Denmark gave place at length to the Oak; and the Oak after flourishing for ages yielded in its turn to the Beech; the periods when these three forest trees predominated in succession tallying pretty nearly with the ages of stone, bronze, and iron in Denmark."

The Common Beech *(Fagus sylvatica)* is indigenous to England and in western Europe as far east as about the old Russian

BEECH, FAGUS SYLVATICA, NEW FOREST, ENGLAND

frontier from Norway and Sweden south to the Mediterranean and it reappears in the Crimea. It is absent from Portugal and is not considered to be wild in Ireland or Scotland though it probably is in the southernmost parts of the latter country. Usually it forms pure forests of considerable extent, some of the finest of which grow on the northern slopes of the Balkans from their base to 4000 feet altitude. Fossil remains of the Beech have been found in neolithic deposits in the Fen districts and elsewhere in England and in the pre-glacial deposits in the Cromer forest-bed. Julius Cæsar stated that Fagus did not occur in England; but apparently the tree he meant was the Chestnut (Castanea). Yet the mistake is a curious one, for the Roman, Pliny, described as Fagus a tree which cannot be anything else than the Common Beech. However, the Fagus of the old Greek philosopher, Theophrastus, was undoubtedly the Chestnut, and Virgil's statement that *castanea* by grafting would produce *fagos* seems to indicate that the name Fagus was in common use among the Romans for the Chestnut.

In all there are ten species of Beech now recognized, eight of which are growing in the Arnold Arboretum, and it is doubtful if any other garden is so fortunate. We are here primarily concerned with the Common Beech but it is not out of place to say a word or two about the other species. They all have the same general appearance and cannot be mistaken for any other tree. All have the same sort of bark—thin, firm, smooth and light gray; the leafage and the character of the branches and their disposition is much the same. They differ one from another in the shape and character of their fruits and in the habit of the bole. In the Common Beech the bole or trunk is single, and this obtains in one Japanese *(F. japonica)* and one Chinese species *(F. lucida)*. In another Japanese species *(F. Sieboldii)* and in the Chinese *F. Engleriana* the trunk divides at or near the base into few or many stems. In the Dagelet Island

F. multinervis and the Chinese *F. longipetiolata* the trunk is usually single, but often divides near the base into several stems. The habit of the rare Formosan Beech *(F. Hayatae)* is unknown to me, also that of the Caucasian *F. orientalis,* though from an account I have read of the latter it would appear to have many stems like the Japanese *F. Sieboldii* and the Chinese *F. Engleriana.* The American Beech *(F. grandifolia)* exhibits even greater diversity in habit. Normally it has a solitary trunk, but in pastures and places where the roots get near the surface, and are consequently exposed and damaged, a multitude of suckers (sprouts) are developed which grow into trees and form a dense copse. Near the foot of the Hemlock Hill by the collection of Arborvitae and Yews in the Arnold Arboretum, there is a splendid example of this type of growth of American Beech.

This distribution of the various species of Beech is remarkable, and is a good illustration of the isolation of members of a single genus. The range of the Common Beech has been given. The American Beech is distributed from Nova Scotia to the northern shores of Lake Huron and northern Wisconsin; south to western Florida, west to southeastern Missouri and Trinity River, Texas. It grows mixed with other trees, and occasionally with Yellow Birch makes nearly pure woods. Outside of America it has not proved amenable to cultivation and in Europe only a few small examples exist. In Japan *Fagus Sieboldii* grows from the southern end of Hokkaido, through Hondo, the main island, and Shikoku, to Mount Kirishima in the south of Kyushu; in places it forms pure woods, though usually it is merely the dominant tree in the mixed forests of certain zones on the mountains. The other Japanese Beech *(F. japonica)* is more rare and I have seen it in the Nikko region only where it grows mixed with Siebold's Beech and other trees at from 3500 to 5000 feet altitude. On the tiny Dagelet Island, a lonely spot in the Japan Sea some fifty miles from the east coast of central Korea, grows an endemic Beech *(F. multinervis)*, recently discovered. It is quite plentiful in forests of mixed broad-leaf trees on volcanic soil. I collected a number of small plants but the time was early June and I failed to get them to America in a living condition. No Beech grows in Korea, Manchuria, nor eastern Siberia. In China, especially in Hupeh, Szechuan, Kweichou, and Yunnan three species *(F. longipetiolata, F. lucida* and *F. Engleriana)* have been found, in fact in Yunnan, in about Lat. 23° N., the Beech finds its southern limit. In western Hupeh and adjoining parts of Szechuan the three species grow together, though *F. longipetiolata* is the more common and occurs at the lowest altitudes. These three Beeches sorely puzzled me (though really they are as distinct as species possibly could be) and it was not until the eleventh and last year of my travels in China that I was able to distinguish them clearly. They were successfully transported to the Arnold Arboretum, where I am happy to say they are all growing today. The Formosan Beech *(F. Hayatae)* is known only from a mountain in the heart of the savage country where I was not allowed to visit. No Beech has been found on the vast Himalayan range, and this is rather curious since so many Chinese types have their western limits of distribution in Sikkim and Nepal. The tenth and last species *(F. orientalis)* is found on the Caucasus, in Asia Minor and in northern Persia; the Caucasus being its centre of distribution. Of these ten Beeches the Dagelet Island and Formosan species are the only ones not growing in the Arnold Arboretum.

All Beeches are lovely trees in their native haunts. Their wood is similar and makes excellent fuel but is not much esteemed otherwise. It is more used in France perhaps than in other countries, and in parts of Buckinghamshire, England, where the manufacture of Beech-wood furniture constitutes a local industry of some importance.

The Common Beech is the only kind whose merit as a planted tree is properly known, and it is one of the very few European trees that thrives in eastern North America. It will grow on almost any soil except pure peat and heavy clay, but prefers dry soil and attains its greatest perfection on calcareous land or on deep loam. On light sandy soils, the bark often splits longitudinally, and the trunks singularly resemble those of Hornbeam (Carpinus). For park and lawn the Beech is a most worthy tree, picturesque, and always gives satisfaction. Very many forms are recognized—the Purple, Copper, Fernleaf, and Weeping being the best known— but as a matter of fact the Beech is more prolific in varying forms than any other broad-leaf tree. Several of these variants call for detailed notice but first a few words on the usefulness of the typical form are necessary.

The Common Beech is an excellent avenue tree provided it be planted thickly, but is perhaps best as a screen tree, and when planted to form pure groves the effect is perfect. Owing to its dense branching habit it is splendid for forming tall, narrow hedges. Under such conditions it carries its leaves, whose russet-brown give a sense of warmth, through the winter. Properly clipped, Beech hedges last for centuries, are impenetrable to man or beast, and form the finest of windbreaks. In Europe, and especially in Belgium and England, they are common. The most famous Beech hedge, probably, is that of Meikleour, in Perthshire, Scotland. It is claimed that this hedge was planted in 1745, and that the men who were planting it left their work to fight at the battle of Culloden, hiding their tools under the hedge, and never returned to claim them. It is 580 yards long and is composed of tall, straight stems set about 18 inches apart and now almost touching at their base. The average height is about 95 feet and branches from the ground up. This hedge is cut periodically, the work being done by men standing on a long ladder from which they are able to reach with shears to about 60 feet. There is also a Beech hedge at Achnacarry, on the estate of Cameron of Lochiel, the history of which is even more remarkable. Here in 1715 the trees were laid in slanting ready to plant when the men were called away to take part in the rebellion of that year. The trees were never planted and have grown up in a slanting position close together just as they were left.

There are in England many fine Beech woods celebrated in song and story, the most famous perhaps being that known as the Burnham Beeches, situated some 25 miles west of London and a few miles from the royal borough of Windsor. This remnant of the vast forest that once stretched across England from the Thames to the Severn covers now about 226 acres. In 1879 it was purchased by the Corporation of London and is a worthy memorial to the wise discretion and public spirit of the city fathers of the time. The age of these venerable Beeches is unknown. They are pollarded trees with huge burked boles and far-spreading umbrageous crowns. 'Neath their shade the poet Gray, author of the immortal *Elegy*, was wont to sit and read his Virgil. Tradition has it that the pollarding was done by Cromwell's soldiers, but much more likely it was the overt act of some greedy lord of the manor at a more remote period for purposes of temporary gain. But, by whomsoever the act was committed, the effect has been remarkable in presenting a spectacle which, taken as a whole, has no parallel elsewhere in the world. In picturesque beauty the Burnham Beeches are unique, and no tree lover should miss a pilgrimage when opportunity offers. It is more than a quarter of a century since I paid my humble tribute to this shrine but the memory of that glorious Saturday afternoon is vivid and undimmed, notwithstanding that I have since seen the forests' glories of half the world.

In Britain grow many famous Beech trees, but none are finer than those in Ashridge Park, Buckinghamshire, where stands the majestic Queen Beech fully 135 feet tall with a trunk straight and branchless for about 80 feet. Except for certain Elms this is the tallest deciduous leaved tree in Great Britain. Incidental mention has been made of the self-layered Beech at Newbattle Abbey. This tree is about 105 feet high and 21½ feet in girth of trunk at five feet from the ground, and has a total circumference of about 400 feet. In Windsor Park, the Royal domain, are many magnificent Beech trees. The finest is near Cranbourne Tower and is about 125 feet tall with a fine, clean bole 15 feet in girth, and is said to be 800 years old. Of inosculated Beeches perhaps the finest is that at Castle Menzies, Perthshire, Scotland, which is 95 feet high. A little above the ground it is forked and then grown together again leaving an opening through which a youth can pass.

The Purple Beech *(F. sylvatica purpurea)* is in my opinion the only tree with colored leaves worth planting. One, possibly two, but not more, properly placed near a house or buildings with plenty of open space around add effective dignity to the surroundings. Unfortunately, however, the use of this tree is all too frequently abused. The Purple Beech is a natural variety of the common European and so far as is known all of them in cultivation have been derived from a single tree discovered in the Eighteenth Century (and still living) in the Hanleiter forest near Sondershausen in Thuringia, central Germany. Propagation has been effected chiefly by grafting and to a less extent by seeds, but only a percentage of the seedlings come purple. This tree grows to as great a size as the parent form and there are specimens in England nearly 100 feet tall. It is popularly supposed that the Thuringian tree is the only wild Purple Beech known. This is not so, neither is that tree the oldest of which records exist, but it is the mother tree of those cultivated in this country and elsewhere. Trees of the Purple Beech grow wild in the Tyrol and at Buch, a village in the canton Zurich, Switzerland, three specimens, growing among the common green-leaved type, Oak and other trees, have been written about since 1680. At one time there were five of these trees and the tradition is that five brothers murdered one another on this spot, and five blood-besprinkled Beech trees sprang up as righteous testimony from God as a lasting witness to so horrible a deed. The armorial shield of the village bears a picture of a Purple Beech and the probability is that its name of Buch, which is the German for Beech, was derived from these trees.

The Copper Beech *(cuprea)* is only a seedling form of the Purple kind with leaves and shoots of a lighter color. It originated about a century ago, presumably in England where there are specimens fully 90 feet tall and 15 feet in girth of trunk. In the sunshine and when the leaves are ruffled by a gentle breeze this tree is strikingly handsome. There is also a weeping form *(purpureo-pendula)* which is of slow growth, and another *(atropurpurea)* with leaves darker than those of the typical Purple Beech; also a variety *(tricolor)* with leaves dark purplish green, spotted with bright pink and shaded with white.

The Fern-leaf Beech *(heterophylla)* has relatively small, variously cut green leaves, and often hairy twigs. Its origin is unknown. At Newport, Rhode Island, there are fine specimens of this distinctly beautiful tree. In England it is known to have been in cultivation for a century. There are forms of this Beech designated by such varietal names as *asplenifolia, comptoniaefolia, incisa, laciniata,* and *salicifolia* which indicate the degrees of lacination

obtaining. Also there is a form *(atropurpurea Rohanii)* with incised leaves of the same hue as those of the Copper Beech.

The Oak-leaf Beech *(quercoides)* has long-stalked leaves,
pointed at the base, with long, drawn-out apex and deeply incised
margins with the individual segments pointed. Other forms with
green leaves are the Crested-leaf Beech *(cristata* or *crispa)* a curious,
small tree with small, shortly stalked leaves crowded into dense tufts
which are scattered at intervals on the branches; *macrophylla* with
very large leaves; *rotundifolia* with small round leaves; *grandi-
dentata* with conspicuously toothed leaves, and several others.

The Weeping Beech *(pendula)* has the main branches very
irregularly disposed and often the outline is rugged. Trees of this
Beech may be tall and slender, or low and broad, or quite irregular
according to the direction of the larger branches which may grow
outward or upward or in almost any direction; the smaller branches
only are uniformly pendulous. The Weeping Beech is a natural
variety and has been found wild in the forest of Brotonne in Seine-
Inférieure, France. Other forms of pendulous habit are *borneyensis,*
which was found wild in the forest of Borney, near Metz, and
is said to have all the lateral and subsidiary branches weeping; *pag-
nyensis,* found in the forest of Pagny, Meaurthe-et-Moselle, France;
remillyensis from the forest of Remilly, near Metz; and *miltonensis,*
with only moderately pendulous branches, found wild in Milton
Park, Northamptonshire, England.

The Parasol Beech *(tortuosa)* is of French origin having been
found in the forest of Verzy, near Rheims, and elsewhere. This
form has a short, twisted trunk and a hemispherical crown with
all the branches directed downward and often touching the ground.
It is seldom more than 10 feet high and more curious than beautiful. A similar form was discovered in Ireland some thirty-five
years ago.

The Fastigiate Beech *(fastigiata* or *dawyckii)* is a remarkable variety with all the branches erect. The original tree grows at Dawyck, Peebleshire, Scotland, on the estate of Mr. F. R. S. Balfour. Finally there are forms with variously variegated leaves of no particular merit, and the Golden Beech *(zlatia)*, discovered in Serbia and introduced to gardens about a quarter of a century ago. I have by no means mentioned all the known forms, but enough has been said to show the adaptable and precocious character of the Common Beech.

The fruit of the Beech is a stalked capsule clothed with simple, pliant prickles, and when ripe it opens at the apex into four divisions and sheds the two nuts each contains. The sharply 3-angled nut is rich in oil and of pleasant flavor. In France, and more especially in former times, the oil is expressed and used for culinary and illuminating purposes. The nuts are greedily eaten by wild pigeons and other birds, and by squirrels, deer, wild pig, and other animals.

The Common Morel *(Morchella esculenta)* a mushroom-like fungus much used in culinary art for flavoring, grows in Beech woods. It is always found in the spring, and in France and Germany the gathering of morels is quite an industry among the peasantry. But more esteemed by the gourmet is the Truffle *(Tuber cibarium)* which grows on the roots of the Beech. This fungus is subterranean in habit and never appears above the ground. It is black, of irregular shape, about the size of a hen's egg, covered with warty excrescences, and possesses a very strong but agreeable odor. It matures in the month of October, and the flesh is brown, veined with white. It is generally found by pigs and dogs trained to search for it. Though by no means confined thereto France supplies commercially the bulk of the truffles of the world.

ARISTOCRATIC MAGNOLIA

RISTOCRATS of ancient lineage possessed of many superlative qualities are the Magnolias. They have the largest flowers and the largest undivided leaves of any group of trees hardy in northeastern North America. No other genus of hardy or half hardy trees and shrubs can boast so many excellencies. Their free-flowering character and great beauty of blossom and foliage are equalled by the ease with which they may be cultivated. As a specimen tree in a conspicuous position on the lawn the Chinese Yulan and its hybrids are unrivalled and as an avenue tree the American *Magnolia acuminata* is hard to excel.

All Magnolias grow naturally in moist rich woods and they detest drought. They will withstand considerable hardships and abuse but the best results are obtained when they are protected from strong winds and are planted in a cool deep soil rich in humus. An ideal place is an open woodland where they suffer less from the inclemency of spring. The best time to transplant Magnolias is late in the spring. They may also be moved successfully in the month of August but after moving they must not be allowed to suffer lack of water and it is advisable to mulch them with well-decayed manure. These are cultural items of the greatest importance which no aspirant to success can afford to neglect. Moreover, such magnificent plants are worthy of a little extra attention which they repay a hundredfold.

Long, long ago Magnolias grew naturally in the forests of Canada and Siberia as they did also in those of Greenland and Europe, but the glaciation of these regions at the end of the Tertiary period

KOBUSHI, MAGNOLIA KOBUS. 40 FEET TALL, TRUNK 9½ FEET GIRTH, SPREAD 50 FEET, HOLM LEA, BROOKLINE, MASSACHUSETTS

destroyed them, leaving only fossil remains to tell the story. Today, Magnolias grow wild in the eastern United States and in eastern Asia from north Japan south and westward to the Sikkim Himalayas with their northern limits in Hokkaido and their southern in Malacca.

The American species all flower after the leaves are unfolded. There are Asiatic species that blossom in this same manner and others which bear their flowers on the naked shoots. It is the latter group that is the most popular and its members are the most conspicuous spring-flowering plants our gardens boast. All the deciduous-leaved American Magnolias, the Japanese and the Korean species are hardy in New England, so, too, are several of the Chinese species, but only one *(M. Campbellii)* of the Indo-Malayan species can be grown out of doors in North America. China is richest in these noble plants and it has been my good fortune to introduce into cultivation from that land no fewer than seven species and two varieties.

The first of all Magnolias to open its flowers each spring is the lovely *M. stellata* of unknown origin and to my mind the most charming of all. It is always a broad, shapely shrub from 10 to 15 feet high and more in diameter; the star-shaped, snowy blossoms are smaller than those of other species but are produced in such profusion as to cover the bush with white. In addition to the type there is a pink-flowered form *(rosea)* which makes a delightful companion.

The typical white-flowered Yulan *(M. denudata,* more generally known as *M. conspicua)* was introduced into cultivation in 1789. It grows wild in the moist woods of central China, though this fact has only recently been made known. This form, however, is comparatively rare in a wild state and that most usually found is the variety *purpurascens* which has flowers rose-red without, rosy pink within. I shall ever remember my first sight of the wild tree of this Magnolia. It was a fine specimen fully 60 feet tall with a broad, more or less pyramidal crown and was laden with thousands of fully expanded blossoms. Never again did I see such a magnificent example of this Magnolia illumining the woodland landscapes of China. Seedlings raised from seeds I collected from this identical tree in 1900 have flowered in an English garden much to the delight of the owner and myself. In the same year I discovered and introduced a distinct white-flowered form *(elongata)* and this has flowered sparsely in the Royal Gardens, Kew, and elsewhere. Both the white and colored varieties of the Yulan are handsome trees from 40 to 60 feet tall with a trunk often 8 feet in girth and a crown of ascending-spreading branches.

In China the Yulan is known to have been cultivated for more than thirteen centuries. Its flower is regarded as a symbol of candor and in paintings, porcelains, and embroideries it has been portrayed by all the best artists of the Orient. A point worthy of remembrance is that this tree has been propagated vegetatively by layering and grafting for we know not how many centuries. This does not appear to have impaired its constitution and accounts for plants less than a yard high flowering profusely.

Less hardy than the White Yulan but a great favorite in gardens is the Purple-flowered Yulan, commonly known as *M. obovata*, *M. purpurea* or *M. discolor*, but correctly as *M. liliflora*. It was introduced from China into England in 1790 but only quite recently has its discovery in a wild state been made. It appears to be always a shrub, and its handsome flowers vary somewhat in color, the finest being a rich wine-red.

Under cultivation several hybrids between *M. denudata* and *M. liliflora* have originated and proved themselves hardier and even better garden plants than their parents. The oldest and best known of these hybrids is *M. Soulangeana* which originated near Paris. It is a vigorous growing tree with flowers suffused with rose-color. Very similar to this are forms known in gardens as *M. speciosa, M. superba, M. cyathiformis, M. Alexandria, M. spectabilis* and *M. triumphans.* Quite distinct is *M. Lennei* with its large blossoms, the outside of the petals of which are port-wine color at the base, and rich crimson toward the tip. It is a late-flowering kind which originated as a seedling in Italy and is regarded as a natural hybrid of the two Yulans. Perhaps the finest of all these hybrids is that known as *M. rustica rubra,* with its large, cheery, rose-red flowers each petal of which is edged with white. It is a chance seedling supposed to be from *M. Lennei* and originated in a nursery in Boskoop Holland, about thirty-five years ago.

The Japanese *M. kobus* is common in forests throughout the greater part of Japan. The southern and typical form is a large bush or low tree, but the northern form *(borealis)* is a fine tree from 60 to 75 feet tall, broad-pyramidal in outline with a smooth trunk 6 feet in girth. This variety is the most northern of all Magnolias and was introduced into America in 1876, and later sent to Europe. It has proved to be the most free-growing of its group, and trees raised from the original seeds are now 40 feet tall with broad, pyramidate crowns. The blossoms are loose-petalled, white and smaller than those of the Yulan. Young trees flower sparsely but with age they are as floriferous as those of any other Magnolia.

Another very charming member of this group is *M. salicifolia,* an inhabitant of mountain woodlands of Japan from the extreme south to northern Hondo and was introduced into cultivation by Professor Sargent in 1892. It is a slender tree with small, white flowers and narrow thin leaves. The shoots when bruised emit a strong smell of camphor; in fact when I first found it wild I took this Magnolia for some member of the Camphor family.

The Himalayan *M. Campbellii* is in flower one of the most gorgeous of all northern trees. It has scented cup-shaped blossoms from deep rose to crimson in color and 10 inches across. It has not proved hardy in the British Isles except in one or two favored places where it has produced rosy pink flowers. A hybrid of this and the Yulan is the new *M. Veitchii* with ivory-white flowers tinged with pink on the outside. Rivalling this Himalayan treasure in beauty of blossom are *M. Sargentiana* and its variety *robusta* which I discovered and introduced in 1908. These are growing in France and in England and so, too, is another new species *(M. Dawsoniana)* of similar origin and distinguished by its lustrous green, leathery leaves. None of these has so far flowered in cultivation.

Of the Asiatic Magnolias which open their flowers after the leaves unfold six species are in cultivation. Perhaps the most striking of these is *M. obovata,* more generally known as *M. hypoleuca,* which in general appearance resembles the American *M. tripetala* and is widely distributed in forests of Japan from the south to the north where it is known as the Honoki. At its best this is a tree 80 feet tall and 7 feet in girth of trunk with smooth gray bark and a shapely crown of stout branches. The leaves are from a foot to a foot and a half long by half this in width at the broadest part, which is above the middle, and are deep green above and silvery beneath. Its flowers are bowl-shaped, 6 to 8 inches across, milk white fading to apricot with a ring of red-purple anthers and are heavily fragrant. It has very large cone-like fruits which are bright scarlet when ripe and very conspicuous. This Magnolia is an important timber tree in the forests of northern Japan, and with *M. kobus borealis* reaches the most northern geographical limits of the family. Closely related to the Honoki is a Chinese species *(M. officinalis)* which is growing in England, where it has flowered, from seeds which I sent there in

1900. In China the bark and dried flowers of this Magnolia are highly valued as tonic medicines.

A Magnolia whose beauty fascinated me in the forests of Korea is *M. parviflora*, which also grows in southern Japan. Its snow-white flowers are egg-shaped in bud and bowl-shaped with infolded petals when expanded, and have scarlet stamens. The specific name is misleading for the flowers are from 4 to 5 inches across. It is a large bush, often 20 feet high, of straggling habit, with ovate leaves each from 3 to 6 inches long and from 2 to 4 inches wide, and is remarkably floriferous. It delights in rocky, granite country and is especially happy by the side of forest streams. On the Diamond Mountains in northeast Korea, where the winter temperature is severe, this lovely Magnolia is a feature, and I have hopes of this Korean form being a better garden plant than the Japanese type in cultivation. There is also in Japan a form *(plena)* with semi-double flowers.

Related to the above but with narrow leaves clothed on the undersurface with pale brown silky hairs is *M. Wilsonii*, native of the mountain fastnesses of the Chino-Thibetan borderland. This is a wide-branching bush or small tree from 10 to 25 feet tall with pendent, pure white, fragrant, saucer-shaped flowers from 3 to 5 inches in diameter. This I discovered and introduced in 1904 and it is now growing happily in several English gardens where it has flowered and won for itself a host of friends.

Of mysterious origin is the rather tender Japanese *M. Watsonii* with leaves larger and thicker in texture than those of *M. parviflora*, and 6 inch broad, cup-shaped white flowers with blood-red stamens and a strong spicy odor.

Perhaps the most delightful of American Magnolias is the Sweet Bay *(M. virginiana,* better known as *M. glauca)* which grows in swamps from Massachusetts south to Louisiana. In its northern limits it is never more than a large bush or small tree but in Louisiana it is quite a large tree, often from 50 to 70 feet tall and from 6 to 10 feet in girth of trunk. It has dark green shining leaves which are silvery white on the underside; they are leathery in texture and in moist sheltered places the plant is sub-evergreen. The bark on the young shoots is a rich apple-green and on the older branches it is gray. The flowers are small, cup-shaped with infolding petals, creamy white, gradually acquiring a pale apricot hue, and are delightfully fragrant, scenting the whole neighborhood. They continue to open in succession from about mid-June until August when the red fruit-cones begin to show in marked contrast against the dark, glossy green foliage. There is not a more delightful North American tree to plant in gardens, nor one that will give larger returns in beauty and fragrance. It is an old garden plant having been discovered and introduced into gardens before the Seventeenth Century. In eastern Florida there is said to grow a dwarf form (*pumila*) which does not exceed 3 or 4 feet in height. A hybrid (*M. major*, better known as *M. Thompsoniana*) between the Sweet Bay and Umbrella-tree (*M. tripetala*) has the general appearance of *M. virginiana*, but larger leaves and larger flowers.

The most stately of the deciduous-leaved American Magnolias is *M. acuminata*, the Cucumber-tree, so-called from the slight resemblance borne by the young fruits to a small cucumber. It is a tree from 70 to 90 feet tall with a stout trunk and ascending-spreading, incurving branches forming a bold broad-pyramidal crown. The leaves are from 6 to 10 inches long, ovate, and pointed, green on both surfaces and slightly hairy below. The flowers are erect, glaucous-green tinged with yellow and are slightly fragrant. It is found wild from southern Ontario and western New York to Ohio and southward. A shapely free-growing tree, it is eminently suitable for avenue-planting and as a specimen tree in parks. It was one of the trees introduced into Europe by the famous John Bartram who sent it in 1746 to Collinson in London, with whom it flowered for the first time on May 20, 1762. There is a form of the Cucumber-tree *(aurea)* with yellow leaves slightly streaked and mottled with green.

Somewhat similar to *M. acuminata* is the yellow-flowered Cucumber-tree *(M. cordata)* whose history is quite romantic. It was originally discovered by the French botanist and traveler, Michaux, in the neighborhood of Augusta, Georgia, some time between 1787 and 1796 and by him (or his son) immediately sent to France. All the trees now in gardens have been derived from the original introduction. Many efforts to rediscover this tree were made but all failed until a few years ago when Mr. Louis A. Berckmans accidentally happened upon it in a dry wood some eighteen miles south of Augusta, Georgia.

Michaux described it as a tree from 40 to 50 feet tall but the rediscoveries were bushes from 4 to 6 feet high; more recently trees of good size have been found. As we know it in cultivation Michaux's plant is a medium-sized tree with a shapely crown and leaves more or less heart-shaped at the base and hairy on the underside. The cup-shaped faintly odorous yellow flowers are about 4 inches across, and have the inner petals frequently marked with reddish lines. It flowers freely about the beginning of June and in wet seasons bears a second crop of flowers in late July and August.

Most remarkable is the Great-leaf Magnolia *(M. macrophylla)* which has the largest undivided leaves of any tree hardy in the gardens of the north temperate regions. The leaves, sometimes as much as 3 ½ feet long and from 8 to 9 inches wide, are obovate-oblong, narrowed and heart-shape at the base, and hairy and white on the underside. The flowers open about the end of June and are fragrant, from 8 to 12 inches across, bowl-shaped, white with a purple blotch at the base of each inner petal. It is not a large tree, seldom exceeding 40 feet in height with a trunk about 3 feet in girth. It attains its maximum development in sheltered valleys and forest glades on the limestones of North Carolina. It is another discovery of the elder Michaux who found it in North Carolina in 1789 and introduced it into European gardens the following year. Naturally with such huge leaves this Magnolia requires protection from the wind and it should be planted in cool, sheltered places. Be it noted that this is a limestone species and, moreover, a much hardier plant than it is generally supposed to be. It is hardy in the Arnold Arboretum and at Rochester, New York; also there are grand trees in the old enclosed garden adjoining Jussieu's garden near the Petit Trianon at Versailles. Such a wonderful tree is worthy of the widest recognition among garden lovers.

Ranking next in size of leaf to the above is the Umbrella-tree *(M. tripetala)* which has leaves from 1½ to 3 feet long, obovate-lance-shaped, tapering at both ends, and clustered at the end of the shoot. The flowers are white, slightly scented and from 5 to 8 inches across. The Umbrella-tree seldom exceeds 40 feet in height, and grows wild on the Alleghany Mountains. It is an old denizen of gardens; having been introduced into cultivation about 1750, it flowered the first time in England on May 24, 1760.

The first of the American Magnolias to open the flowers each year in Massachusetts is *M. Fraseri,* the Ear-leaf Umbrella-tree. It is native of the southern Appalachian region but is quite hardy in the Arnold Arboretum. A slender tree, rarely more than 40 feet tall, it has an open crown of long branches, foot-long leaves, oblong-obovate and spatulate in shape, deeply cleft at base, green above and glaucous below. Its flowers, which are very conspicuous by reason of their standing well above the end of the branches, are creamy white, sweet-scented and from 8 to 10 inches across; they

PINK YULAN, MAGNOLIA SOULANGEANA, HOLM LEA, BROOKLINE, MASSACHUSETTS

open about the end of May. This tree was discovered by W. Bartram as long ago as 1776 and introduced into Europe about 1784 by John Fraser. Closely related to the above but smaller in all its parts is *M. pyramidata* which grows wild in the extreme southwestern corner of Alabama and adjacent Florida.

Of the evergreen Magnolias the only Asiatic species calling for mention here is *M. Delavayi*. This has ovate, pointed, leathery leaves, dull green above and pale below, and in size larger than those of any other evergreen tree that can be grown in the cool-temperate lands. The flowers are fragrant, white, cup-shaped, from 6 to 8 inches across, and are followed by large red, cone-like fruits. A native of Yunnan, southwest China, it is a broad, much-branched tree fully 50 feet tall. I had the pleasure of introducing this Magnolia into English gardens by means of seeds sent in the late autumn of 1899. Plants raised from them flowered for the first time in Kew Gardens in 1908. This is a splendid evergreen tree for California and the warm states.

One of the noblest of all evergreen trees is the Bay Laurel or Bull Bay *(M. grandiflora)* native of southeastern United States. It is worth a journey to Louisiana to see this tree luxuriating on its native heath where it is sometimes 100 feet tall and 12 feet in girth of trunk. It has many relatively short, spreading branches which form a bell-shaped crown. The leaves are of good size, glossy green above, gray to rust-red on the underside. The cup-shaped flowers are fully 8 inches across, white fading to cream with a rather heavy spicy odor. Like other American Magnolias it was early introduced into Europe; it was in England in 1737 but is only properly hardy in the most favored parts of that country. In Europe a great many seedling forms have appeared differing in trivial characters, chiefly those of the leaf. The most marked are varieties *angustifolia, ferruginea, lanceolata* and *obovata*.

HANDSOME HORSECHESTNUT

F A census of opinion were taken as to which is the most handsome exotic flowering tree in the eastern part of the United States there is little doubt but that it would be overwhelmingly in favor of the Horsechestnut. In Europe also the same would be true. For no other tree is a day specially set apart in England as is Chestnut Sunday for this famous exotic. According to season this is a rather movable feast but it is usually between May 19th and May 26th, when from London and its suburbs people journey in thousands to bask in the glory of the avenue of Horsechestnut trees in Bushey Park, on the banks of Father Thames.

The width of the avenue is 170 feet and its length about one mile. It was planted by the celebrated architect, Sir Christopher Wren in 1699. There are one hundred and thirty-seven trees on each side and they stand 42 feet apart in the line. A quarter of a mile from the Hampton Court Palace end of the avenue a round pond 400 feet in diameter, with a noble fountain in the centre, forces the Horsechestnut trees from line to circle with great enchantment of effect. Some of the larger trees have died and have been replaced by young ones, but the show of blossoms is wonderful year after year. The largest trees are fully 100 feet tall and from 10 to 20 feet in girth of trunk, with handsome crowns, the lower branches of which sweep the ground.

The tree is so common a feature of the landscape in the British Isles that a majority of the people take it for granted that it is a native tree. With schoolboys it is a great favorite for does it not furnish the seeds used to play the famous game of Conquerors? Among my earliest recollections is that of a grove of trees in an ecclesiastical seminary, and much I used to appreciate a generous gift of nuts from the student priests. How carefully one used to bore a hole through them—a horseshoe nail being a favorite tool—dry them afterward, and test their strength in battles with other boys. Some were clever in hardening them by roasting, but, so far as memory serves, mine always burst when placed in the oven. Many a mile do boys in England walk to gather the Horsechestnut seeds and when seven or eight years old my proudest possession was a long rope of them. Young schoolboys can scarcely be expected to be interested in trees for their beauty alone. Of fruit as something to eat it is quite a different matter, and I know of no other tree that boys take interest in unless to satisfy their appetite. Deer greedily eat the nuts of the Horsechestnut but cattle leave them alone.

Considering its striking appearance, its handsome flowers, and its general popularity, comparatively little has been written about the tree. No poet or writer of prose has immortalized it in the sense that the Holly, Yew, weeping Willow, not to mention the Rose, have been immortalized. Some have seen in its prodigality of blossoms and the manner in which they strew the ground a symbol of ostentation, but surely this is harsh judgment. Should it not with more propriety be likened to the exuberance of joyous youth—healthy, carefree, and overflowing with happiness as schoolboys on a holiday? Of all trees the Horsechestnut is most fitting to be regarded as an emblem of vigorous youth. An alien to the parks and gardens of western Europe and to those of this country it came, and by merit of its hardiness, its sturdy growth, and lovely flowers it conquered, established itself among us and holds its own among the wealth of indigenous trees.

In literature and art Greece has given much to the world, and the western world gladly acknowledges the debt it owes. It is less generally known that to her many other gifts Greece added the Horsechestnut, but the fact is established after a lapse of three and a half centuries. Western Europe's first knowledge of the Horse-chestnut was of trees cultivated in Constantinople—just as was the case with the Lilac, most familiar of garden shrubs. The two discoveries almost synchronized. The Lilac was sent from Constantinople to Vienna by Dr. von Ungnad, Imperial Ambassador to the court of Suliman II, and a tree was raised by the celebrated Clusius. But a Flemish doctor, one Quakleben, who was attached to the embassy of Archduke Ferdinand I at Constantinople, in 1557 first mentioned the tree in a letter to Mattioli as told in the letters, *"Epistolarum medicinalium libri quinque,"* published in Prague in 1561. Later Mattioli received a fruit-bearing branch and published the first description of the tree with a good figure of the leaves and fruit on page 212 of his *Commentarii in libros sex Pedacii Dioscoridis De medica materia,* which was published in Venice in 1565. Mattioli called it *Castanea equina* because the fruits were known as At-Kastan (Horsechestnut) to the Turks who found them useful as a drug for horses suffering from broken wind or coughs. Here then we have the origin of the popular name which has remained unchanged to this day. The generic name Aesculus, from *esca,* nourishment, was adopted by Linnaeus, but was first given by Pliny to a kind of Oak having an edible fruit. The specific name Hippocastanum was also adopted by Linnaeus in 1753, and is the vernacular name latinized. The tree raised in Vienna by Clusius grew rapidly and is mentioned by him, with a good figure of the leaves and fruit and the history of its introduction to Vienna, on page 7 of his work entitled *Rariorum Plantarum Historia,* published in 1601.

To France seeds were brought from Constantinople by Bachelier

Horsechestnut, Aesculus hippocastanum, 70 feet tall, trunk 10 feet girth, spread 80 feet, Salem, Massachusetts

in 1615. It was probably introduced to England about the same time, for in Johnson's edition of Gerarde's *Herbal*, published in 1633, it is stated that the Horsechestnut was growing in John Tradescant's garden at South Lambeth. In the original edition, published in 1597, Gerarde mentions it as a tree growing in Italy and sundry places of the eastern countries.

In the early struggling days of this country its English settlers found time to introduce many plants of esthetic value as well as those of purely economic worth. But, unfortunately, dates are so often lacking that exact history is seldom available. Were these more ascertainable the romance of familiar garden flowers and crops would be apparent. History in general as taught in schools may be as "dry as dust," but the salient historical facts appertaining to the commonplace things of every-day life and acquaintance are rich in interest. And, moreover, their teaching is not without its direct value in present day affairs. Our ancestors sought food for the body and things of beauty to delight the soul even as we do today. We enjoy the results of their labors, and it is our bounden duty to hand them on, and in increasing worth, to the generations that succeed our immediate own. Whether this is done through selfish or altruistic motives it matters not at all in the practical results which accrue. And it will be done though in a measure unconsciously. Improved strains of wheat, pulse, cotton, of Roses and new flowers, of everything which increases the food resources or ministers to the soul have today, as they always have had and must ever have, not only immediate but progressive value to the human race.

As we realize what our forebears did under adverse conditions the question as to what we are doing naturally presents itself. After all the present generation is not a slothful, heedless one; selfish and thoughtless it may be but the fault is not deliberate on its part. Ignorance is not yet eradicated neither is it ineradicable, but instruction is needed today just as it always has been needed. Every father has thoughts of providing toward the future welfare of his children, and if these thoughts tend more to their material advancement in bodily comforts it is not that he wishes to starve their minds. From personal experience every present-day father knows the need of the one, fewer know the needs of both. As the race develops so a proper appreciation of the needs of body and mind will be attained, and the fact clearly appreciated that mind is greater than matter and its needs even more important. In God's great book of Nature will be found food essential to the full and proper development of the human race. All this may seem to belong more to the realm of philosophy than to the matter of the Horsechestnut, and yet the story of this tree is, after all, the commonplace story of the triumph of the beautiful over the sordid cares of life. And it demonstrates anew the truism that beauty is transcendental.

Thanks to the letters published by William Darlington in his *Memorials of John Bartram and Humphry Marshall* in 1849, the story of the introduction of the Horsechestnut into America is on record. Thus page 146, London, September 16, 1741: "I have sent some Horsechestnuts which are ripe earlier than usual; hope they will come fit for planting." P. Collinson, p. 175; April 16th, 1746: "I have some hopes of the Horsechestnut though most of them were blue-molded yet some seemed to be pretty sound." J. Bartram.

And finally, p. 252, London, August 4, 1763: "But what delights me is, to hear that our Horsechestnut has flowered. I think it much excells the Virginia, if the spikes of flowers are as large with you as with us. To see a long avenue of these at Hampton Court— of trees 50 feet high—being perfect pyramids of flowers from top to bottom, for all the spikes of blossom are at the extremities—is one of the grandest and most charming sights in the world." P. Collinson.

I have had some experience in sending seeds from distant lands and consider the Horsechestnut among the most difficult to transport safely. I marvel that in those days of slow sailing ships it should have been successfully done. From the lapse of time between Collinson's reply it may be inferred that more than one consignment was sent. But sticking to it does wonders, and today we benefit from these grand old plant lovers' successful efforts. In this one accomplishment they made the American people their debtors—such debts are pleasant to acknowledge and to bear.

So well known is the Horsechestnut that it seems superfluous to attempt a description of the tree. It will grow well on sandy or on calcareous soils but luxuriates best in rich, cool loam. Given plenty of room in park or on lawn it will exceed 100 feet in height and 20 feet in girth of trunk. Its massive branches with their laterals form a splendid oval or bell-shaped crown and sweep the ground. In spring pyramids, each fully 10 inches high, of flowers are upthrust from the ends of thousands of branches. No tree is more spectacularly beautiful. The petals are erect and tend to curve backward, the stamens—seven in number—and the style are slightly curved and projected forward, and serve as a platform for bees— their chief visitors. On the face of the upper petal are yellow spots which later turn red and are called honey-guides. A closer inspection will reveal other interesting facts. In each thrysoid inflorescence the upper flowers open first and are potentially male; the lower flowers are perfect, but the pistil matures first and is ready to receive the pollen immediately the flowers open; the stamens in these flowers are at first bent down below the style, later on they move up to its level. We see here a provision for cross-pollination from the upper male flowers and, if this fails, self-pollination is assured by the rising of the stamens in the same flowers. The scent of the flowers is remotely like that of the Hawthorn and is not particularly pleasant. The bright green leaves unfold slightly before the inflorescence appears and are full grown when the flowers are wholly expanded. The leaves are disposed in opposite pairs on the shoots, have a long, stout stalk, and the blade is of from five to seven separate leaflets radiating from a common base like fingers of the hand. When the leaves fall in the autumn they leave prominent scars on the shoots. The winter-buds are large, chestnut-brown, and are covered with resinous scale-leaves; they contain next year's shoots in an advanced state including the flowers. If sliced vertically all this may be clearly seen in winter; in spring the buds expand very rapidly as the least observant must have noticed, a whole shoot from 1 to 1½ feet long being fully developed inside of three weeks. These viscid winter-buds are a character of importance. In eastern North America several species of Horsechestnut grow wild. Here they are known as Buckeyes; and is not Ohio the Buckeye State? But all these have gray winter-buds, perfectly free of any suspicion of resin. The Old-World species, of which there are six (one in Japan, two in China, two in India, and one in Greece), and the one which grows wild in California have viscid winter-buds.

The large, nearly globular, fruit with its prickly studded shell is well known. It splits and falls when ripe and liberates the seeds which vary from one to three and are glossy, shining brown with a broad pale gray base. The Horsechestnut is easily raised from seeds, grows rapidly, and is readily transplanted. In dry summers and in towns its leaves turn brown early and for this reason, and also on account of its fruit, it is not a good tree for street planting. It is, however, for specimens and for avenues and parks, exemplary.

The wood of the Horsechestnut is soft, lacks strength and durability, and is of little or no value. It burns badly and is not much good as fuel. The bark contains gallic acid and a bitter principle, which gives its value as a tonic equalling that of the Willow. The seeds have many uses besides that employed by schoolboys, and the ancient one of the Turks. Their taste is at once mild and bitter and they are rich in starch. Reduced to powder they serve as soap; roasted they are used as coffee; fermented they yield a spirituous liquor which yields alcohol by distillation. The young aromatic buds have been substituted for hops in the manufacture of beer. During the Great War the nuts were tried in England for the preparation of acetone by the fermentation process, and it was considered that the difficulties attendant on their use for this purpose were in a fair way of being surmounted when the armistice was signed.

Until comparatively recently the Caucasus, Persia, northern India, and Thibet were variously given as the supposed home of the Horsechestnut. On the authority of Doctor Hawkins, Sibthorp in his *Flora of Greece*, published in 1806, states that this tree is wild on Mt. Pelion in Crete but later investigations have decided that it was only planted there. Trees introduced into Greece by the Turks are always found in the neighborhood of towns, and it is doubtful that the ancient Greeks had any knowledge of the Horsechestnut. For centuries the native country of this tree was a matter of doubt and the question was not settled definitely until 1879, when Theodor von Heldreick published a full account of it. It is now known to be wild on the mountains of Thessaly, Epirus, and other parts of northern Greece. In 1897 it was found growing wild on precipices in the district of Janina in Albania, below the lower limit of the coniferous belt.

Quite naturally in a tree so long cultivated several varieties have been detected and perpetuated by vegetative propagation. Among the most distinct are the varieties *pyramidalis, umbraculifera, tortuosa* and *pendula,* sufficiently described by their names. A form

with leaflets incised into narrow lobes has been distinguished as
laciniata; another with short-stalked, yellowish variegated leaves
suggests a diseased condition and ought to be discountenanced. A
variety with double flowers *(Baumannii),* however, has merit since
the flowers last longer than those of the type, and as it bears no
fruit it may be planted where the type is objectionable. In 1822,
near Geneva, a Mr. A. M. Baumann discovered on an ordinary
Horsechestnut-tree a single branch which bore double flowers. This
branch was propagated by the Bollweiler Nursery in Alsace, and
this is the source of all the plants of the double-flowered variety in
cultivation.

To many people the name Horsechestnut stands only for the
great tree from the mountains of Greece, but there are many other
Horsechestnuts, both trees and shrubs, some with yellow, some
with orange and others with red flowers of various shades. These
sorts with colored flowers are all natives of this country, where they
are generally known as Buckeyes, but some of the handsomest are
hybrids in which the American and European species have been
blended. The best known is the red-flowered *Aesculus carnea,* a
hybrid probably between the Common Horsechestnut and the red-
flowered *A. Pavia* from the southeastern United States, although
the actual history of its origin is unknown. These hybrids and varieties of the American Horsechestnut were popular garden plants
in France in the first half of the last century but they have now
largely disappeared from cultivation and are difficult to obtain. The
flowers vary from flesh-color to deep red and handsomest of all the
forms being known as *A. carnea Briotii,* which is one of the most
beautiful of all flowering trees hardy in Massachusetts.

The yellow-flowered *A. octandra* is the largest of the Buckeyes
and blooms a little later than *A. carnea.* The best known, in books
at least, of the red-flowered southern Buckeyes is *A. Pavia,* tender

in New England. An even more beautiful plant, is the red-flowered
A. discolor mollis, which is generally distributed from the coast of
North Carolina to southern Arkansas and western Texas, and in
flower one of the most brilliant plants of the South. A recently
described species from the southeastern states is *A. georgiana,* a
broad, round-topped shrub, growing from 5 to 6 feet tall with large,
red and yellow flowers in long compact clusters, and a plant of much
promise as a garden ornament. From eastern Texas hails the yellow-
flowered *A. arguta,* a small shrub, and from the southern and southwestern states *A. austrina,* a beautiful red-flowered shrub or small
tree.

Harbison's Buckeye *(A. Harbisonii)* is the latest species to
unfold its leaves, which do not appear until those of most of the
other trees and shrubs of its family are nearly full grown. It is a
good garden plant which has proved itself perfectly hardy in the
Arnold Arboretum, where it has flowered regularly for many years.
The stem and branches of the flower-cluster and the calyx are rose
color, and the petals are canary-yellow slightly streaked with red
toward the margins; the lateness of their appearance adds to the
value of this shrub. By the middle of July the last of the Buckeyes
(A. parviflora) is in flower. This native of the southeastern states is
a broad, round-topped, much branched shrub from 6 to 10 feet high,
and every branchlet terminates in long, narrow, erect spikes of small
white flowers in which the stamens are long exserted. This shrub
requires good soil and a moist situation and is well suited for planting in large masses or as a single specimen.

All the Horsechestnuts demand a deep cool loam which should
be liberally enriched with fertilizer from time to time, cow manure
and bonemeal being their favorite foods. While the Common Horsechestnut is a familiar subject in this country, it is by no means over
planted. At the same time, it has been placed where it cannot do

itself justice. As a street tree, it has no value. In the first place, owing to under drainage, lack of air, and food, and smoke and gas-laden atmosphere, the foliage turns brown early in August and the tree becomes unsightly. Moreover, it fruits freely and these are not only a temptation to boys to climb and break the trees but are a nuisance as they litter the streets. For the large garden or especially in the park, either as a specimen tree or an avenue, it cannot be excelled. The yellow, pink, and red-flowered forms are splendid for the small garden, being trees of moderate size, but the bush sorts are best employed on the margin of woods or on the outskirts of a garden.

Nurserymen have neglected these handsome trees, all of which are easily raised, the species from seeds, the hybrids by grafting on understocks of the Common Horsechestnut. The French are the people who properly appreciate our colored Horsechestnuts and it is high time the American public awoke to the value of these native trees and their hybrid progeny. Their season of blooming is a lengthy one, starting about mid-May according to climate and extending in succession well into July. They are permanent plants that repay the good food they demand.

FRAGRANT LINDEN

HE first northern tree of the year to open its blossoms is the Silver Maple *(Acer saccharinum,* more
widely known, perhaps, as *A. dasycarpum),* a magnificent tree which grows to a large size in rich bottom
lands of eastern North America. The flowers are formed in knot-like
clusters along the shoots in late autumn and any time after mid-
February when the weather is mild they may open. The last of the
trees to bloom is an Asiatic Elm with small leaves known as *Ulmus
parviflora.* In both cases the flowers are inconspicuous, which is
true also of a majority of northern trees outside of the members of
the great Rose family. As April approaches various Cherries put
forth their delightful flowers in utmost profusion and competing
with them we have the Magnolias, followed by Almonds, Peaches,
Plums and the whole of the great Crabapple family. Throughout
April and May there is a plethora of bloom on bush and tree but
as mid-June arrives blossoms become less plentiful. However, there
are a number of trees, some native, others exotic, which have their
season of flower at high summer. The leaves in every case open first
so the flowers are seen to best advantage against a foil of rich green.
These trees have a special value in gardens, being well-suited for a
place on the lawn, large or small, and for parks and pleasure resorts.

The most important summer-flowering trees are the Lindens
(Tilia) whose fragrant flowers perfume the air during a large part
of the month of July. Usually the trees of eastern Asia are more
successful in this climate than those of the same genus from Europe,
but to this general rule Tilia is an exception. All the European

species and their hybrids and varieties flourish in New England, but the Asiatic species are bad growers there, and only *Tilia japonica* really flourishes. This is a late-flowering species with drooping branches and light green foliage and is conspicuous in early spring as it unfolds its leaves a week or two before those of other Lindens.

The most widely distributed of European Lindens is *T. platyphyllos*, which may be recognized by the yellow tinge of the leaves and by the thick covering of short hairs on their lower surface. It is not the handsomest of the European Lindens, but it is the tree which is usually sold by American nurserymen as the European Linden. There is a variety with leaves larger than those of the type (*grandifolia*), another with erect branches forming a broad pyramidal crown (*pyramidalis*) and others with variously divided leaves (*lacinata* and *vitifolia*). A handsomer tree is *T. cordata*, the common Linden of northern Europe, where it sometimes grows to a large size. This may be recognized by its small, thin, more or less heart-shaped leaves which are pale on the lower surface and furnished with conspicuous tufts of rusty brown hairs in the axils of the principal veins. Unfortunately, it has been rarely planted in this country although it is the latest of the Lindens to flower and especially valuable for supplying bees with food after the flowers of other species have faded.

The finest of the Lindens of western Europe is considered a natural hybrid between the two species already described, and is variously called *T. vulgaris, T. europaea, T. intermedia* and *T. hybrida*, the first name having preference. Although widely distributed in Europe, this tree appears to be much less common than either of its supposed parents. It is a tall round-headed tree, and noble specimens can be found in New England, where formerly it must have been more often planted than any of the other foreign Lindens.

EUROPEAN LINDEN, TILIA VULGARIS, 85 FEET TALL, TRUNK 12 FEET GIRTH, SPREAD
60 FEET, HOPE HOUSE, EASTON, MARYLAND

EUROPEAN LINDEN, TILIA VULGARIS, 85 FEET TALL; TRUNK 12 FEET GIRTH,
HOPE HOUSE, EASTON, MARYLAND

Two Lindens occur in eastern Europe, the Silver Linden *(T. tomentosa)* and *T. petiolaris*. The former is a tree with erect-growing branches which form a broad, compact, round-topped, rather formal head, and roundish leaves dark green above and silvery white below. This distinct-looking tree is not very common in Massachusetts, but it can be often seen in the neighborhood of New York and Philadelphia. A more beautiful tree is *T. petiolaris* which also has leaves silvery white on the lower surface, but, drooping on long slender stalks, they flutter gracefully in the slightest breeze. The branches, too, are drooping and form a narrow head. This tree is not known in a wild state, and all the plants in cultivation have been derived from a single individual found many years ago in a garden in Odessa. A supposed hybrid of this tree and *T. glabra* is *T. Moltkei*, often sold in nurseries as *T. alba spectabilis*, one of the most beautiful of all Lindens with leaves in size and shape like those of *T. glabra* but silvery white on the lower surface. In Europe much attention is paid to another supposed hybrid Linden, *T. euchlora*, or as it is more generally known, *T. dasystyla*. This is a fast-growing, pyramidal tree with lustrous dark green leaves and is now largely planted as a street tree in Germany and Holland. It is hardy here and promises to be a useful ornamental tree in New England.

The common Basswood *(T. glabra)*, better known as *T. americana*, is a common northern tree, growing, probably, to its largest size along the northern borders of the United States from Nova Scotia to Minnesota, and easily distinguished by the green and shining lower surface of the large leaves which have no hairy covering with the exception of the conspicuous tufts in the axils of the principal veins. The leaves of this tree cultivated near cities are often made brown, especially in hot, dry summers, by the red spider, which, however, can be controlled by spraying with sulphur dust.

Michaux's Basswood *(T. Michauxii)* is a common tree in the northern states and is distributed from the valley of the St. Lawrence River to the mountains of North Carolina and to Missouri and Arkansas. It may be readily distinguished by the thin covering of pale brownish hairs on the lower surface of the leaves. The third of the Linden trees of the northern states is *T. monticola,* which is found from western New York to northern Alabama, and through Kentucky to southern Indiana and Illinois, reaching its largest size and greatest beauty in the forests which cover the high slopes of the mountains of North Carolina and Tennessee. The leaves of this tree are larger than those of the other American Lindens, oblong in shape, very oblique at the base and silvery white on the lower surface, and, hanging on long slender stalks, the slightest breeze makes them turn first one surface and then the other to the eye. This beautiful and perfectly hardy tree appears to be rarely cultivated.

One of the noblest trees of the Orient is *Acanthopanax ricinifolius,* which covers itself with broad, terminal clusters of small, white flowers during the month of August. This tree is found in China and in northeastern Asia generally, reaching its greatest size in the forests of Manchuria and northern Japan, where it is often 100 feet tall with a trunk 15 feet in girth. It has palmate leaves on long stalks singularly resembling those of the Castor Oil plant (Ricinus), hence its specific name. The bark is dark gray, deeply fissured and both trunk and branches are studded with short, stout prickles. The small, white flowers are produced in a compound, flattened truss at the ends of each shoot and they are very speedily followed by small fruits which at first reddish change to black. It is one of the hardiest of all trees, delighting in a rich soil and a cool situation. It is easily raised from seed and after the first few years grows rapidly. So far as I know it is not attacked by any disease or insect pest. The wood also is valuable and at one time it was much exported from Japan to Germany under the name of Sen. For the colder parts of this country and the St. Lawrence Valley and Canada I know of no more hardy flowering tree. Its large foliage has quite a tropical appearance, but, unfortunately, it assumes no autumn tints. On account of its prickles it should make a useful street and park tree, since small boys and others are not tempted to climb into its branches.

A close relative of the above is *Aralia chinensis*, the Angelica-tree. This is a small tree, seldom exceeding 15 feet in height with a thin trunk and few branches, all armed with sharp prickles. The much divided leaves are armed here and there with stout prickles. They are of enormous size, being sometimes as much as a yard long and broad. The inflorescence is terminal, huge in size and consists of a compound, paniculate mass 1½ to 2 feet through. The individual flowers are small, pure white and are rapidly followed by small, red, changing to black, berries. The plant suckers freely and is apt to become a nuisance unless planted by itself. On the edge of a cool woodland or by the side of a pond half a dozen of these trees make an arresting picture in August. This oriental tree is widely spread in China, Japan and Korea and several forms are known but the differences that distinguish them are purely technical. A related species is *A. spinosa*, the Devil's Walking-stick, which grows on the southern Appalachian Mountains. It is a more slender tree, somewhat taller than its oriental relative but is less hardy.

A handsome Korean tree which flowers in the first half of August is *Evodia Daniellii*, a member of the Rue family. It is a smooth-barked tree, seldom more than 30 feet tall, with a flattened round crown and a wealth of pinnate, Ash-like leaves, which, if crushed, give off the well-known odor of rue. The flowers are white with prominent yellow anthers and produced many together in flat, terminal corymbs. Some trees produce male flowers only, whereas, in others the flowers are hermaphrodite. In case of the perfect flower truss dry capsular fruits containing jet black, shot-like seeds form in September and are almost as handsome as the flowers. I have noted that the male flowers are particularly attractive to bees. This, like the Acanthopanax, is not subject to disease or insect attacks and has proved very hardy.

Maackia amurensis is a tree often 60 feet tall and flowers in July. It has dark green, pinnate leaves which fall in the autumn without much change of color. The flowers are borne in erect, cylindrical racemes, which, branching at the base, form candelabra-like masses. The individual flowers are cream-colored, pea-shaped with a much swollen calyx; the standard is strongly recurved and greenish, while the keel opens to display the orange-red anthers. The fruit is a dry, thin pod and possesses no ornamental qualities. More handsome is the variety *Buergeri*, which differs in having the leaflets hairy on the underside.

One of the first trees of the Orient to be introduced into cultivation was *Sophora japonica*, the Pagoda-tree, which was sent to France so long ago as 1747. It is much cultivated in the Far East, being usually associated with Buddhist temples and other religious sanctuaries but its real home is northern China. It is well known in gardens and valuable on account of its late-flowering qualities. Moreover, it seems to withstand city conditions better than the average tree, as specimens in the Public Garden, Boston, Massachusetts, well demonstrate. The leaves are pinnate, dark green above, gray on the underside, and the bark is deeply fissured and corrugated giving old trees the appearance of the White Ash. The flowers, which appear in early August, are cream-colored and borne in large, much-branched panicles at the end of every shoot and are followed by slender, jointed pods which, if crushed, are soapy to the touch. In the Orient trees 80 feet tall with a trunk 12 feet in girth and an abundance of gnarled, wide-spreading roots are frequently to be seen. There are several horticultural varieties, the most distinct being that with pendent, crowded branches *(pendula)*. Grafted high as a standard, this makes a picturesque tree.

Koelreuteria paniculata, often but erroneously called Varnish Tree, is one of the handsomest flowering trees hardy in North America and, except the Laburnum, the only tree with yellow blossoms that can be grown in New England. It is a flat-topped tree, seldom 40 feet high but with a crown more than this in diameter, and dark green, pinnate leaves with incised leaflets. The flowers are borne in enormous compound, paniculate masses at the end of every shoot. They are similar in shape to those of the Horsechestnut, but are clear yellow in color with prominent orange-red markings at the base of the petals. The fruit is top-shaped and bladder-like; at first white it ultimately changes to pink and brown. Native of northern China, this tree was brought into cultivation more than a century and a half ago but is by no means as widely grown as its merits deserve. Like *Sophora japonica* it thrives in town gardens and parks better than a majority of trees and on this account is doubly valuable. It is easily raised from seed and there is no reason why it should not be readily obtainable.

The western Catalpa *(Catalpa speciosa)* is a magnificent flowering tree native of the Mississippi Valley, where it is often more than 100 feet tall with a trunk 12 feet in girth. It has broad, heart-shaped, long-pointed leaves and terminal clusters of large blossoms. The Pentstemon-like corolla has fringed lobes and is more or less striped and dotted with brown-purple on the lower half and marked within the tube with yellow. For park or large garden this is an excellent tree but it has no place in the suburban lot and much less should it be used as a street tree, its disadvantages being that the leaves unfold late and fall early without any change of color, and for much of the year the tree is gaunt in appearance. A related species, which is more common in gardens, flowers later and is distinguished by its smaller flowers, is C. *bignonioides*.

Oxydendrum arboreum, the Sorrel-tree or Sourwood, is one of the few tree members of the great family to which belong the Rhododendrons, Kalmias, Ericas, Vacciniums and other familiar plants. Native of the southeastern United States, it is a tree from 30 to 50 feet tall with a straight trunk clothed with dark gray, furrowed bark. The pointed leaves are oblong-lance-shaped, finely serrated along the margins, bright green on both surfaces and have a pleasant acidulous taste, from which character the tree derives its generic name. The urn-shaped flowers, borne in loose, spreading panicles at the end of every shoot, commence to open towards the end of July. As the corollas wither, dry, white fruits simulating the flowers in appearance speedily form and remain attractive late into the fall. Among native trees none assume more brilliant autumn tints of orange and crimson and from the time the flower buds appear in mid-July until the leaves fall in late October the Sourwood is decidedly ornamental.

Another late-flowering tree worthy of a place in gardens is *Rhus javanica*, better known as *R. Osbeckii* or *R. semialata*. This is seldom more than 20 feet tall with a wide-spreading, flattened crown and erect, terminal clusters of white blossoms. It has handsome pinnate foliage and is one of the most ornamental of its group.

After the last flower has disappeared from the common Lilac its kinsmen, the Tree Lilacs, claim the field. These have large terminal trusses of pure white flowers, resembling magnified infloresences of the Privet, borne above dark green leathery foliage which sets them off to great advantage. These trees are natives of the Orient and three species are known. The most familiar, perhaps, is *Syringa japonica*, a shapely tree sometimes 40 feet tall with smooth, polished bark and a round-topped crown. Very similar is *S. amurensis*, different in being perfectly smooth in all its parts. These inhabit the cold regions of Manchuria, Korea and northern Japan and are perfectly hardy well north into Canada. The third species is *S. pekinensis* found widespread throughout northern China and distinguished by its smaller leaves and its deeply corrugated bark.

GRACEFUL BIRCH

IRCHES are graceful, fast-growing trees to which greater attention ought to be paid in landscape plantings. There is much character in the bark, and the slender branches form a light and feathery crown of singular grace and charm. The genus is essentially a northern one, ranging from the Arctic Circle to the Tropic of Cancer with its greatest development in cold temperate regions. Its southern limits are the Yunnan province of southwestern China and the Himalayas. About forty species are recognized and nearly all are in cultivation. Some like *Betula nana, B. glandulosa, B. fruticosa, B. humilis* and *B. pumila* are low, broad bushes; *B. Potaninii* is prostrate, the branches often hanging down the face of cliffs. But the great majority are trees of varying size, some quite large, and it is with these that this essay deals.

Two low-level Himalayan species *(B. alnoides* and *B. cylindrostachya)* are not properly hardy in northern lands and some of the Chinese species like *B. Fargesii* and *B. insignis* are little known and not in cultivation, but the majority of Birches are boreal trees, hardy and amenable under northern skies.

The one deciduous-leaved tree most readily recognized is surely the White Birch, Lady of the Woods, of which there are half a dozen species. In size and timber value the White Birches are exceeded by many others but in distinctiveness, in grace and in beauty they are certainly not surpassed. The White Birches of Europe and north-western Asia *(B. pendula* and *B. pubescens)* of northeastern Asia *(B. japonica)* and of North America *(B. populifolia* and *B. papyrifera)* inhabit the open waste places of the northern hemisphere where they cover vast areas and often form pure forests of great extent. Moreover, they, like the Aspens, are natural nurses for more valuable trees such as Larch and Spruce.

The genus is singularly well equipped to perpetuate and spread itself though it is a light demanding tree. The male and female flowers are borne in catkins, separately but on the same individual; they are pollinated by the wind and the fruit ripens early and disintegrates. The seeds are very light, are provided with wings and are easily transported by the winds. Many of the White Birches flourish on the poorest of gravelly soils and being of gregarious habit quickly form thickets and woods. All the species should be raised from seeds and it takes but a few years to obtain trees of good size. Sow the seeds on the surface of prepared light soil, throw a thin layer of brush wood over the beds beneath which the seeds will vegetate freely and the seedlings make rapid growth. Transplant in nursery rows and later into final positions. Nothing in the art of raising trees is simpler than the requirements of Birch. Forms of special merit, pendulous, cut-leaf, etc., should be grafted on the parent species. Though many White Birches will grow in the poorest of gravelly soil they do not object to good loam, a soil best suited to the members of the genus at large.

Under the name of *Betula alba,* Linnaeus confused the two White Birches so abundant in Europe and northern Asia far into Siberia. These are known as *B. pubescens* and *B. pendula,* the former being distinguished by its hairy and the latter by its warty branchlets. *B. pubescens* is the smaller and less important tree and is partial to moist places. On mature trees the bark is dark, fissured and rugged at the base of the trunk. The best form is the variety *urticifolia,* a native of Sweden and characterized by its long drawn-out leaf apex. *B. pendula* has silvery white bark on the trunk and main branches, polished red-brown branchlets clothed with glandular warty excrescences and pendent tips. There is no more graceful and beautiful tree than this Lady of the Woods which, though usually about 60 feet, is sometimes as much as 100 feet tall. There are several named varieties including one *(fastigiata)* with erect branches and columnar in habit like a small Lombardy Poplar. Another, Young's Weeping Birch *(Youngii)* is singularly charming with its slender hanging flagellate branches and is the best of several weeping forms. A good variety found wild in Sweden is *dalecarlica* with deeply laciniated and coarsely-toothed hanging leaves and pendent branchlets.

The American homologue of the White Birch is *B. populifolia*, the Gray Birch, a small tree rarely more than 30 feet tall with a slender trunk, tumid at the base and often with a cluster of stems diverging from a common rootstock; the bark is compact, firm, dull chalky white, bright orange on the inner side with dark triangular markings at the insertion of the branches, shallowly fissured and nearly black at the base of the trunk. Very abundant from Nova Scotia southward through New England and westward this has triangular lustrous green leaves and is a most aggressive if short-lived tree springing up in quantity on abandoned farm lands and in fire-swept forest areas, growing rapidly in the poorest of soils and forming a useful nurse to the seedlings of more valuable trees. Very similar is *B. coerulea*, the Blue Birch. This is also a small tree native of Canada and northern New England.

Stateliest of all White Birches is *B. papyrifera*, the Canoe or Paper Birch of North America with polished creamy white bark freely separating into thin layers. It is not a very tall tree for it seldom exceeds 70 feet in height but the trunk is thick, from 7 to 10 feet in girth, and is clean of branches for three-fourths of its height. It has a small crown of comparatively few thick branches and it is the stout tall white-barked trunk that is so striking. The bark

EUROPEAN BIRCH, BETULA PENDULA, 60 FEET TALL, TRUNK 6 FEET GIRTH,
ARNOLD ARBORETUM, JAMAICA PLAIN, MASSACHUSETTS

River Birch, Betula nigra, trunk 7 feet girth, Arnold Arboretum, Jamaica Plain, Massachusetts

is tough, durable, impervious to water and from immemorial time has been used by American Indians for making canoes and miscellaneous utensils and to cover their wigwams in winter. It is the conspicuous tree of the boreal forests of North America, being found across the continent from the Atlantic to the Pacific.

The White-bark Birch of northeastern Asia *(B. japonica)* is found over an immense area from the higher mountains of western China northeastward and throughout Japan northward to Kamtschatka. The foliage varies a great deal and a number of named forms are recognized but all agree in having a pure white bark easily separating in thin layers. At its best in the forests of northern Japan this Birch approximates in size to the American Canoe Birch but the finest form is that named *szechuanica* from the high mountains of extreme western China which has thick, bluish green leaves and very polished red-brown branchlets and an open crown of wide-spreading branches. Trees raised from seeds I collected near Tachien-lu have grown well in America and Europe and proved a decided acquisition.

One of the least known of all Birches is the white-barked species of the northwestern Himalayas *(B. Jacquemontii)* native of Kumaon, Kashmir and Afghanistan. It is in cultivation at Kew and there are small plants growing in the Arnold Arboretum but beyond the fact that the bark is white and peeling little is known about this tree.

The most common Birch in Japan and one found in great quantity throughout Korea and northeastern Asia generally is *B. Ermanii* which has a greater altitudinal range than any other oriental species It also grows to a larger size than any other Birch of eastern Asia with the possible exception of *B. grossa,* but in the alpine zone of the higher mountains of northern Japan it is reduced to a low, very broad shrub with branches prostrate on the ground. I saw it on the higher mountains northward from those of the Shinano province in central Hondo; it is common in the Nikko region and most abundant in Hokkaido and Saghalien. In Hokkaido it is known as Gambi (White Birch) and the wood with that of *B. japonica,* which is known by the same name, is, like that of *B. Maximowicziana,* exported in quantity to America and Europe and used for making furniture. Soot obtained by burning the bark of this Birch is used by Ainu women in tattooing themselves. Growing in such a wide area and under such diverse climatic conditions, this species naturally exhibits much variation. The trees differ in habit; the leaves vary greatly in size and in degree of dentation and considerably in shape also. The bract of the female flowers varies enormously both in size and shape. The bark is grayish, sometimes suffused with red-brown, or it may be white; it is exfoliated in thin sheets or the sheets may remain on the tree in shaggy masses. The fruit is always erect. Usually the trunk divides a few feet from the ground into several massive stems and these branch to form a wide-spreading crown, but when the trees grow crowded together in rich woods the trunk is relatively slender and very tall and the branches are thin and short. During 1914 I paid much attention to this Birch in Japan, but I failed to discover any constant character by which any variety or form could be definitely distinguished in the field. Its variability notwithstanding, *B. Ermanii* is a well-marked species. The variety found around Nikko *(subcordata),* with a tall trunk clothed with peeling gray-white, pink-tinted bark, is the most handsome of the many forms of this Birch.

A lovely Birch abundant on the highest mountains of Central China is *B. albo-sinensis.* This is a tree up to 80 feet tall with a clean trunk sometimes 10 feet in girth which grows mixed with other deciduous leaved trees, though occasionally it forms pure woods. The bark is singularly lovely, being a rich orange-red or orange-brown and peels off in sheets, each no thicker than fine tissue paper, and each successive layer is clothed with a white glaucous bloom. It is in cultivation from seeds I sent from China in 1910. For some unknown reason it has not grown well in the Arnold Arboretum and I hope better fortune has attended it in other gardens for it is a most capitivating ornamental tree. A presumed variety (septentrionalis) is very common on the mountains of the Chino-Thibetan borderland where it grows 100 feet tall with trunks from 12 to 15 feet in girth. The bark varies from orange-brown on young trees to orange, orange-yellow or orange-gray on old trees. It exfoliates in thin sheets which persist as shaggy masses on old trunks and branches. The bark lacks the white glaucous bloom of the central China Birch and in my opinion it represents another species, but whatever its identity it is a most worthy tree and from youth to middle age its smooth polished orange-brown bark is most attractive. In the spring of 1909 I saw growing in the Botanic Garden at St. Petersburg a Birch with the same characteristic bark and I am sure it is my friend of the Chino-Thibetan forests. It was called *B. utilis* and under this name several writers have referred to it. The authorities at the time could not tell me of its origin but I doubt not that Russian explorers had sent back the seed from the Thibetan Marches. The true *B. utilis* is a Himalayan species introduced into England by Sir Joseph Hooker in 1849 but to this day remains a little known tree. From what one can learn it appears to be tender in Britain and, moreover, there is a confusion with *B. Jacquemontii* not yet properly unravelled.

The common low-level Birch of central China is *B. luminifera,* which under the name of *B. alnoides pyrifolia* is growing in England from seeds which I collected. This has a firm smooth dark red-brown bark which becomes dull brown or even yellowish gray on old trees. It is a common tree, rarely 75 feet tall with a trunk from 3 to 8 feet in girth. The foliage varies a great deal in shape and serration and the clustered catkins are often more than 3 inches long. It has not proved hardy in the Arnold Arboretum but is growing well at Kew where it promises to be a useful addition to the arboretum.

The Red Birch of northern Japan *(B. Maximowicziana)* has the largest leaves and longest catkins of all known hardy Birches. In Hokkaido where it is at its best I have seen trees fully 100 feet tall with a trunk 12 feet in girth and clean of branches for 50 feet and more. But such trees have a roundish mop-like crown, gray-brown or gray unattractive bark split into long, broad thin sheets which cling to the tree in shaggy masses. The young vigorous trees are of open habit with trunk and principal branches clad with firm smooth snow-white bark. Introduced in 1893 into cultivation by the late Professor Sargent this Birch has proved a hardy, vigorous, quick growing tree, distinct and markedly handsome.

A semi-aquatic Birch and lover of rich alluvial soil is *B. nigra,* the River Birch, abundant in eastern United States from the Atlantic seaboard to west of the Mississippi River and found in its greatest size in the lowlands of sub-tropical Florida. It is a large tree from 80 to 90 feet tall with a trunk 15 feet in girth which divides some 10 to 20 feet above the ground into from two to several massive diverging limbs. The bark on young trees is shining light reddish brown and separates freely into large thin papery scales which curl and remain on the tree for many years in shaggy masses. On the trunk of old trees the bark is fissured and broken on the surface into thick closely appressed scales dark red-brown in color. This Birch is most strikingly distinct and picturesque in appearance.

Speaking of the River Birch reminds one of *B. davurica* so abundant in northern Korea which has a similar bark, curled and shaggy but rather thicker and deeply fissured into irregular squares that are blackish on the lower part of the trunk of old trees. On the volcanic soils of northern Korea this and an Aspen *(Populus tremula Davidiana)* are the natural nurse trees of Larch. However, it is by no means confined to volcanic soil and is found west into north China and east into Japan where it occurs as a rare tree on the Shinano Alps. This Dahurian Birch grows from 50 to 80 feet tall and has a short trunk from 5 to 10 feet in girth, which forks after the manner of its American relative. On trunk and branches the reddish gray bark either peels off or remains in loose untidy masses. The tree grows well in the Arnold Arboretum, but in the British Isles like other boreal continental types is apt to start into growth early and to suffer from subsequent late frosts. It ought to be a useful tree to associate with Larch in the Highlands of Scotland.

A conspicuous and characteristic tree of the mixed forests of northern Korea is *B. costata* with white papery bark. It grows from 40 to 80 feet tall and has a trunk from 3 to 8 feet in girth which on old trees is clad with pale gray, loose, scaly bark. The leaves are ovate, long pointed, sharply toothed, lustrous green, with prominent nerves; the fruit is erect stout, barrel-shaped with long pointed scales. This Birch has been much misunderstood and often confused with the Black Birch of Japan *(B. grossa)* and with *B. Ermanii*, both very different species. It is doubtful if it ever had been in cultivation until I sent seeds to the Arnold Arboretum in 1918 from Korea. With its polished foliage and rugged trunk it is a decidedly ornamental tree.

Another little known Birch is the Japanese *B. corylifolia* with smooth fine silvery gray bark, broad ovate to obovate, coarsely toothed leaves with prominent veins, gray on the underside and clothed when young with silky appressed pale gray hairs. The fruit is cylindric, stout and ascending, with very long pointed scales. The leaves except for their large teeth suggest those of the European

Beech but the important point is that the twigs have an aromatic odor like those of the American Sweet Birch *(B. lenta)*; this is the only Birch with white bark that has this peculiarity. This distinct and interesting Birch is fairly common on volcanic soils in central and northern Japan, but I have not seen it wild elsewhere. I introduced it in 1914 but it has failed to make itself at home in the Arnold Arboretum.

The Yellow Birch *(B. lutea)* which has aromatic bark is one of the largest trees of northeastern America. In moist uplands where rich soil obtains this tree is often 100 feet tall with a trunk 12 feet in girth. On young trees the bark is shining pale orange or yellowish gray separating into loose persistent scales which are more or less rolled on the margins. On old trees the bark is darker, irregularly fissured into large thin plates. This persistent bark rolled and bunched into masses of no particular shape gives the naked trees an uncouth appearance. The young leaves as they unfold are reddish passing to bronze-green and in the autumn turn a clear yellow.

It is passing strange that the foliage of all the Birches changes to shades of yellow in the autumn but in none is the tone richer or purer than in the Sweet Cherry, or Black Birch *(B. lenta)*. This is a very common tree in the forests of eastern North America, growing from 60 to 80 feet tall with a trunk from 6 to 15 feet in girth. The branches are relatively slender, spread horizontally and are pendulous toward the ends forming an open, narrow bell-shaped crown. The bark is smooth, firm, dark brown almost black tinged with red beneath and on old trees furrowed and cracked into thick irregular plates. The black trunks are sombre and in strong contrast with the gray of Oak and Maple and the white of the Canoe and Gray Birches among which it grows. In autumn its splashes of pure yellow illumine the forests. By fermenting the sugary sap of this tree the birch beer of the Indians and early colonists was obtained and by distillation is yielded an oil used medicinally.

The Japanese Cherry or Black Birch *(B. grossa)* very closely approximates to its American relative but in habit is a less attractive tree. It has similarly aromatic bark, dark, firm and fissured on old trees but the trunks are apt to divide into two or three massive stems and the shape of the crown is more open and less shapely. It is common in the mixed forests of Japan and in Hondo grows to a larger size than any other Birch except *B. Ermanii.* Other names of this species are *B. carpinifolia* and *B. ulmifolia.* Like all Birches it varies considerably in shape of leaf and bract and in degree of pubescence but the color and character of its bark and its aromatic taste and odor afford ready means of identification in the forests.

The wood of all the Red and Black Birches is valuable, quite a little of it being used in furniture making, more especially for cutting mahogany veneers. The most valuable of all is that of *B. Schmidtii,* the famous Pak-tal of the Koreans. This has pale brown wood, heavier than water and very much used in Korea for making rollers, mallets and other implements; it is exported in quantity to Manchuria and China for making axle-trees and felloes of carts. This Birch seldom exceeds 60 feet in height and has a short stout trunk clothed with thick, dark flaking bark and a broad crown of no particular shape made up of massive branches. The fruit is narrow, cylindric and erect. This Birch is very common on steep cliffs and is especially abundant on the Diamond Mountains where its clear yellow autumnal tints contribute very largely to the autumn glory of that beautiful region. It crosses to Japan where it is a rare tree in the Nikko region, a volcanic area. In Korea it loathes volcanic soils and so far as I know is never found growing in them. The Pak-tal is growing fairly well in the Arnold Arboretum but it needs planting thickly to develop a trunk for like *B. grossa* it has a strong tendency to start life as a shrub rather than a tree. The wood and bark of the very different *B. chinensis* is almost identical with that of *B. Schmidtii* and the Koreans designate it the lesser Pak-tal. This is always a small tree, indeed, very often a bush, and in Korea is found at low altitudes and on any kind of soil. It has small broad ovoid fruits, hairy branchlets and small leaves.

Lengthy as the above list is, it is by no means exhaustive but if it draws tree lovers' attention to a rather neglected group of useful trees its purpose will have been served. I may mention once again that apart from their own ornamental value in bark and habit of growth and their quite useful timber Birches are admirable nurses for various Conifers like Larch, Spruce and Fir and also for the slow-growing hardwood trees. They are also very useful shade trees for Rhododendron and other broad-leaf evergreens. Furthermore, such species as the European Silver Birches *(B. pubescens* and *B. pendula)*, the American Gray Birch *(B. populifolia)* and the oriental *B. japonica* are of northern trees the best suited for reclaiming sandy, gravelly wastes unprofitable for agriculture or for the growing of first-class timber trees. There is much waste land in northern regions that might well be planted with these White Birches and the common Aspen *(Populus tremula)*—the Birch wood for fuel, that of the Aspen for match-splints. Many may laugh at the last mentioned use, for the Great War is over and some of its afflictions together with many of the lessons it should have taught, forgotten, but if inquiries be made the dearth of match-splints will be made known and for this purpose there is no other wood so good as that of the Aspen.

LOVELY HOLLY

Oh! lovely Holly tree, how cheering thou to me
When winter's howling tempests drive around.

OLLIES constitute the genus Ilex and are found universally distributed through the forested regions of the temperate and tropical parts of both hemispheres. They are perhaps most abundant in South America where is found *Ilex paraguariensis,* the Mate, which is economically the most important member of the genus, an infusion of its leaves furnishing a much appreciated beverage similar to tea. Hollies are bushes or trees of moderate size, some of them deciduous but a majority evergreen. Both groups are represented by species indigenous to eastern North America, including the New England states. Of the some three hundred known species only a few are in cultivation in northern gardens. Climate alone is responsible, for Hollies are popular plants wherever they can be grown.

In general, Hollies are dense of growth, possessed of handsome foliage long retained and often lustrous, and have red or black berry-like fruits. The common Holly of Europe *(I. Aquifolium)* is one of the oldest of cultivated trees and the finest broad-leaved berried evergreen grown out of doors in the gardens of the British Isles. Either as a specimen or as a hedge plant the Common Holly is the pride of a thousand English gardens and the envy of garden-loving visitors from this country. The climate of Oregon is so much to the liking of the English Holly that it grows and fruits there as luxuriantly as on its native heath. Fortunate are the people among whom this beautiful evergreen flourishes. Those who garden in Maryland and south, and in other favored climatic regions of these

United States may also enjoy the common Holly of Europe but we of New England and places of similar climate are denied this noble, lustrous leaved evergreen with its clustered scarlet-hued berries.

Hollies love a cool, well-drained, loamy soil but some grow in quite swampy places and others in dry limestone regions. As a matter of fact, when once established they are not particular as to soil provided they get a proper supply of water at the roots. Many of the sorts, and these include the Common Holly, do not move readily unless abundance of soil be retained about the roots and the moving done when the ground is warm. In the north September or May are the best months for moving Hollies but in warmer regions this can be done at almost any time during the winter months. Once established Hollies are among the most accommodating of plants and those with thick, glossy green leaves withstand in an astonishing manner the smoke laden atmosphere of towns and cities. In the heart of England's capital, London, amazingly fine Holly hedges flourish, fog and smoke notwithstanding. The leaves of the Common Holly have this advantage, that being perfectly smooth and glossy smoke and dust are more readily washed away by the rains than from the leaves of less fortunately provided plants.

The Common Holly with its brilliant berries has been associated with Christmas since early Christian times. The custom would appear to have been borrowed from pagan festivals for the Holly was particularly associated with the festival of Saturnalia. In literature mention of the Holly dates back to Pliny although it is some question whether the Holm Oak (*Quercus ilicifolia*) was not confused with it in Roman times. Be this as it may, in plant mythology, legendary lore, and poetry the Holly has figured as a favorite subject for a thousand years and more. In old books on medicine a number of healing properties are attributed to it and at one time

AMERICAN HOLLY, ILEX OPACA, 25 FEET TALL, DIXWELL ESTATE, JAMAICA PLAIN, MASSACHUSETTS

its bark was considered a certain cure for coughs. Most of these uses have long since been discredited or abandoned, but until quite recent years a mucilaginous substance for snaring birds was prepared from its bark. Speaking of the bark, it will be well to emphasize that Hollies resent injury to their bark more than almost any other tree, the reason being that it is produced from the outer layer of living cells which if injured die and cannot give rise to other bark-forming cells so the injury is permanent and ends in death.

Under long cultivation the Common Holly has given rise to innumerable forms. In one book, almost solely devoted to this tree, no fewer than one hundred and two varieties are enumerated; they vary in habit of growth, size and character of their foliage, degree of spinyness and some are variegated with white and others with yellow. In short every conceivable variation is to be found in the varieties of this valuable tree. To enter into detail would be tedious; it is sufficient to say that apart from the type the weeping form *pendula,* the golden Aurea Regina, and the Silver Argentea Regina, are worth a place in every garden where the climate enables them to be grown. Even more handsome than the forms of the Common Holly are those of its hybrids with *I. perado* and *I. platyphylla,* of which the Dutch Holly *(I. belgica),* the large-leaved form *(camelliaefolia),* the Highclere Holly *(I. altaclarensis),* and Sheperd's Holly *(I. Sheperdii)* are noteworthy examples. The common Holly and its progeny are long-lived trees, the type and its more vigorous descendants being sometimes 80 feet tall with a smooth-barked trunk 6 feet in girth and a long oval crown densely branched and luxuriously furnished with leaves. In a young state all the leaves are spiny but as the trees grow into size and come to maturity the spiny character becomes less and less and in time those on the upper parts of the tree are totally devoid of spines. Individual Holly trees may bear male, female, or hermaphrodite flowers and so in purchasing specimens, since it is the berries that are wanted, it is well to buy one furnished with fruit in the first instance.

In the British Isles the Common Holly is the favorite hedge plant and has been for some centuries. Today Holly hedges hundreds of yards long are the pride of many an old estate. If desired they may be kept from ten to twenty-five feet in height and much the same in width and there is no reason why in Oregon and other climatically genial states similar Holly hedges should not be had. To keep a Holly hedge in good order it is necessary to clip the sides and top at least once a year. April is a good time since young growth then quickly appears and hides the mutilated leaves. Some old writers recommend cutting hedges back with a knife to save the disfigurement of the leaves, but this is impracticable where larger hedges are concerned. If early cutting back is persisted in a Holly hedge soon becomes very dense and it is almost impossible to see into it much less through, indeed, no subject makes a denser and finer hedge than the Common Holly—a hedge that neither man nor beast can penetrate and, moreover, a thing of beauty at all times. Of all the plants the gardens of Great Britain boast we of New England envy them most the Common Holly.

The American Holly *(I. opaca)* is at best a poor substitute for the common Holly of Europe but being hardier its berried twigs may be enjoyed by those who live so far north as Boston, Massachusetts. The leaves similar in shape and equally spiny are dull green and lack the cheerful appearance of its European relative. At best the American Holly is a tree some 50 feet tall with a smooth-barked trunk 15 feet in girth and a shapely ovoid crown. More usually, however, it is a small tree furnished with an irregular mass of branches. In some districts such as Hog Island, Virginia, this Holly is plentiful and during the winter months when laden with berries highly attractive.

The only evergreen Holly perfectly hardy in northern New England is the native *I. glabra,* known as the Inkberry, which is found wild near the coast from Nova Scotia south to Florida. This is a bush of dense, twiggy habit with upright stems and small, lustrous, black-green foliage. The small white, star-like flowers which crowd the axils of the leaves are not unattractive, but are far less beautiful than the shining black berries which later take their place. Although cultivated since about 1759, the Inkberry is by no means so common in gardens as its merits deserve. There are so few broad-leaved evergreens capable of withstanding New England winters that each and every one that does is a jewel beyond price. The Inkberry is not only handsome massed by itself but makes a very useful low screen.

Another black-fruited Holly, precariously hardy so far north as Boston but perfectly all right on Cape Cod and southward, is *I. crenata,* native of Japan. A bush or small tree, much branched, and of irregular outline, this has crowded, black-green leaves, each usually less than an inch long, variable in shape and blackish green in color. As it becomes old and assumes tree-like habit the branches are short and irregular giving the crown a stiff but picturesque appearance. The leaves vary considerably in shape and in one variety *(variegata)* are spotted with yellow. Perhaps the most attractive form is *nummularia,* better known as *Mariesii,* which is low-growing and has convex leaves, rounded and lustrous. From its behavior in the Arnold Arboretum this would appear to be hardier than the type.

A considerable number of species of Holly are natives of China and several of these have been recently introduced into cultivation. None has proved perfectly hardy in the Arnold Arboretum though it is questionable if any has enjoyed a fair test. On Cape Cod and Long Island two or three of them are quite at home and promise to be as useful and as hardy as the Japanese *I. crenata*. Most pleasing of these new Chinese sorts is *I. Pernyi*, a bush or small tree, pyramidal in habit with ascending-spreading branches crowded with more or less rhombic, spiny, shining dark green leaves. The berries are relatively large, stalkless or nearly so, bright red and clustered in the axils of the leaves. The branches are rigid and the spines on the leaves remarkably sharp, affording effectual protection from onslaughts of man or beast. Discovered so long ago as 1858, it was not introduced into cultivation until 1900 when I sent seeds to England. In central China this Holly is common in thickets on the mountain slopes, especially in the vicinity of streams and also in moist woods. Shapely of habit, its cheery green, formidable armed leaves attracted me the first time I set eyes on the plant; later when laden with its fruit I fell further in love with it. Looking down a vista of nearly thirty years I still consider *I. Pernyi* the handsomest and the most useful of Chinese Hollies. It is perfectly hardy in England and I believe will withstand the climate of New England as far north as Massachusetts if planted under the same conditions as one would plant Boxwood. Very different in every way is another Chinese species *(I. Fargesii)* which I also introduced into cultivation in 1900. This is a shrub or tree from 10 to 20 feet tall with few branches and narrow, 2 to 5 inch long leaves, finely toothed above the middle and not spinescent. It bears clusters of fragrant white blossoms and large, short-stalked, deep red berries. Except when in fruit there is little about this plant that suggests a Holly. A neat and charming Holly of my introducing is *I. yunnanensis*, twiggy of habit with short-stalked, shiny green ovate leaves seldom an inch long, crenated along the margin, and thickly crowded along the twiggy upright branches. This is a bush of irregular habit, usually about 10 feet tall, in many ways not unlike the Japanese *I. crenata* but characterized by its small, bright red fruits. The oldest Chinese

Holly in cultivation is *I. cornuta* which was introduced so long
ago as 1846 and is occasionally seen in California gardens. This is a
bush or sometimes a small tree 10 to 15 feet tall, of dense habit,
usually but slightly higher than broad. The leaves are leathery,
dark glossy green, more or less rectangular, suggestive in outline of
a flying bat with four large spines at the corners representing the
outstretched limbs; there is also a terminal spine and sometimes
two pairs of smaller spines projecting from the margins. The
fruit is globose, red and similar to that of the Common Holly. On
the margins of woods in eastern China, southern Korea, and southern
Japan grows the handsome *I. rotunda* with smooth, roundish, dark
green leaves and abundant axillary clusters of small, bright scarlet
berries. This is a large tree sometimes 60 feet tall with a dense crown
as much in diameter, flattened and tabular in appearance and a
smooth barked trunk 12 feet in girth. In some old temple and castle
grounds in Japan magnificent specimens of this Holly may be seen.

In Japan grows the noble *I. latifolia*, the Tarajo of the Japanese or the Magnolia-leaved Holly of our gardeners. Native of
the warmer parts of Japan and of southern Korea this is a tree
often sixty feet tall with large lustrous leaves more or less ovate,
serrated on the margin, each from four to five inches long and two
to three inches broad. It has the usual bright red fruits of its relatives but its value is in its noble evergreen foliage. This, of course,
is a subject for the warmer states. Where the Tarajo can be grown
so, too, can *I. insignis*, its Himalayan relative, whose leaves are
among the largest in the genus, often measuring from 7 to 10
inches long and 3 to 4 inches in width. This, too, bears red berries.

For those who garden in California and other warm states three
species of Holly native of the southeastern United States are well
worth attention. Taking them alphabetically, the first we mention
is *I. Cassine*, the Dahoon, which is a small evergreen tree, some-

times 30 feet tall, but often a low tree-like shrub. The leaves are thick, glossy green, entire or slightly spiny on the margin, more or less oblong in shape and each from 1½ to 3 inches long by 1 inch wide. The fruit is red, globose, produced in the axils of the leaves. With its glossy foliage and bright red fruits this is a very ornamental Holly. The second is *I. lucida* which may be compared with the Inkberry and like that shrub has black fruits. The leaves, however, are much larger, more coriaceous and, as the name suggests, shining green. Finally there is *I. vomitoria,* known as the Cassena or Yaupon, a small, much-branched tree with rigid, horizontally spreading branches, small, oblong, crenately margined shining leaves and abundant clustered scarlet fruits. In habit of growth and in appearance except for the color of its fruit it resembles the Japanese *I. crenata.* These three Hollies, plentiful in moist places in the warm southeastern states, have been too long neglected by nurserymen and landscape gardeners.

The group of Hollies that lose their leaves in the autumn was at one time distinguished as a separate genus under the name of Prinos but except in their deciduous character the members differ in no important respect. From a garden point of view, however, they are totally distinct and in garden making serve other purposes. The best known species of all have bright red fruits, either clustered in the axils of the leaves or suspended on slender stalks. Unfortunately, the plants are usually of two sexes and so in buying persons should be careful to select, say of a dozen, ten that are fruiting plants, the other two males, which if planted among them should be sufficient to insure fruit. In moist places, wayside thickets and on the margin of pond and lake from Canada to Florida and west to Wisconsin and Missouri, one of the most common of native shrubs is the Black Alder *(I. verticillata).* A spreading shrub often 10 feet tall and correspondingly broad, its twiggy branches in autumn and far into the winter are studded with small, shot-like, scarlet berries which make a brilliant showing on the naked shoots. Why this plant is not more commonly used in gardens is a mystery but, maybe, the fact that it is a common native shrub is against it. I can think of no other reason since it is accommodating, not particular as to soil, long-lived and free-fruiting. There are two or three forms of it; one *(chrysocarpa)* with yellow berries is well worth growing. Closely related and found wild from Maine to Virginia is *I. laevigata,* commonly known as the Winterberry. On the whole this a smaller shrub than the Black Alder but it has lustrous leaves and larger, orange-red fruits, solitary in the leaf axils. The two species are closely related but readily distinguished in the autumn when before the leaves fall they change to clear yellow in the Winterberry, whereas, those of the Black Alder turn black or brown after the first frost. One of the most delightful of Japanese shrubs in the winter and one whose twigs are much used in household decoration is *I. serrata.* This is a large bush or small tree with rigid slender branches and thin, more or less ovate leaves, each about an inch long, dull green above and hairy on the undersurface. The fruit is round, shot-like, brilliant red and clustered in greatest profusion in the leaf axils. No Holly fruits more abundantly than this. There are one or two varieties, among them a yellow-fruited sort *(xanthocarpa)* and another rather anemic sort with white fruit *(leucocarpa).* Very different from the above is another Japanese species *(I. geniculata)* in which the scarlet globose fruits hang suspended on thread-like stalks. In this plant the fruit ripens in August and generally falls about the same time as the leaves change to yellow. Of twiggy habit, with erect and spreading stems, this is a shrub up to 10 feet tall and when in fruit one of the most charming of its tribe. Indeed, during September no berried shrub attracts greater attention in the Arnold Arboretum than this comparatively newcomer from the Land of the Rising Sun. Another deciduous-leaved Holly less hardy than the above is *I. decidua*, native of Virginia and southward. It is usually a small tree 25 feet tall with spreading branches and more or less clustered obovate leaves; the fruit, relatively large, is orange to scarlet in color. In Virginia and Louisiana grows *I. Amelanchier* with large, solitary, scarlet fruits suspended on long stalks. As its name implies, it suggests a Shadblow. For those who garden south of Washington it is a useful shrub. There are others but this list may close with mention of *I. dubia*, native of eastern North America and represented in Japan by a variety called *macropoda*, at least such is the opinion of botanists though to the layman it seems impossible that a shrub native of Eastern North America should grow also on the mountains of Japan. A tree or tree-like shrub of irregular habit, this has rather large leaves and stalked clustered orange-red fruits. One and all of these deciduous leaved Hollies are worth a place in gardens. Placed where they can be seen from the windows of the house their berried twigs cheerfully light up winter landscapes.

STATELY PINE

INUS is the largest genus of coniferous trees and the one with which people of the northern hemisphere are most familiar. Their long, slender, needle-like, **gray or dark** green leaves arranged in bundles of two or more, according to species, and their woody, usually long persistent cones are characters which distinguish them from all other trees. Their appearance is so distinct that the least observant has no difficulty in recognizing a Pine tree. The genus is essentially northern. In America it is distributed from the Arctic Circle south to the West Indies and Guatemala. In the Old World species of Pine are known from the Arctic Circle south to the Canary Islands, northern Africa, Himalayas, Burma, the Philippine Islands and one species crosses the Equator to Sumatra. In all some eighty species are known, the greatest number being native of western North America including Mexico.

Pine trees grow from sea level to high up on the mountains. They are social trees and form more or less pure woods or forests of vast extent. Often, however, they are associated with other coniferous and broad-leaved trees. The genus contains some of the most important timber trees of the world and in the temperate regions wherever trees are planted either for ornamental or for forestry purposes members of the Pine tribe are in request. In South Africa, in Australia, and in New Zealand, where no species of Pine is indigenous, millions have been planted. Of the species employed the California *Pinus radiata* is the most useful. Indeed, it promises to be the greatest blessing among trees that the north has contributed to the southern hemisphere.

The wood of Pines is straight grained, easily worked, resinous and is employed for an immense number of purposes. Turpentine is one of the products of the Pine tree, particularly of *P. palustris* and *P. caribaea*. One group of them known as Nut Pines have edible seeds which in Siberia, Korea and in parts of western North America are important articles of human food. In Europe and the Orient the planting of Pine trees for the production of timber has long been practiced and is now being carried out in this country. For ornamental purposes, in parks and gardens of all temperate lands, different species of Pine trees have for immemorial time been in request. In many respects it is the most accommodating as well as the most useful of all the Conifer tribe.

In the Arnold Arboretum some thirty species and thirty-eight varieties of Pinus are growing and about half this number of species may be said to thrive. They are all to be found in the pinetum, which is well worth a visit at any season of the year, but especially during the autumn and winter months. Of the thirty species seven of them are natives of northeastern North America, nine of western North America, eight of the Far East, one of the Himalayas, and five of Europe. The varieties are mostly sports which exhibit different types of growth. Some of these have been found in a wild state but the majority have appeared in gardens where Pine trees have been raised from seeds over a long period. These curious forms must be perpetuated by grafting, but for the species the best and, indeed, the only practical way of raising Pine trees is from seeds.

Of the eastern North American species the best and most beautiful is the White Pine *(P. strobus)*, one of the most common and most valuable of native trees. No lengthy description is necessary since it is known to all who love American trees. Its leaves are gray with silvery lines, slender, and arranged in bundles of five. The branches spread more or less horizontally to form a pyramidal crown, the leaves hanging somewhat giving the tree a graceful outline. For planting as specimens, as forest trees or as shelter belts, the White Pine is for eastern North America the most valuable Pine tree, the threat of blister rust notwithstanding. It is the most important timber tree of northeastern North America and has played a conspicuous part in the material development of the country. The vast forests which formerly existed have been felled and the great trees, once the pride of the northern forests, no longer exist. However, it is still plentiful, regenerates readily in open country, and the sylvan landscapes of New England owe much of their peculiar charm to the widespreading, gray-green crowns of this tree.

Owing to the value of its timber it was early carried to Europe and was cultivated at Badminton in 1705. It was abundantly planted for forestry purposes, especially by Lord Weymouth, and in England it is known today as the Weymouth Pine. Like certain other trees of eastern North America it did not prove at home in the climate of the British Isles and for forestry purposes has proved a failure.

There are several varieties of the White Pine in cultivation, the most useful being the dwarf variety *nana* and the upright branched form *fastigiata*. The dwarf form makes a broad, more or less round-topped bush of dense habit, seldom more than 6 feet tall but twice that in diameter. Distinct and decidedly ornamental is the variety *fastigiata*, which has ascending stems forming a columnar crown, the loose arrangement of its foliage taking away the stiffness so usual in upright-growing trees.

An excellent species is *P. resinosa*, the Red or Norway Pine, so named for a small village in Maine where once this tree was abundant. This is a handsome tree sometimes 80 feet tall with a straight trunk clothed with light, reddish brown, rather thick bark. The leaves, two in a sheath, are long but the branching of the tree is light and open. For ornamental purposes in eastern North America it is comparable with but superior to the Austrian Pine. The Jack Pine *(P. Banksiana)* and the Jersey Pine *(P. virginiana)* can be recommended for planting on rocky waste lands. They are similar in habit of growth but the cones are quite distinct. In the Jack Pine it is oblong, points towards the apex of the branch and remains closed for many years. In the Jersey Pine the cone-scales open at maturity. This species is a feature of the Pine-barrens of New Jersey, growing in almost pure sand. The Jack Pine is found as far north as latitude 65. It attains its greatest size and beauty in the region around Lake Winnipeg, where it covers great areas of sandy, sterile soil. The Pitch Pine *(P. rigida)* is an unlovely tree, readily recognized by the presence of green sprouts on the trunk. Except that it will grow where lashed by the sea, it has little garden value. The other two species, *P. pungens,* the Hickory Pine of the Appalachian Mountains, and *P. echinata,* the Short-leaf Pine, only exist in the climate of Massachusetts.

The best of the western North American species is *P. monticola,* the White Pine of the Rocky Mountains. In many respects this resembles *P. strobus* but has thicker leaves which give the crown a heavier appearance. It grows more slowly than its eastern relative, which is the more ornamental species. *P. ponderosa,* the Yellow or Bull Pine grows quite well in the Arnold Arboretum, its long, dark green thick foliage giving it, as its specific name indicates, a ponderous appearance. There is a form with hanging branches known as *pendula,* which has a distinct place in the garden. The variety *Jeffreyi* is one of the few Pacific coast Pines that thrives at all decently in New England. The Sugar Pine *(P. Lambertiana)* grows very slowly and gives no promise of ever becoming a useful

WHITE PINE, PINUS STROBUS, 110 FEET TALL, TRUNK 14 FEET GIRTH, WEST OSSIPEE, NEW HAMPSHIRE

JAPAN RED PINE, PINUS DENSIFLORA, 75 FEET TALL, TRUNK 9 FEET GIRTH,
PUKCHIN, NORTH HEIAN, KOREA

ornamental tree. The Limber Pine *(P. flexilis)*, although of slow growth is perfectly hardy and happy in the Arboretum. Its relatively long, plume-like branching gives it a characteristic appearance. The related *P. aristata,* and *P. Balfouriana* the Fox-tail Pine, do poorly.

Of the Far Eastern species the Japanese White Pine *(P. parviflora)* and the Korean Nut Pine *(P. koraiensis)* grow well in Massachusetts. In Japan the first named is often grafted on *P. Thunbergii,* the result being a stunted, short-needled plant of value only for Japanese gardens. Raised from seeds, it is a free-growing tree with wide-spreading rather rigid and stiff branches and retains its cones over a long period of years. The Korean Pine for eastern North America is better than the Swiss Pine *(P. cembra)* which it strongly resembles. It grows faster and its dark and thick needles give it a very handsome appearance. This is the best of all the oriental Pines from the point of view of its timber. The Red Pine of Japan *(P. densiflora)* is also quite at home in eastern North America. It has short gray-green needles and reddish brown bark. The Black Pine *(P. Thunbergii)* with thick black-green leaves and long pure white winter buds is excellent for planting by the sea. Its branches are apt to grow crookedly when the tree assumes the appearance one is familiar with in Japanese paintings and embroideries. The White Pine of China *(P. Armandi)* and the Bhotan Pine *(P. excelsa)* suffer from boring insects and neither promise to make a tree here.

Of the European species three with numerous varieties do very well in Massachusetts. The Austrian Pine *(P. nigra)* and its several varieties grow rapidly and with their dense rather heavy black-green foliage are decidedly ornamental. They stand salt spray and strong gales well and for seashore gardens and wind breaks this species and its forms have great value. The Mountain Pine of central Europe *(P. mugo)* is one of the most useful dwarf Pines for garden purposes that can be grown in eastern North America. Its dark foliage and compact habit make it most adaptable for small gardens and for foundation plantings. Of the several varieties, *compacta, mughus* and *pumilio* are the best known. All are well worthwhile. The Macedonian Pine *(P. peuce)* grows slowly and does not promise to be of much ornamental value. The Scots Pine *(P. sylvestris)* perhaps the most useful of all European species, is not a success in eastern North America. It grows rapidly when young but after about twenty years becomes stunted and subject to insect attacks and fungous diseases. No one Pine has been more abundantly planted in this part of the world and it is more than probable that many will rue the day they set it out in expectation of its value as a timber producing tree. This species has an immense distribution in Europe and Siberia and some of its geographical forms behave differently under cultivation. In the Arnold Arboretum the best trees were raised from seed collected in Finland and represent the variety *lapponica*. For the small garden there is a variety *(Watereri)* of dense, columnar habit with short, steel blue leaves that is well worth a place.

FIR AND SPRUCE

HE Firs and Spruces are among the most valuable timber trees of the northern hemisphere and the most important of ornamental narrow-leaved evergreen trees.
In boreal regions they cover vast areas often forming
pure forests enormous in extent. In both hemispheres the Firs
find their southern limits just within the Tropic of Cancer,
but the Spruces keep within the temperate regions. Both Firs
and Spruces in northern regions grow at sea level but in temperate, and more especially warm-temperate, regions they are
restricted to the higher mountains, the Firs being more alpine
in character than the Spruces. The Firs form the genus Abies
and the Spruces that of Picea. They bear a close resemblance one
to another, indeed, there is much confusion in the lay mind as to
their distinctive characters. In the Firs the cone is always erect and
falls to pieces when ripe; in the Spruces the cone is pendulous and
does not disintegrate at maturity. Another distinction is that in
dried specimens the leaves of Spruce always fall from the branches,
whereas those of the Abies remain attached. As timber producing
trees the Spruces are more important than the Firs but for ornamental purposes the opposite obtains. All are tall trees, those of some
species approaching 200 feet in height and ranking among the loftiest
and most impressive of Conifers, but in the boreal regions they are
reduced to scrub. Lovers of regions where the air is pure and where
they enjoy abundant moisture at the root, neither Firs nor Spruces
are suitable for planting in cities or manufacturing towns. There
are species suitable for almost any climate where at least a moderate

177

rainfall prevails but none are desert plants, although a number withstand extremes of both heat and cold. Obviously those native of the mountains bordering the tropics are not suitable to the gardens of New England, neither do the more alpine species thrive at sea level. Moreover, the natives of different regions of the world behave quite differently under cultivation in eastern North America. Speaking in general, the more than fifty years' experience of the Arnold Arboretum is that the Firs and Spruces of Europe and western Asia, those of Japan and Korea, and those of Colorado grow well in Massachusetts. In western North America grow some of the noblest, tallest, and most beautiful of all the Firs but none of these is at home in the Arnold Arboretum. The two species of Fir *(Abies balsamea* and *A. Fraseri)* native of eastern North America are not happy in the Arnold Arboretum though Fraser's Fir does splendidly a few miles to the north. Of the three native species of Spruce *(Picea glauca, P. mariana* and *P. rubra)* the first-named only does moderately well in the Arnold Arboretum where the summers are a little too hot and dry for its well-being. The other two merely exist and are not worth their board and room. The Arnold Arboretum's work in the acclimatization of Conifers during more than fifty years ranks among its most important contribution to dendrology and landscape gardening. A visit to the pinetum at any season of the year is interesting and instructive to all lovers of these trees since they may see for themselves how particular species behave in the climate of Massachusetts and judge which are of greatest value.

Of Firs or Silver Firs, as they are usually called, there are growing in the Arnold Arboretum twenty-five species and sixteen varieties. Of these, four species and three varieties are native of Europe and western Asia, five are Chinese, eight with four varieties are indigenous in Japan and Korea, six species and four varieties have their home in mid-western and western North America, while two species

COLORADO WHITE FIR, ABIES CONCOLOR, 65 FEET TALL, ARNOLD ARBORETUM,
JAMAICA PLAIN, MASSACHUSETTS

NIKKO FIR, ABIES HOMOLEPIS, 55 FEET TALL, TRUNK 4 FEET GIRTH, BRISTOL NECK, RHODE ISLAND

and five varieties are native of the Atlantic seaboard. Of the twenty-five species, eleven appear to be first-class ornamental trees but of these *A. chensiensis, A. Fargesii* and *A. recurvata* are comparatively new introductions from China, and *A. holophylla* and *A. koreana* from Korea which have not been with us sufficiently long for a definite opinion to be expressed. The remaining six species of Fir have proved their value over half a century. One only of these is American, two are Japanese, and three hail from southwestern Europe and western Asia. First of these six Firs must be placed *A. concolor* the Colorado White Fir, of which there are specimens in the pinetum more than 65 feet tall, symmetrical in outline with branches sweeping the ground and well-clothed with long spreading glaucous-gray leaves. A worthy partner of this White Fir is the Nikko Fir *(A. homolepis,* more widely known as *A. brachyphylla),* a Japanese species with wide-spreading branches densely furnished with black-green leaves silvery on the under surface. The three Eurasian Firs *(A. Nordmanniana, A. cilicica* and *A. cephalonica)* are of about equal value, each and several being of distinguished appearance and highly ornamental. The sixth Fir is *A. Veitchii* of Japan, a tree less tall than either of the above with a smooth, pale gray bark and short, horizontally spreading branches clothed with dark green leaves silvery on the lower surface. Of the Chinese Firs *A. Fargesii* with its mahogany-purple shoots and long black-green leaves silvery on the under surface is of much promise. So, too, is *A. koreana,* which in habit of growth somewhat resembles its relative *A. Veitchii.*

The Spruces are richer in species than the Firs but from the point of view of ornamental horticulture less valuable since they do not grow old so gracefully. One and all have weak points, not the least of which is their habit of sooner or later losing their lower branches. From the point of view of producing timber this is a great advantage but for ornamental purposes it is a bad defect. In the Arnold Arboretum some twenty-six species and sixty-one varieties of Spruces are growing but of the varieties no fewer than forty-one are referable to the Norway Spruce *(Picea Abies)*. Of the twenty-six species, eleven give promise of being first-class ornamentals but of these the Chinese *P. asperata, P. Balfouriana* and *P. Wilsonii* have not been in cultivation long enough for a definite statement to be made and the same is true of the Japanese *P. Koyamai.* However, in reference to these four species it may be said that they promise well; they grow freely and have withstood with impunity the severest of New England winters experienced since their introduction some twenty years ago. Of the seven remaining Spruces, each of which has been tested for half a century in the Arnold Arboretum, the Caucasian *P. orientalis* ranks first in ornamental qualities. This tree has short, shining dark green leaves, densely arranged on the plumose branches which spread outward and downward and are upturned at their extremities. The whole tree is a symmetrical pyramid of lustrous dark green at all seasons of the year. Next in merit ranks the flat-leaved Serbian Spruce *(P. omorika)*, a narrow tree with horizontally and down-spreading branches tilting upward at the tips and clothed with black-green leaves silvery on the under surface. This is a rather narrow tree but of arresting character. Its weak point is that the leading shoots, especially of young trees, suffer from boring insects. The Norway Spruce does not grow old gracefully, becoming scrawny and, where it is exposed to the strong winds, its leading shoots are killed and the tree dies from the top downward. However, under favorable circumstances for fifty to seventy-five years its ornamental qualities can be depended upon and if planted on a lawn where it will have plenty of room its lower branches will remain sweeping the ground for a longer period than those of any other Spruce. This well-known tree is, when in good

SERBIAN SPRUCE, PICEA OMORIKA, 50 FEET TALL, OAKDALE, LONG ISLAND, NEW YORK

BLUE SPRUCE, PICEA PUNGENS, 80 FEET TALL, BRISTOL NECK, RHODE ISLAND

health, strikingly beautiful with wide-spreading horizontal branches from which long branchlets hang suspended. Probably of all Spruces none has been more widely planted than the Colorado Blue Spruce *(P. pungens)*, especially its glaucous form *(coerulea)*. Undoubtedly, this Spruce has been greatly overplanted and, moreover, has been placed in positions totally unfitted for it, but these are faults of the landscape gardener rather than of the tree itself. Rightly placed, a Blue Spruce is a thing of beauty and for northern gardens and parks is well entitled to rank in the first half dozen Conifers. Its neighbor, *P. Engelmannii,* is also a first-class ornamental. At one time it was hoped that this species would hold its lower branches permanently when placed in open situations but experience has shown that it is no more constant in this than the Blue Spruce. In the neighborhood of Boston, Massachusetts, the summers are a little too hot for the well-being of the Canada Spruce *(P. glauca)* but the Japanese Tiger-tail Spruce *(P. polita)* is quite at home. With its stout, pungent, dark green leaves this tree has a rather sombre appearance but is undeniably handsome. Of the sixty-one varieties of Spruce, the majority are dwarfs and among them are some delightful rockery plants. Of all the dwarf Spruces, and indeed of all the lesser Conifers, the most beautiful is the curious form *(conica)* of the western variety *(Albertiana)* of the Canadian White Spruce. This plant, the proper name of which is *P. glauca conica,* forms a dense tower-like mass of pellucid green ultimately 5 to 8 feet tall, suggesting a gigantic moss plant. No other dwarf tree resembles it in appearance or in delicacy of leafage.

There is one Conifer which although it is neither a Fir nor a Spruce is among the most ornamental and useful of all narrow-leaved evergreens, namely the Douglas Fir or Oregon Pine *(Pseudotsuga taxifolia)*. This tree is widely distributed in western North America from British Columbia south to New Mexico, reaching its greatest development on the shores of Puget Sound, where trees 200 feet are plentiful. It crosses the Rocky Mountains into Colorado which is very fortunate for those who garden in New England where the Pacific coast type is not hardy. The Rocky Mountain form, however, grows freely and is perfectly at home even in northern New England. The Douglas Fir is a shapely tree with plumose branches densely clothed with dark green to glaucous green foliage silvery on the reverse. Its cone is pendulous with exserted bracts and with the sharp-pointed winter buds afford ready means of distinguishing this tree from its relatives, the Fir and Spruce proper. When raised from seed it exhibits a considerable amount of variation especially in the color of its foliage and one type with pendulous branchlets that has originated this way is among the most lovely of all Conifers.

INDISPENSABLES

OTHER NATURE will smile at the egotism which attempts to select the best and most useful of her trees, for to the Mother all are best. She plays no favorites; all are important in her scheme of things but man in assuming the rôle of lord of the earth appraises Nature's other children chiefly on the basis of their usefulness to him. No fault can be found with this utilitarian viewpoint since to exist is the endeavor of all forms of life. At a very early period in his history man discovered the roots and fruits good to eat and capable of nourishing him. Wherever he has found himself, man has discovered and made use of the plants yielding food and stimulating drink. Moreover, the discovery was made at so early a period that its history is lost to oblivion. It is greatly to be regretted that the written records of man concern themselves so very largely with his quarrels and so very, very little with the history of his crafts and arts. Could any plant useful to man speak it could tell more of the real history of the human race than all the written records extant.

So far as vegetable foods are concerned the Christian era has seen no discovery of raw supplies. The discovery of new lands by voyagers of East and West caused the universal dispersal of plants yielding food materials, but did not result in the actual finding of any food plant absolutely unknown to mankind. The recent centuries, more prolific in invention than any the world has ever known, has found new methods of preparing raw foods but has discovered no new plant yielding them. On the other hand by selection and hybridization the plant breeder has improved vege-

183

tables and fruits to such an extent that with rare exceptions the cultivated plant has but a remote resemblance to its feral ancestor. As a mark of progress the fact that never in the world's history did the human family enjoy fruits, vegetables and cereals of the quality it does today is worthy of record.

Modern science has discovered new worlds, new minerals, new gases, new forms of locomotion, new methods of communication drawing the human family more closely together, new methods of utilizing the earth's raw products but she has discovered no new form of wild fruit or vegetable unknown to early man. This is worth pondering thoughtfully for it should increase respect for our primitive ancestors.

The association of man and the plants indispensable to him dates from remotest antiquity and in many instances we know not the continent of their origin. Savants have written learnedly on the subject but their conclusions are usually at variance one with another and in most cases are at best merely plausible. Such investigations have a peculiar fascination for some of us, but for the purpose of this essay the question of origin may be discreetly sidestepped and the facts as they exist today accepted.

That it is a difficult task to set forth the ten most useful trees of the world the reader will readily agree, and in any such selection there is sure to be two or three whose standing others may question. From a universal viewpoint the most important tree in all the world is the Coconut Palm, for to millions of folks this tree supplies all their needs from birth until death. Fringing the coast, this Palm is the outstanding feature of the tropics of both hemispheres. It luxuriates everywhere; it fringes the surf-wracked strand, the sides of the brackish lagoons, and fresh water streams; and yonder forms orchards miles in extent. Its slightly leaning cylindrical trunk is capped full 60 feet aloft with a feathery crown of rich green, arch-

COCONUT, COCOS NUCIFERA, ROAS BAY, SOLOMON ISLANDS

ing leaves in the axils of which cluster the familiar fruits in all stages of development from the tiny young grass green nutlet to the huge egg-like golden ripe fruit. Every part of this tree has its uses. The stems are used as uprights in rough construction work; and the wood is often made into chairs and other useful articles; the leaves are employed in roofing native huts and to make hoods for native carts; from the husk of the fruit the well-known coir-fibre is obtained; the sap within the nut serves as a refreshing beverage and when fermented yields a potent spirit; the hard shell of the nut is made into drinking cups and may yet be useful in button manufacture; the white flesh is a valuable article of food, and when split and dried forms the copra of commerce so much used in soap-making and in other industries. No other tree has so many valuable uses and no tree is more abundant on tropical shores than the lovely Coconut Palm—Queen of The Tropic Strand.

Next to the Coconut I place the Orange-tree, followed by the Apple, the Mango, Para-rubber, Date Palm, Bamboo, Cocoa, Olive and Cinchona. The Cocoa-tree, Para-rubber, and Cinchona are natives of the South American tropics, which also have strong claims to being the birthplace of the Coconut. The Apple and Olive are Eurasian in origin, the Orange is Chinese, the Bamboo hails from the Orient in general, the Mango from India and the Date Palm from north Africa and Arabia. Five of these most useful trees—the Apple, the Orange, Olive, Date Palm, and Bamboo—are successfully grown in this country. The Apple, Orange, and Olive rank as three of the great orchard crops of America. The other five, Coconut, Para-rubber, Mango, Cinchona, and Cocoa, are grown in the New World tropics but with the exception of the Cocoa-tree not so abundantly as in the tropics of the Old World.

To the people of the warm-temperate regions the Orange is the most highly prized fruit, and to us of the north it has become a necessity. The Citrus family to which the Orange belongs claims also the Grapefruit, Lime and Lemon, which in parts of the world run the Orange closely, but the latter is nevertheless the brightest jewel in the family crown.

Authorities consider that the real home of the Orange is China and that ages past it was carried westward to India and from there by Alexander the Great to the shores of the Mediterranean. It was introduced into lower California and Florida by the Spaniards very soon after the discovery of America. The industry has waxed mightily during the last few decades, and today the orange crop of California and Florida is annually worth many millions of dollars. An enormous quantity is produced in the Mediterranean region and the industry flourishes in Australia and in South Africa. The yearly yield of oranges throughout the world is fabulous but the human family absorbs it all and like Oliver Twist asks for more. An interesting fact about the Orange is that in the tropics proper although the fruit ripens the skin remains green in color. As a matter of fact within the tropics the Orange is not happy. It is essentially the fruit tree of the warm-temperate parts of the world.

There are varieties of oranges with tight and loose skins; there are sweet oranges and bitter oranges, navel oranges, seedless oranges and many other sorts. The Orange is extraordinarily fruitful and as many as twenty thousand oranges have been picked from a single tree. I know of no more beautiful sight than an Orange-tree laden with ripe fruit and those who have seen the Orange groves of California, Florida or elsewhere will surely agree.

To the people of this country the most important tree beyond shadow of doubt is the Apple-tree, and among the fruits of cold-temperate climes the apple is pre-eminent. Brought from Europe by the early settlers it has been a favorite here since earliest colonizing days. Its cultivation has spread from East to West and every year sees its boundaries extended. Not alone in this country is the apple abundantly grown but in all temperate parts of Australasia and South Africa and in Europe and western Asia it has been grown from earliest times. In the spring few trees equal in beauty the Apple-tree in blossom; in the autumn bowed down by the weight of yellow, russet or ruddy fruits it is monarch of the orchard.

To the three hundred millions of people that crowd the Indian Peninsula and many other millions throughout the East and West Indian tropics the Mango is far more important than the Apple is to dwellers in the north. For centuries the people of India have held it sacred and celebrate annual ceremonies in its honor. Long ago a Persian poet wrote, "The Mango is the pride of the garden, the choicest fruit of Hindustan." The Mango is a large tree with gray bark, ascending-spreading branches which form a round topped crown and lustrous dark green, 8-inch long lance-shaped leaves. The foliage is shed at the approach of the dry season and later succeeded by another crop of leaves, pink-hued when unfolding. The flowers are borne in a large, much-branched panicle at the ends of the branches and are followed by a cluster of egg-shaped fruits, yellow, orange, or reddish in color, and varying in weight according to variety from six ounces to three pounds.

The Mango has been cultivated from immemorial time and was brought to the American tropics soon after their discovery. A long cultivated fruit tree, varieties in great numbers have originated and hundreds of different sorts are recognized in India. The best mangoes have a subtle blending of many agreeable flavors, but in the inferior sorts the flavor of a mixture of tow, turpentine and molasses is prominent. The best sorts are without fibre in the pulp, and are eaten with a spoon like custard. Some fibrous sorts are celebrated for their delicious piquant flavor and are eaten by sucking the pulp pressed out through a hole in the skin. It is facetiously stated the proper place to eat mangoes is in the bath tub, which saying unwittingly pays compliment to the juiciness of this most excellent fruit.

Para-rubber is one of the wonders of the age we live in and one of today's indispensables. With its multitude of familiar everyday uses it is difficult to realize that this rubber is to us comparatively a new discovery and that it is only since this century dawned that it has come into such enormous usage. The tree itself is a native of the forests of the mighty Amazon valley in South America. The early nineties of last century saw the beginning of plantation-rubber which is now one of the tropics' greatest sources of wealth.

It is said that the properties of rubber, long known to the South American Indians, were first made known to the west by a sailor, who with a piece of rubber showed how pencil marks could be erased from paper. At first the world's supply of rubber came from the Amazon valley, being collected from wild trees by the natives. The bicycle created a new demand for rubber and this demand increased enormously as the automobile came into being. Today the rubber annually used in the world is valued at hundreds of millions of dollars.

The story of the transport of the Para-rubber tree from its native home to the tropics of the Old World is like a story from *The Arabian Nights*. More or less surreptitiously seeds were procured in Brazil by Mr. H. A. Wickham and taken to the Royal Gardens, Kew, England. These seeds were sown and the plants raised were shipped to Ceylon and the Strait Settlements in 1896. This was the beginning of the plantation rubber industry. Many other plants produce rubber but in none does the quality approach that of the Para-rubber plant. The technical name for the Para-rubber tree is *Hevea brasiliensis* and it is, strange to relate, a relative to the humble Spurge plant of our northern waysides.

GIANT BAMBOO, GIGANTOCHLOA ATER, PERADENIYA, CEYLON

TREE BAMBOO, DENDROCALAMUS GIGANTEUS, PERADENIYA, CEYLON

A fast growing tree, Hevea attains the height of 70 to 100 feet and has gray bark, a round topped crown, and leaves not unlike those of the Horsechestnut but more pointed. The rubber is contained in a milky juice present in all parts of the tree. It is obtained by slicing through the bark of the trunk, a process technically called tapping. The cuts are made in a herringbone fashion. The milky juice, called latex, is collected in little jars which are fastened at the base of the incisions. Afterwards it is taken to the factories where the moisture is evaporated and raw rubber prepared. The tree grows with a remarkable rapidity and is ready for tapping within a few years from seed.

The importance of Para-rubber is so great and the profits so large that the tree has been planted in great abundance throughout all the tropics, but the tree flourishes best in Ceylon and Malaysia. Throughout Malaya one may travel for days and never be out of sight of plantation-rubber for the virgin forests of this region have been ruthlessly destroyed to make room for King Rubber.

To the Arabs, Bedouins and other wandering tribes of the hot arid regions of northern Africa and Arabia, the most important food is the fruit of the Date Palm *(Phoenix dactylifera)*. To them it has been the chief necessity of life from the earliest times. As every reader of travels knows the Date Palm marks the wells and oases of those arid regions where the camel is the principal beast of burden. The tree is happy under the most roasting heat conditions and withstands the scorching winds and the blinding dust storms which characterize the regions bordering the Red Sea. It has been cultivated by the Arabs from immemorial time with the result that many different kinds have arisen varying in the size, quality and abundance with which the fruits are borne.

In recent years, through the activity of the United States Bureau of Plant Industry some of the better sorts of the Date Palm have been introduced to the hottest parts of southern California. The experiment has been a success and today those parts of the United States are yielding fruit superior in quality to that of northern Africa.

The Date Palm is a tree up to 40 to 50 feet tall with a naked trunk clothed with a crown of fathom long feathery leaves. From the axils of these leaves the fruit is produced in large, much-branched clusters.

Probably the most important softwood timber tree of this country is the Oregon Pine or Douglas Fir as it is often called (*Pseudotsuga taxifolia*), although that of certain true Pines and Spruces have strong claims. Commercially, Teak (*Tectona grandis*) is the most valuable hardwood timber tree though Oak, Ash, and Hickory are well in the race. No genus of trees yield such variety of timber as does the Eucalyptus of Australia. None of these trees, however, are so important to millions of mankind as is the Bamboo to the peoples of the Orient, and to the Chinese particularly. The uses to which the Bamboo is put in China are indeed limitless. It supplies many of the multifarious needs of the people with whose everyday life, from birth to death, it is inseparably entwined. From bamboo stems are fashioned the various household utensils, furniture, the house itself, many agricultural implements, masts, and gear for boats, rafts, ropes, bridges, irrigation-wheels, water-pipes, gas-pipes, tubes for raising brine, sedan-chairs, tobacco and opium-pipes, bird-cages, snares for entrapping insects, birds, and animals, umbrellas, rain-coats, hats, soles for shoes, undershirts, sandals, combs, musical instruments, ornamental vases, boxes, and works of art, the pen (brush) to write with, the paper to write upon, everything, in fact, useful and ornamental, from the hats of the highest officials to the pole with which the coolie carries his load. Formerly the records of the race were written on bamboo tablets which were strung together at one end like a fan. Records of this description, dug up in A. D. 281, after having been buried for 600 years, were found to contain the history of Tsin from 784 B. C., and, incidentally, also that of China for 1500 years before that date. Bamboo shavings are used in caulking boats and for stuffing pillows and mattresses. The young shoots are a valued vegetable and according to popular belief, in times of scarcity a compassionate Deity causes the Bamboo to flower and yield a harvest of grain to save the people from starvation.

The plants which yield tea and coffee are best regarded as shrubs, but cocoa, the third of the world's great beverages, is the product of a tree of moderate size. This tree, technically known as *Theobroma cocao,* is native of the forests of the Amazon and Orinoco rivers and their tributaries. It occurs as an escape from cultivation from Panama to Guatemala and was probably introduced into Central America and the warm regions of Mexico before the discovery of America by Europeans. At any rate the Cocoa was grown in Central America and Yucatan when the Spaniards first visited those regions and the seeds were sent into the highlands of Mexico and even used as money so greatly were they valued. The custom of drinking chocolate was universal and the name of this excellent drink is Mexican. In more recent times it has been carried to Ceylon, Java and other islands of the Malay Archipelago, and to the tropical parts of Africa.

The plant has adapted itself to the tropics of the Old World and these today supply about half of the world's demand. The tree seldom extends 40 feet in height and begins to bear when it is six or seven years old and not more than 8 feet tall. The small and insignificant flowers are borne on the trunk and the bare parts of the older branches and are succeeded by enormous pods the shape of a short thick cucumber. Each pod is about 6 or 8 inches long, furrowed and yellow to reddish in color, and closely packed within are bean-like seeds immersed in a fatty pulp. By drying, curing and grinding, cocoa and chocolate are prepared. As a beverage cocoa may rank well behind tea and coffee, but no one will question that chocolate ranks as the world's premium candy and sweetmeat. How much the ancients thought of it is emphasized by its name Theobroma which is derived from two Greek words signifying "Food of the Gods."

Olives, the fruits of *Olea europaea*, are nowadays a very important Californian crop. The industry has waxed mightily during the past half century and is a splendid illustration of what can be done in that wonderful climate of California. The original home of the Olive tree is probably the countries bordering the eastern limits of the Mediterranean. To the people of Syria, Greece, and Palestine, the olive has always been one of the indispensable fruits. It is eaten ripe or unripe, raw or pickled and from it is obtained the finest of all salad oils. How highly it was valued by the Jewish people is shown by the frequent references to it in both the Old and New Testaments. It may be remembered that the dove liberated by Noah from the Ark returned bearing an Olive branch in its beak. Also it may be mentioned that olive oil is not only used in culinary purposes but by the Jews was in great request for anointing the body.

The Olive-tree is exceedingly slow growing with wide branches clothed perennially with narrow dark green leaves. On the islands of the Greek Archipelago there are Olive trees claimed to be two thousand years old. Nowadays culinary oils are obtained from a variety of plants but that of the Olive still stands pre-eminent.

Of all the vegetable drugs of service to man quinine is the greatest for as a prophylactic, it has gone a long way toward making the tropics safe for the white man to live in. The human

PARA-RUBBER, HEVEA BRASILIENSIS, SUNGEI BULAH, FEDERATED MALAY STATES

ANCIENT OLIVE-TREE, OLEA EUROPAEA, GARDEN OF GETHSEMANE, PALESTINE

family has probably suffered more from malarial fevers than from any other disease or illness and in quinine a cure has been found. So highly is quinine esteemed by the British Government that in India there is an organized system by which this drug may be obtained for a cent or so at any town throughout the length and breadth of India so that it is within easy reach of the millions of people.

The value of quinine became definitely known to the outside world in 1638 when the Countess Chinchon, wife of the Viceroy of Peru was cured by its use. Quinine is an alkaloid obtained from the bark of several species of small trees, technically known as Cinchona. It is obtained by stripping the bark from the trees and drying. Some fifty years ago Cinchona plants were introduced into Ceylon and parts of India by the British Government. Later some were taken to Java where great attention to the cultivation of this plant has been paid with the result that today Java enjoys a monopoly.

In extending the Cinchona industry to the tropics of the Old World and thus rendering the drug available to all, an Englishman, Sir Clements Markham, played a leading rôle. In recognition of this great service to mankind the Peruvian Government has recently presented a bust of the deceased gentleman to his motherland.

FRUIT TREES

T HE origin of our common fruit trees is lost in the dust of antiquity. Some—the Damson, for example—can be traced in old Greek literature back to the Sixth Century before Christ. But they are much older, for charred remains of the Apple and stones of the Bullace (Yellow Plum) have been found in the pre-historic lake-dwellings of Switzerland. They are, of course, the oldest trees cultivated by man, and did we know just where the human race had its cradle we might be a little more sure of the birthplace of our Plums, Apples, Pears, and Cherries. Books in general make them of Eurasian origin giving their distribution as from southeastern Europe, through the Asiatic shores of the Black Sea, to the Caucasus, Persia, Kashmir and north to Bokhara. Doubtless this vast and vague area includes the home of some of our fruit trees but nothing is definitely known. Possibly some, like the common Plum, were first cultivated on the shores of the Caspian Sea and on the plains of Turan where the Huns, Turks, Mongols, and Tartars, flowing back and forth in tides of war-like migration, maintained in times of peace a crude agriculture long before the Greeks and Romans tilled the soil. All that can be stated definitely today is that our common fruit trees are native of those parts of the Old World west of the highlands of central Asia.

In North America grow wild more species of true Plums than are found in Europe and Asia, but the cultivation of none was attempted until early in the Nineteenth Century, and even today their true worth is not sufficiently appreciated. The native Apples and Cherries of this country have no value as fruit trees, and America's only contribution to the fruit trees of the world are her Plums. So small a part do these play even in American orchards that it is correct to write that this country owes all her fruit trees to Europe and Asia. The introduction of these trees began with the earliest settlers; in Massachusetts some were planted by the Pilgrims, for Francis Higginson, writing in 1629 says: "Our Governor hath already planted mulberries, plums, raspberries, corrance, chestnuts, filberts, walnuts, smalnuts, and hurtleberries." John Josselyn, writing of a voyage to New England in 1663 says: "the Quinces, Cherries, and Damsons set the dames a work, marmalade and preserved Damsons are to be met with in every house." In the voyages undertaken for exploration and commerce soon after the discovery of America by Columbus the Peach was introduced by the Spaniards, for immediately after permanent settlement had been made in the South colonists found this fruit in widespread cultivation by the Indians, and its origin could only be traced to the Spaniards who earlier visited Florida and the Gulf region. As early as 1682 William Penn wrote, "there are very good peaches in Pennsylvania, not an Indian plantation is without them."

In the northern hemisphere, during the course of ages, two forms of civilization have developed. They are commonly expressed as that of the west and of the east, *i.e.*, that of Europe and that of eastern Asia whose dominant factor has been China. So, too, have two distinct stocks of fruit trees. There is the Eurasian group of apples, pears, plums, and cherries and there is the Chinese group of these same fruits. They are separate and distinct one from another, and have been evolved independently from the wild species found in areas separated by the high tableland of central Asia. This important fact only quite recently has been properly established. It has been my privilege and good fortune to discover in China and Korea the wild types of the apples, pears, cherries, and plums of the Orient.

The Peach is of Chinese origin and probably the Apricot also, though there is still doubt about the real home of the latter. The Peach and Apricot have been grown in this country since the early times of settlers; the oriental Plum, under the name of the Japanese Plum, for nearly three-quarters of a century, but the pears, apples and cherries of the Orient have received scarcely any attention here.

Since the wild habitat of certain of our fruit trees is not clearly known it will occasion no surprise to learn that botanists differ in opinion as to the species to which some of our domesticated fruits belong. Naturally these have become so vastly changed under long cultivation that they bear but a remote resemblance to their ancestral forms. Another fact that adds enormously to the difficulty is that parts of Europe, western Asia, and the Orient where they are supposed to have had their home have changed completely under the long, if intermittent, practice of agricultural husbandry. The ravages of a thousand wars and the migration to and fro of peoples down the ages have likewise profoundly influenced the problem. In the case of the Common Apple and the Domestica Plums it is doubtful if we shall ever be absolutely sure of the original habitat and identity of the wild types. Crabapples, or reversions toward the wild type or types, are found everywhere in the world where Apples have been long cultivated, and casual observers have concluded that they are truly wild whereas *naturalized* is the correct term to employ. In this connection it must be confessed that often it is well-nigh impossible to distinguish between naturalized and spontaneous plants. Let us take the case of the Common Apple. Loudon in his *Arboretum et Fruticetum Britannicum*, II, 894, says, "the Apple grows spontaneously in every part of Europe except the torrid zone. It is found throughout western Asia. . . . In the north of Europe it is found as far west as Finland in Lat. 62°;

APPLE, SEEK-NO-FURTHER, 35 FEET TALL, TRUNK 10 FEET GIRTH, SPREAD 60 FEET, MARSHFIELD HILLS, MASSACHUSETTS

APPLE SEEK NO FURTHER, TRUNK 10 FEET GIRTH, BRANCHES 3 FEET FULL. See Mr. STUART IV, c. 2, No.

in Sweden in Lat. 58° or 59°; in central Russia to 55° or 60°. In Britain, the Apple is found in a wild state in hedges, and on the margins of woods, as far north as Morayshire. It is found wild in Ireland, but it is rare there." The latest authority as represented by Bailey's *Standard Cyclopedia American Horticulture*, V. 2870 (1916), gives southeastern Europe to western Asia as the home of the principal, or supposed principal, parent of the Apple and western and central Europe for its other and lesser parent. The Apple, according to the best authorities, was introduced into France and Britain by the Romans, as was also the Pear; and like that fruit probably reintroduced by religious houses on their establishment, after the introduction of Christianity. Others claim that the Apple was to the Druids a sacred or semi-sacred tree, that it was cultivated in Britain from the earliest ages, and that Glastonbury was called Apple Orchard, from the great quantity of apples grown there previous to the arrival of the Romans.

The Apple-tree is mentioned by Theophrastus and Herodotus, and is also distinguished by legends in the mythologies of the Scandinavians, and the Druids. Hercules was worshipped by the Thebans under the name of Melius, and apples or quinces were offered at his altars. The ancient Welsh bards were rewarded for excelling in song by "the token of the Apple spray." In the Apple growing parts of England many quaint ceremonies were in olden times practised. In Devonshire on Christmas Eve the farmers and their men used to take in state to the orchard a large bowl of cider with toast in it, and salute the Apple trees with much ceremony in order to induce them to bear well the next season. The farmer and his men each took an oblation of the cider, threw some of it about the roots of the tree, placing bits of toast on the branches; then forming themselves round the most fruitful Apple-tree sang:

> Here's to thee, old Apple-tree,
> When thou mayst bud, and whence thou mayst blow;
> And whence thou mayst bear apples enow.
> Hats full! caps full!
> Bushel-bushel-sacks full!
> And my pockets full, too!
> Huzza!

In other parts of the country this ceremony took place on Twelfth-Night-Eve, and roasted apples took the place of toast. The song varied somewhat in different parts of the country but everywhere fecundity was invoked. Putting roasted apples in ale was another old English custom. Shakespeare alludes to it in *Midsummer Night's Dream,* where Puck says:

> Sometimes I lurk in a gossip's bowl,
> In very likeness of a roasted crab;
> And, when she drinks, against her lips I bob,
> And on her wither'd dewlap pour the ale.

A large volume would be required to record the folk-lore and facts that have accumulated round our premier fruit and then much would be omitted.

The species thought to be the principal parent of our favorite orchard fruit is known as *Malus pumila,* and is characterized by having its branchlets, leaves, inflorescence, and sepals covered with woolly hairs. It is considered to be wild from southwestern Europe to the Caucasus. Another species from which a few kinds of apple have been derived is *M. sylvestris,* which is nearly smooth and hairless in all its parts, and is regarded as indigenous in western and central Europe. The apples of the Orient have been derived from *M. prunifolia rinki* which grows wild on the margins of woods and on the banks of mountain torrents in Hupeh, central China, where I discovered it in 1907. In habit, general appearance, and flowers it resembles *M. pumila,* but the fruit-stalk is longer and more slender, and the fruit, which is small, is not impressed at the apex but has the calyx raised, thickened and fleshy at the base.

When the Chinese first began to cultivate the Apple is not known, but it was long, long ago. From China it has been introduced to Korea and Japan where, however, it is fast being displaced by apples of the European type introduced from America. The Chinese apple is small, ripens early, is greenish to greenish yellow and rosy on one side; occasionally it is nearly all red; the flavor is pleasant and bitter-sweet. It ripens its fruit in the hot, moist Yangtsze Valley round Ichang in July, and on the mountains, where the climate is severe, in early September. As a fruit it has no particular value to recommend it to western gardens but since it thrives under extremes of climate it may be useful to the hybridist.

The history of the Common Pear closely parallels that of the Apple but there is much less folk-lore gathered round it. In Britain, until about a century ago, it was more valued for making perry than for dessert. In fact, many of the best varieties were originated in France and Belgium, especially in gardens attached to religious establishments of which Louvain was among the chief, and were introduced into general cultivation after the battle of Waterloo. The Pear is less hardy than the Apple, and in England the better sorts are grown against walls and on sheltered trellises. The Common Pear is mentioned by the earliest writers as common in Syria and Greece, and from the latter country it appears to have been brought to Italy. The Romans introduced it into France and Britain, and it was brought to this country by the early settlers. Theophrastus speaks of the productiveness of the Pear-tree, and Virgil mentions some pears which he received from Cato. Pliny in his fifteenth book describes the varieties in cultivation as being exceedingly numerous. In Gerarde's time the Katherine Pear, a small red, early sort, was considered the best, and it remained a market variety in England down to about 1840.

The parent of our pears *(Pyrus communis)* is undoubtedly of

Eurasian origin, being found over a considerable portion of Europe and eastward to the Caucasus and northern Persia, but it is difficult to distinguish between naturalized escapes from cultivation and true wildings. A variety *(cordata)* sometimes regarded as a distinct species is indigenous to western France and England, and has a round, or slightly turbinate, fruit about half an inch in diameter. The Pear in a wild and naturalized state is pyramidal in habit and is armed with spines.

The pears of the Orient are flattened and depressed top and bottom like our apples, and not of the familiar pear-shape; a few are egg-shaped. They are very firm and gritty in texture, rich in a sweet watery juice, and one group is generally known as sand pears. At present it is certain that two species *(Pyrus serotina* and *P. ussuriensis)* have been concerned in their evolution, but whether other species have played a part or whether there are hybrids between the above-named species has yet to be determined. Much attention is now being given in parts of this country to these pears for under stocks on which to work our own pears and for breeding purposes. We are entirely without knowledge as to how long the Chinese have cultivated their pears but three thousand years is not an exaggerated estimate. The Sand Pear was introduced into Japan more than a thousand years ago and is very extensively cultivated there to this day, for the Japanese, like the Koreans and Chinese, prefer its fruit to that of our Pear trees.

The sand pears, of which there are brown and green-skinned kinds, are characterized by the absence of the calyx. They have apparently all been derived from *P. serotina,* a common wild tree in the woods on the mountains of the province of Hupeh in central China, where I discovered it in 1900 and introduced it into the Arnold Arboretum in 1909. Though widely cultivated over the greater part of China, Korea, and Japan it has not been found

wild except in central China. The other species *(P. ussuriensis)*
is more northern, being abundant in central and northern Korea,
and in Manchuria also; it has recently been found wild in Japan
in the region around Mount Fuji, and on the mountains of Shinano
province in mid-Japan. In this species the skin is green, russet-
green, or rosy; the calyx is usually persistent but sometimes it is
deciduous. Many varieties of this Pear are grown in Korea and
Manchuria, and in the more northern parts of China. Around
Peking a variety bearing a delicious little apple-shaped pear of a
pale yellow color is much grown and is known as the White Pear.
In parts of Japan it is called the Stone Pear and is not esteemed.
There are a few hybrids between the Sand Pear and the European
Pear the best known being the Kieffer and Le Conte.

There are many other species of Pear trees in Eurasia and the
Orient which some day may be found of value in the pear industry
in western lands. One *(P. Calleryana)* with minute fruits, which
I introduced to the Arnold Arboretum from central China in 1909,
is already achieving prominence as the most resistant to the dreaded
Pear blight of all the species and in consequence a valuable under
stock on which to work our garden pears.

The Quince *(Cydonia vulgaris)* is nowadays more esteemed in
New England than in Britain. A low tree with tortuous branches,
and considered native of southern France and central Europe, it
was known to the Greeks and Romans and by both nations held
in high esteem. By the ancients it was considered the emblem of
love, happiness, and fruitfulness and was dedicated to Venus. The
Nuptial chambers of the Greeks and Romans were decorated with
the fruit, and the bride and bridegroom also ate it so soon as the
marriage ceremony was performed. In eastern Asia grow three
species of Quince but their fruits are of little value; they are, however, very decorative garden plants. Another old fruit-tree seldom

seen nowadays is the Medlar *(Mespilus germanica)* whose fruit is not eaten until it is in a state of incipient decay, when it is very agreeable to some palates.

Now let us consider the stone fruits which, like the preceding, all belong to the great Rose family. At the head of these stands the Peach *(Prunus persica)* which, as previously stated, was introduced to this country by the Spaniards soon after Columbus' time. The Romans, during the reign of the Emperor Claudius, received the Peach from Persia and for centuries it was considered native of that country and received its specific name to that effect. Present-day authorities, however, are pretty well agreed that its real home is China, though undisputable wild trees have never been discovered. Nevertheless, it is found naturalized over the greater part of China where it has been cultivated for its fruit as far back as records go. In Chinese folk-lore, in arts such as porcelain-ware, wood-carving, embroidery, and painting it figures largely. Personally, I think there can be no doubt about its Chinese origin, and am convinced that it reached Persia and the Caspian region through seeds carried by the old trade-route across central Asia. In China are grown today freestone and clingstone varieties with white reddish, or yellow flesh; also a curious variety having the fruit compressed top and bottom and known as the "pien-tao" or flat peach. The smooth-skinned Peach or Nectarine likewise is of Chinese origin and seems to prefer a rather warm climate. It is much grown in northern Formosa. From China the Peach was long ago taken to Korea and to Japan where today a great many local varieties are cultivated. Into France and Britain it was introduced by the Romans, but in England it was not much cultivated before the Sixteenth Century. The Spanish introduced it into South America. It has been planted in the more temperate parts of Africa (the famous missionary traveler, Livingstone, planted it by the Victoria Falls on the Zambesi

KOREAN PEAR, PYRUS USSURIENSIS, 60 FEET TALL, TRUNK 14 FEET GIRTH, SPREAD 75 FEET, NR. SHINAN, KOGEN, KOREA

River), and in Australasia; indeed, no fruit tree is now more widely grown. There is no need to tell of the importance of the Peach industry in this country, where probably high-class fruit is produced in greater quantity than in any other land, but a real desideratum is a Peach bud—hardy in northern New England. I think there is a possibility of this being found through the medium of the Peach which is semi-wild on the mountains west of Peking.

Two other species of Peach grow wild in China, namely, *P. Davidiana* and *P. mira*. The first-named is native of the cold northern provinces of China and although the fruit is of no value the plant is favored in parts of this country as an under stock for varieties of the common Peach. The other is native of the alpine regions of the Chino-Thibetan borderland, where I discovered it. This has a palatable white-fleshed fruit and an exceedingly small, perfectly smooth stone. I had high hopes of it being useful to the hybridist when introducing it to the Arnold Arboretum in 1908, but apparently its alpine character is against its successful acclimatization in New England.

The Apricot *(Prunus Armeniaca)* is another fruit-tree whose specific name is a geographical misnomer. Originally considered native of the Caucasus and Armenia it is now pretty generally accepted as being of Chinese origin. Its history is similar to that of the Peach. The Romans cultivated it and it is described by Pliny and Dioscorides. To France and England it was almost certainly carried by the Romans though the first mention of its being in England is in Turner's *Herbal* published in 1562. In China I know it only as a cultivated tree but many travelers have seen it wild in the northern provinces. It is much grown in Korea and, though I have not yet had time critically to compare the material, I am inclined to think that an Apricot I gathered on cliffs in northern Korea, and unquestionably wild there, represents this species. It may, however, belong to *P. sibirica,* by some considered merely a variety of *P. Armeniaca.* In Japan the Apricot is much cultivated, and the fruit is pickled and eaten as a relish. Its Japanese name is Ansu and there are many beautiful garden forms with white, pink to rose-red, single and double flowers. In Afghanistan and other regions of the northwestern Himalayas the fruit is preserved by sun-drying, and dried apricots are an article of commerce through High Asia and Thibet. I have eaten fruits of such origin in the frontier town of Tachienlu, situated on the Chino-Thibetan borderland. Apricots make a delicious preserve and to my thinking are very much better as jam than as fresh fruit.

In central Korea the Manchurian Apricot *(P. mandshurica)* is a common wild tree and grows to a very large size. Its fruit is similar to that of the Common Apricot but the leaves differ and its bark is thick, corky, black outside and red beneath. Then there is the so-called Black Apricot *(P. dasycarpa)* of uncertain origin but probably west Asian. It was introduced into England in 1800, has white flowers produced very early, and purplish black fruit. There is a strong family likeness among all the Apricots and what is needed is to get all the kinds together in one place and study them comparatively. In any case this would serve to provide the hybridist with material for further effort to improve the existing races.

The Cherry trees cultivated in gardens and orchards of the West for their fruit are the product of two species *(Prunus avium* and *P. Cerasus,* respectively the Sweet and Sour Cherries), both of Eurasian origin. They have been cultivated from very early times and their history is very similar to that of the Apple and Pear. The Sweet Cherry, Mazzard or Gean, from which the Heart and Bigarreau Cherries have been derived, is a native of western Europe, including England and Norway and eastward to Asia Minor and the Caucasus, but is rare in a wild state in Spain and Italy; in

Russia it is apparently confined to the southwestern provinces and to the Crimea. It favors well-drained light soils on the margins of woods, and especially among Beech trees. It is a handsome, more or less loosely pyramidal tree from 80 to 90 feet tall and 10 feet or more in girth of trunk. In Beech woods on the Chiltern Hills in England it grows to perfection. It is less hardy than the Sour Cherry, suckers little from the roots, and from the fact that birds favor its fruit it owes its specific name. The Sour or Pie Cherry from which the Kentish Cherries and Morellos have been derived is native of southeastern Europe, Asia Minor, and the Caucasus, and in this country is a much hardier tree than the Sweet Cherry. It is a low tree, rarely 40 feet tall, with a broad, wide-spreading crown and suckers freely. It is naturalized in the colder states of this country and over a great part of Europe. A variety *(marasca)*, native of Dalmatia, is worthy of mention as the source of Maraschino, a distilled liquor much used in Europe and elsewhere, and in America in the preparation of maraschino cherries.

Theophrastus in his *History of Plants,* written some three hundred years before the Christian era, gives a good description of the Sweet Cherry but in ancient Greece it was little esteemed as a fruit-tree. Pliny states that Lucullus, the Roman soldier and epicure, brought them to Rome 65 years before the birth of Christ; but that Pliny was in error is proved by the illustrious Roman scholar, Marcus Terentius Varro, who in his book on farming written in 37 B. C., treats of them as commonplace orchard trees of the period and tells when and how to graft them. The Romans carried cultivated varieties of cherries to England and this fruit tree became well established in Kent during their occupation of Britain. In the time of Henry VIII and Queen Elizabeth the cherry was a highly favored fruit and an excellent account of it is given by the Elizabethan herbalist, Gerarde.

The Cherry was one of the first fruit trees planted in this country and was brought to New England by the earliest settlers. Francis Higginson, writing in 1629, states that the Red Kentish was the only Cherry cultivated in Massachusetts. In 1641 Cherry trees were on sale in a nursery in Massachusetts. John Josselyn, who made voyages to New England in 1638, 1639, 1663, in his *New England Rarities discovered* says: "It was not long before I left the country that I made Cherry Wine, and so may others for there are a good store of them both red and black. Their fruit trees are subject to two diseases, the Meazels, which is when they are burned and scorched with the sun, and lowsiness when the woodpeckers jab holes in their bark; the way to cure them when they are lowsie is to bore a hole in the main root with an augur, and pour in a quantity of Brandie or Rhum and then stop it up with a pin made of the same tree."

In China, cherries are the product of *Prunus pseudocerasus,* a small tree, wild in the woods of the province of Hupeh, central China. It is not very hardy but is cultivated over a considerable area in China, and also in the warmer parts of Korea and southern Manchuria. Formerly it was much grown in Japan, but its place has been taken by European Cherries. The Chinese Cherry has a sweet red fruit of little flavor, suggesting a White Heart cherry in miniature. It was introduced into England about 1822 but was soon lost or nearly so. It has not proved hardy in the Arnold Arboretum but has fruited in Chico, California.

Much more valuable is the Bush Cherry *(P. tomentosa),* a common wild shrub in central and western China and much cultivated in northern China, Manchuria and Korea for its fruit. It is a very hardy plant and will thrive in the coldest parts of the United States. It has short-stalked, globose, scarlet fruit, very juicy and pleasantly acid. The plant seldom exceeds 6 feet in height and as much in diameter, and has leaves clothed with gray, woolly hairs on the underside. The Sand Cherry *(P. pumila)* of eastern North America and its western relative *(P. Besseyi)* have received a little attention from fruit breeders during recent years and may ultimately prove of some value, but their fruits are decidedly astringent.

The consensus of opinion is that our common Plums have been evolved by long cultivation from two Eurasian species, *P. insititia* and *P. domestica.* To the first-named belong the damson, bullace, mirabelle, and St. Julien plums; the second is the more important of the two and here belong the greengages (Reine Claude plums), the prunes, the perdrigon plums, the yellow egg plums, the Imperatrice, and the Lombard plums. The Insititia Plum was mentioned by the old Greek poets Archilochus and Hippona in the Sixth Century B. C. and has been cultivated from the earliest times. Nowadays it grows wild in all the temperate parts of Europe, and in western Asia to the Caspian region. The Damsons derive their name from the old city of Damascus, and ancient works on pomology state that Alexander the Great brought these plums from the Orient after his expedition of conquest and that some centuries later Pompey, returning from his invasion of the near East, brought plums to the Roman Empire. It may be assumed with reasonable probability that the Syrians and Persians were the first to cultivate these Plums.

The Domestica Plums were apparently first known and cultivated in the Transcaspian region and did not reach Europe until after the dawn of the Christian era. Pliny is the first to give a clear account of these and he speaks of them as a new introduction from Asia Minor. The prune group of the Domestica Plums are rich in sugar which enables them to be preserved by drying without removing the stone. They probably originated in Turkestan in early times and were brought to Europe by the Huns, becoming established in Hungary where in the Sixteenth Century they were an important trading commodity. When and where the Reine Claude plums originated nobody knows. The name commemorates Queen Claude, wife of Francis I, the fruit having been introduced into France about the end of the Fifteenth Century. The English synonym, Greengage, is named for the Gage family who procured them from the Chartreuse Monastery in Paris early in the Seventeenth Century. The Perdigon Plums are an old group and take their name from an ancient geographical division of Italy. Of the Egg Plums the Imperial or Red Magnum Bonum was known in England in 1629 and the Yellow Egg is described by Rea in 1676. Parkinson in 1629 describes half-a-dozen sorts of Imperatrice plums distinguished by blue-black bloomy fruits. Both Insititia and Domestica Plums were among the earliest fruits planted by the settlers in this country but they have never attained the importance here that they hold in Europe.

Before leaving the subject of Eurasian Plums mention ought to be made of *P. cerasifera,* the Myrobalan Plum, native of Transcaucasia, northern Persia and Turkestan. It is a hardy, handsome tree but its fruit is much inferior to that of the two already mentioned so it is but little grown.

The Plum cultivated in the temperate parts of eastern Asia is *Prunus salicina,* better known as *P. triflora* and in the vernacular as the Japanese Plum. It is indigenous in central China where I have found it to be fairly common, but it is unknown in a wild state from any other region. Curiously enough it is the only true Plum known from all that vast area. In China it has been cultivated from time immemorial and there are varieties in quantity, some with greenish, others yellow, red, or bloomy black fruits. From China it has been taken to southern Manchuria, Korea, and Japan where today it is extensively cultivated. From Japan it was intro-

BLACKHEART CHERRY, PRUNUS AVIUM, 50 FEET TALL, TRUNK 8 FEET GIRTH, ACCORD, MASSACHUSETTS

PL. LVIII.

St. JULIEN CURZON. DRYING APPLES. A shady orchard. A lean-to shed.

duced into this country about 1870 by a Mr. Hough, of Vacaville, California, through a United States Consul to Japan, Mr. Bridges. The first ripe fruit of these east Asiatic Plums was produced in the grounds of Mr. John Kelsey, Berkeley, California, in 1876. So impressed with their value was Mr. Kelsey that he urged others to take them up and this resulted in their propagation being undertaken on a large scale by Messrs. W. P. Hammon & Co., Oakland, California, about 1883. Today about one hundred varieties of Japanese Plum are grown in this country. It reached Europe, where it is less valued, later, and by way of America.

A hybrid between a cultivated form of the east Asiatic Plum and the common Apricot, known as *Prunus Simonii,* has been cultivated for nobody knows how long in the provinces of Shantung and Chili. It was introduced to France in 1867 and has since been much grown in this country. This Plumcot is short-lived and of no particular value.

Authorities are not yet agreed as to the exact number of species of plums found wild in this country and Canada but undoubtedly they exceed in number the total found in the rest of the world. Virtually all have fruit useful for culinary purposes if not for dessert and were so employed by the early settlers. The Indians knew their value and utilized them. In recent years different Agricultural Experimental Stations have undertaken proper investigations with promising results. By selection and hybridizing there is much promise of future usefulness, and especially for the prairie states and those of the Mississippi Valley where European plums do not succeed. The best known is *Prunus americana* which is distributed from the Atlantic Coast to the Rocky Mountains. It was known in Europe before 1768 when it was mentioned by Duhamel under the name "Prunier de Virginie" but has never become important there. Among the oldest known is *Prunus nigra,* the Canada Plum, first described in 1789, and its fruits were the dried plums Jacques Cartier saw in the canoes of Indians, on his first voyages of discovery up the St. Lawrence in 1534. These primitive prunes were a staple article of diet among the Indians in those early times, and it is possible that they planted trees of this species about their habitations. The comparatively recently recognized *P. hortulana* and *P. Munsoniana* are perhaps the most promising and valuable of American plums, especially for the more southern states of the Middle-West. The Pacific Plum *(P. subcordata)* is one of the staple foods of the Indians east of the Coast Range from southern Oregon to central California, being eaten raw or cooked and is sometimes dried in quantity. The Chicasaw Plum *(P. angustifolia)* and the Beach Plum *(P. maritima)* were both named by Marshall in 1785 and were known to the earliest settlers along the Atlantic seaboard. There are several other named species and numerous varieties, and intimate study will assuredly result in new discoveries. A century hence these American plums will probably be in the first rank among the stone-fruits of this country.

In northern China a Jujube *(Zizyphus sativa)* is very extensively cultivated and the varieties are very numerous. Some of the best of these have been introduced into this country by the late Frank N. Meyer for the Department of Agriculture and may eventually rank among the fruits of America. The most popular fruit in China, Korea, and Japan is the Persimmon *(Diospyros kaki)*, and several of the best kinds have been also introduced by Meyer, but there has not yet been time to establish the industry here. Were unlimited space at my disposal I would tell of the Fig and other fruits but there must be an end to this essay. The attempt has been to set forth some of the more interesting facts centered around our common fruit trees. The practical side of pomology is not part of the scheme but in emphasizing the ancient character of the cult, its remote and crude beginnings, it is obvious that the end is not yet. Even as we now enjoy fruits in greater variety and of a quality superior to those of the Roman period, so also will the fruits of the future assuredly be better and of greater variety than those of today.

NUT TREES

UT-BEARING trees were among the first trees planted by man and nuts of various sorts have been eaten by the human family from the earliest times. The Pecan-tree was probably the only tree planted by the North American Indians; in the tropics the Coconut and in the temperate regions the Walnut and Hazel-nut trees have long been grown for their nuts and the industry is of great commercial importance. Today in America nut-growing is steadily increasing and must in time become an industry of first magnitude. On the whole, however, the growing of nuts has lagged so far behind that of succulent fruits that in importance the two industries bear no comparison. Possibly they never will, but it is safe to assert that nuts are destined to play a more important part in our diet in the future than they do at the present time.

In the case of succulent fruits man has from the long distant past striven to improve their size and flavor, and his efforts have been abundantly rewarded. With nut fruits the story is different though undoubtedly primitive man ate the Acorn, Walnut, Hazelnut, Pecan, and Pine-nut long before he did succulent fruits. The acorn has fallen into disfavor although that of *Quercus ballota* is still eaten by the peasants in Spain as it was in the days of Don Quixote. North American Indians also eat the acorns of certain Oaks, but so far as American people are concerned the acorn will never come back as an article of food. The nuts of the Beech-tree are sweet and good flavored and are eaten sparingly; the seeds of the Swiss-pine *(Pinus cembra)* are eaten in Europe, and in Siberia they are a very important article of food. The same is true of the Korean Nut-pine *(P. koraiensis)*, the kernels of which mixed with honey make a delicious sweetmeat. In Mexico and in western North America the seeds of several species of Pine are eaten, including those of the Sugar-pine *(P. Lambertiana)*.

The European Hazelnut has been improved and such forms as the Cob and Filbert established; probably the Common Walnut *(Juglans regia)* has been subject to like treatment, but for all practical purposes selection and cross-breeding among nut fruits has only recently begun. In this country the growing and breeding of nut trees are beginning to receive attention and the future will see a tremendous advance in this work.

The most valuable nut in the world is the Coconut, the product of a tropical maritime Palm *(Cocos nucifera)*. Many other nuts are grown within the tropics but few only find their way into our markets. The Brazilnut *(Bertholletia excelsa)* is familiar to all, and in recent years the Pili-nut *(Canarium commune)* from the Philippines has been not uncommon in city stores in this country. But this résumé deals only with those grown in temperate lands, the number of which is quite limited. The most important are the Walnuts of which, if we include the Butternuts, there are about a dozen species. The most valuable is the Common Walnut *(Juglans regia)*, the classical "Jovis glans" and the "Nux" of Greek poets. It grows wild in the Balkan peninsula and eastward through Asia Minor to the Caucasus, Persia, Afghanistan, Kashmir, and northward to near Bokhara and Ladak. From western Asia it was long ago carried to China where it is abundantly cultivated throughout the cooler parts of that land and here and there naturalized. From China it has been taken to south Manchuria and Korea where it is abundantly grown and to Japan where it is only sparingly cultivated. It is much in evidence throughout the temperate region of the Himalayas and is grown in quantity in all but the coldest regions of Europe and Asia and likewise in this country, especially in California. No other nut tree is so much appreciated as an article of food in temperate lands. An important desideratum is a type of this Walnut which would be perfectly hardy in northern New England. A few trees are known in Massachusetts but properly speaking the tree is not hardy there. From the colder parts of western China I sent seeds in the hope of securing a perfectly hardy type, but I am not sanguine although one tree has done fairly well in the Arnold Arboretum.

The Common Walnut is one of the noblest of northern trees; at its best it grows 100 feet tall with a broad, rounded crown of massive branches and a bold, often gnarled, trunk fully 20 feet in girth. Through long and wide cultivation many varieties have originated and the nuts vary much in size, shape, sculpturing and thickness of shell. The most superior kinds have a thin shell and are fully 2½ inches in length. By careful selection it is possible that even greater improvement will result. A very interesting variety and one that deserves to be better known is *praeparturiens*, which originated in the nursery of Louis Chatenay at Doue-la-Fontaine, France, about 1830. Monsieur Chatenay found among a batch of seedlings of *J. regia* three years old an individual plant which bore fruit. This variety was propagated and put on the market by Mons. Janin of Paris. The nuts are generally thin-shelled and, although small, of good flavor. It is necessary to propagate this variety vegetatively since it does not breed true from seeds.

From the viewpoint of nuts the next important Walnut is the Japanese *J. Sieboldiana* which was first introduced into Leyden, Holland, about 1864 by Von Siebold and from there to France in 1866. There is good reason to believe that it was introduced into this country by Dr. G. R. Hall in 1862, but the largest tree

PECAN, CARYA PECAN, TRUNK 16 FEET GIRTH, OLDEST AND LARGEST PLANTED
SPECIMEN KNOWN, EASTON, MARYLAND

BRAZIL-NUT, BERTHOLLETIA EXCELSA, 80 FEET TALL, TRUNK 8 FEET GIRTH, BOTANIC GARDEN, SINGAPORE

I know of is in the Arnold Arboretum where it was raised from seeds received from France in 1879. In Japan this tree is known as Kurume and is distributed from south to the bitterly cold regions of central Hokkaido. The Kurume is a much smaller tree than its European relative with the fruit in long racemes and ovoid or globose nuts rounded at the base and pointed at the apex, very slightly wrinkled and pitted, not ribbed, and rather thick-shelled. Much cultivated in central Japan is the variety *cordiformis*, characterized by its heart-shaped, much-flattened, sharply two-edged nut which is smooth and rather thin-shelled. Raised from seed the variety *cordiformis* cannot be depended upon to come true, for many revert to the wild type. In this country the best results in walnut-growing will probably be obtained by hybridizing *J. regia* with the Japanese *J. Sieboldiana* and its variety *cordiformis*, which are hardier, the importance of which fact cannot be over-estimated for what is needed is a hardier race of thin-shelled walnuts.

The Black Walnut (*J. nigra*) is a magnificent tree producing valuable timber but its nut is small, has a very hard shell and is comparatively of little economic value. The Texan Walnut (*J. rupestris*) is a tree of quite moderate size and bears small nuts of no particular use. The two Californian Walnuts (*J. californica* and *J. Hindsii*) are large trees but their fruits are poor. The Formosan species (*J. formosana*) is a large tree but the fruit is small, and, moreover, the plant will be hardy only in the warmer parts of this country. It is growing in California from seeds I gathered in 1918.

The other species of Juglans to be considered are classed as Butternuts, and the best known and most valuable is the American *J. cinerea*. This is a tree occasionally 100 feet tall and 10 feet in girth of trunk with a broad, round-topped crown and is distributed in eastern North America, from the valley of the St. Lawrence River southward. It was introduced into England with the Black Walnut so long ago as the middle of the Seventeenth Century. The ovoid, pointed, ribbed nut has a thick shell but the flesh within is sweet. The Chinese *J. cathayensis* is a bush or slender tree with a small, very rough nut of no particular value. I introduced it into cultivation in 1903 but it has not proved properly hardy in the Arnold Arboretum. The Manchurian *J. mandshurica* rivals the American Butternut in size and the nut shows a decided approach to that of the true walnuts. The shell is very thick and the flesh limited in quantity. It is a common tree in the forests of Korea and is very hardy. The little-known *J. stenocarpa* of Russian Manchuria is probably a form of *J. mandshurica*.

Having dealt with the species of Juglans within our province it remains to say a word or two about the hybrids though none is valuable for its nuts. A supposed hybrid between *J. nigra* and *J. cinerea* was described as long ago as 1857 from a tree in the Botanic Garden at Marburg in Germany. The other hybrids, and there are several, are between the Common Walnut *(J. regia)* and the American species. One of these, a cross between *J. regia* and *J. nigra*, is known as *J. intermedia Vilmorineana*. This originated at Verrieres les Buisson, near Paris, about 1885. The original tree is now nearly 100 feet tall and 10 feet in girth; in bark, branchlets, and winter buds it is intermediate, but in habit and nut it resembles the Black Walnut. Another hybrid of the same parentage is *J. intermedia pyriformis* which has pear-shaped fruits.

Of *J. intermedia* there is on Rowes Farm, James River, opposite Brandon, Virginia, a magnificent specimen which must rank with the largest Walnut trees known anywhere; the trunk at 2 feet from the ground measures more than 31 feet and at 6½ feet, 25 feet in girth. The spread of branches is enormous but the height I have not been able to ascertain.

In the neighborhood of Boston, Massachusetts, a number of

trees of *J. regia* x *J. cinerea* are known. The name of this hybrid is *J. quadrangulata.* In California are grown several hybrids between *J. regia* and *J. Hindsii,* one of them, which Burbank claimed to have originated, is named Paradox. Another which Burbank named the Royal is said also to be a cross between *J. nigra* and *J. Hindsii* and to fruit freely. All these hybrid Walnuts are fast-growing, handsome trees and like the species the wood of all is valuable. However, for nuts the breeder will do well to stick to the European and to the Japanese species and its variety. By intermingling these valuable and more hardy races of Walnuts will result.

The most famous and oldest cultivated nut tree native of this country is the Pecan *(Carya pecan),* which grows in the valley of the Mississippi River, in Louisiana, Oklahoma and Texas. The latest authorities consider that it was planted by the Indians in the Mississippi Valley and elsewhere, and it is therefore not easy to determine the natural distribution of this tree. The Caryas are among the noblest trees of North America and furnish tough and valuable timber. A few years ago a species *(C. cathayensis)* was discovered in eastern China, but until that time the genus was considered peculiarly North American. The Pecan probably exceeds all other Hickories in size for in rich alluvial soils trees 175 feet tall by 16 feet in girth of trunk occur. In the Arnold Arboretum grows one healthy young Pecan-tree and this is one of our proudest possessions for its hardiness is a surprise. In this connection it seems necessary to emphasize the fact that the Pecan is a southern tree which cannot be expected to be hardy in the cold northern states. There is a wide region in this country where Pecans can be successfully grown but it is not New England nor any of the cold northern or middle-west states. If intending nut growers will properly appreciate this fact, they will be saved money and disappointment. Pecan nuts are variable in size, and the best forms are about

2 ½ inches long and 1 inch broad and have a thin red-brown shell and a sweet flavored reddish brown kernel. They are borne in clusters of from three to twelve; each is contained within a thin, brittle, dark brown, 4-angled husk which is coated with yellow hairs and when ripe splits nearly to the base.

The next Hickory in importance is the Shagbark *(C. ovata)* distinguished by its thin-shelled nut, its leaves of five, rarely seven, leaflets, its flaking bark, and other less obvious characters. It is a northern tree, being distributed from the neighborhood of Montreal and southern Minnesota southward to the Carolinas, east central Mississippi, southern Arkansas, Louisiana, and eastern Texas, where it is rare. It is common in the New England and other northern states and in Livingston County, western New York, a natural hybrid between it and the Kingnut *(C. laciniosa)* named *C. Dunbari* occurs. There are several varieties of the Shagbark distinguished by the shape of their leaves or fruit and a number of selected named forms valued for the size and quality of their nuts. In the type the fruit is short-oblong to sub-globose and depressed at the apex. Of much potential value is *C. Laneyi,* a natural hybrid between *C. cordiformis* and *C. ovata,* which has a nut with the thin shell of the Bitternut and the large sweet kernel of the Shagbark. The nut of *C. Laneyi* keeps remarkably well and this hybrid is probably one of the most valuable of all that have been found. The type tree grows in the Riverview Cemetery, Rochester, N. Y.

A third species of Hickory is *C. laciniosa,* the Kingnut or Big Shellbark. This is essentially a tree of the central states, being particularly abundant in the river swamps of central Missouri and of the Ohio basin. It exceeds 100 feet in height by 10 feet in girth of trunk. The fruit is solitary or in pairs, about 2 inches long with a hard, woody shell; the nut is compressed, four-to-six ridged with a bony shell and a light brown, sweet kernel.

As nut trees the Pecan, the Shagbark and the Kingnut are the most important of the fifteen species of Carya now recognized in this country. In several others the kernels are sweet though the nuts are small. Several natural hybrids have received names and there are probably others yet to be distinguished. In the hands of the hybridist other superior forms will assuredly appear.

Hickories and Pecans are easily raised from seeds but the seedlings develop long, thick tap-roots and in consequence are difficult to transplant. The best plan is to sow the nuts and leave the seedlings to develop *in situ*. The better varieties are increased by grafting and budding and old trees can be headed back and top-worked in a satisfactory manner in the warmer states. In the north the propagation is more difficult but yearly it is becoming better understood and in time will probably become as easy as that of the Apple and Peach. In the Arnold Arboretum the Bitternut *(C. cordiformis)* has been found to be the best under stock. The work is done under glass in January and side-grafting close to the collar of the stock is favored. The Pecan industry is well established in the warmer states but it can never become profitable in New England nor in the colder parts of this country. But there seems to be no reason why Hickory orchards cannot be successfully established in regions where the Pecan is not hardy.

To write of the Chestnuts when those in this country are fast disappearing through disease is not a pleasant task. No cure has been found for this fatal disease, and it looks as if in a few years one of the valuable timber trees in eastern North America will have vanished. It is sad, but we may as well realize that it cannot be helped. Thousands, yes, billions, of types have arisen and disappeared since first organic development began, for the fittest only survive. The Chestnut blight is a new and deadly thing in this country, but it is a disease old in the Orient. In Korea it has existed beyond the memory of the oldest inhabitant yet there are today millions of Chestnut trees in Korea, where the nut is a staple article of food. The same is true of Manchuria, but in Japan the blight appears to be a comparatively recent visitant and is deadly. In Korea and Manchuria the older and larger trees are more resistant than saplings. Doubtless, the fungoid Chestnut blight *(Diaportha parasitica)* rages in a cycle and when the zenith of the curve is reached decreases in virulence. Let us heartily hope that this zenith may be reached while yet a goodly number of trees remain to us. Meanwhile, the hybridist should be busy endeavoring to breed Chestnuts immune to the blight. Some good work in this direction was done by the late Dr. Van Fleet working with the Chinquapin *(Castanea pumila)* and an Asiatic species, but it is desirable that additional workers take up the burden for the task is heavy.

The fruit of all the Chestnuts, and there are eight species, is edible. In eastern Asia grow four species, in this country three, and in southern Europe, Asia Minor, the Caucasus, and northern Persia, one species. There is a strong family likeness among all the Chestnuts so much so that many botanists have united them into one species, but the eight species may be distinguished by the absence or presence and distribution of minute, scale-like glands and of hairs on the leaves, and by other less obvious characters. The European *Castanea sativa* is the best known and the most famous of all Chestnuts but, unfortunately, it is not hardy in the colder parts of this country. It is much cultivated in Italy, Spain, and France, where the nut is a staple article of food. This Chestnut is often 100 feet tall and 20 feet in girth of trunk with a wide-spreading crown of massive branches; the nuts are usually three in each spiny, round husk, occasionally more, sometimes one only. There are many garden varieties and some with very large-sized nuts are grown in Madeira.

Rivaling the European species in size of nut is the Japanese *C. crenata,* wide-spread in Japan and in Korea and hardier than the European Chestnut but prone to disease. It is not a very large tree but some of the named sorts like Tamba or Mammoth have huge nuts but of rather inferior flavor. The type and the best known varieties have been introduced into this country, where the trees grow rapidly and fruit at a comparatively early age; it is regrettable that they are not more disease resistant.

More valuable is a Chinese Chestnut *(C. mollissima)* introduced into this country from Peking by the late Professor Sargent in 1903. The nut is rather smaller than those of the preceding species but is sweet and of excellent flavor. It is a tree of moderate size, wide-spread in China from east to west and northward into Manchuria; it is cultivated in northeast Korea, where it is esteemed above the native species. Long, shaggy hairs on the shoot distinguish this species from all others. Though subject to Chestnut blight in the Orient this species seems to be moderately immune in this country, and this combined with its hardiness makes it a most useful tree for breeding purposes. The largest of the Asiatic Chestnuts is *C. Henryi,* which is occasionally 100 feet tall and 18 feet in girth of trunk and is characterized by having normally a solitary, ovoid nut in each spiny husk. The leaves are smooth, without glands, and the lateral nerves project beyond the margin in long, hair-like points; the petioles and shoots are quite smooth and dark colored. The nut, though small, is very sweet and of most excellent flavor. It is common in central and western China growing in mixed forests on the higher mountains. I introduced it in 1907 into the Arnold Arboretum where it has proved quite hardy.

We need say nothing about the American *C. dentata* but a passing word is due the American Chinquapin or shrubby Chestnut *(C. pumila)*. This bush or small tree is distributed from southern Pennsylvania to northern Florida and westward to southern Arkansas and eastern Texas. Usually it bears in each husk a single nut which though small is sweet and good to eat. This species in the hands of the hybridist may be the progenitor of a race of Bush-chestnuts bearing fruits as large as the European and Japanese kinds, and as sweet in flavor as the Chinese.

In the southeastern United States, in the neighborhood of the coast from North Carolina to western Florida and west to Louisiana grows the dwarf *C. alnifolia* in which the husk is only sparingly clad with spines. This is a shrub or low tree from 10 to 30 feet tall. There is in China a Bush-chestnut *(C. Sequinii)* which ought to be re-introduced in quantity into our gardens. Robert Fortune introduced it into England in the fifties of the last century, but it was soon lost for its value was unappreciated. I introduced it into the Arnold Arboretum in 1907, but the plants were afterward destroyed by a grass fire caused by a careless visitor. This Chestnut is abundant on the hills throughout the Yangtsze Valley and there should be no difficulty in securing seeds though they travel badly. It forms a bush from 10 to 18 feet high and is sometimes a tree; the husk contains from three to six small nuts which have a peculiarly sweet and pleasant flavor. I never saw it attacked by the Chestnut blight. Summing up the question of the Chestnuts it would appear that in hybridizing the large fruited tree forms with the three bush forms there is a field of much promise.

The genus Corylus which yields the hazel-nuts is spread throughout the northern hemisphere. Some twelve species and several varieties are known, three species in this country, four in eastern Asia, two in the Himalayas, three in Europe and Asia Minor. Three of them *(C. colurna, C. Jacquemontii,* and *C. chinensis)* are large trees; the others are best described as large bushes though occasionally they form small trees. The Oriental C. *chinensis* is a very large tree and I have a vivid recollection of one giant, growing in central China, fully 120 feet tall and 18 feet in girth of trunk with a broad oval crown. The nuts of all the species are edible but in the tree species the shell is very thick. For orchard culture the European C. *avellana* only has so far received attention. This is much grown in Italy, Spain, France, and the county of Kent in England, but the bulk of the nuts in commerce are shipped from the Spanish port of Barcelona, hence the name Barcelona-nut. This species is wild in the hedgerows and coppices of Europe, and the nuts of the wild plants are excellent eating and in England are much sought after by country people. According to French authorities the nuts of Provence and Italy are preferable to those of Spain and Levant. A number of varieties are grown and in France the better kinds are called Avelenes. The best sorts are known as Full-beards or Filberts and Cob-nuts. The first-named has an elongated nut enclosed within the long, tubular husk which is contracted above the apex of the nut. There are several forms differing in the shape of the nuts and the relative length of their husks. The red and white filberts are similar in external appearance but in the former the pellicle which covers the kernel is red and in the latter pale gray-brown. According to the books the Filbert was first known from Pontus on the Asia Minor shores of the Black Sea, and was known to the ancient Greeks as *Nux pontica*. The Cob-nuts are short and roundish and have a thick shell, the most familiar being the Barcelona nuts of commerce. A form with large nuts is known in England as the Kentish Cob. Some consider the Cob-nuts to belong to a separate species known as C. *pontica,* but this seems to be doubtful. Another European species *(C. maxima)* is a large shrub confined to southern Europe and has a husk contracted above the apex of the nut into a short tube. A recent view is that the Filberts are hybrids between this species and *C. avellana.* There is also a hybrid between the common *C. avellana* and *C. colurna (C. intermedia)* which has been known in Europe since about 1836 but is still rare. It is fairly intermediate in character though the nut is more like that of *C. colurna.*

Of the three American Hazel-nuts *C. rostrata* is most widely spread for it grows throughout Canada from the east coast to British Columbia and in this country as far south as Virginia and west to Minnesota. It is a bush of moderate height producing suckers freely; the husk completely encloses the nut and is contracted beyond into a long tube. Another species *(C. californica)* which grows in Colorado and westward through northern California, Oregon, and Washington, differs in having the husk terminate in a very short tube. The third species *(C. americana)* has a roundish nut contained in an open husk with jagged, almost fringed, margins and is a broad shrub from 5 to 12 feet tall, distributed from New England southward to West Virginia and westward to Mississippi, Arkansas and South Dakota. These native species of Hazel-nut have been neglected and ought to be taken in hand for orchard culture. The three Tree-hazels all have roundish nuts with thick, hard shells and small kernels and need to be much improved before they have value as nut trees. The Himalayan *C. ferox* and the Chinese *C. tibetica* have spiny husks resembling those of the Chestnut and are unpromising subjects for the nut growers.

The two Bush-hazels of eastern Asia *(C. heterophylla* and *C. Sieboldii)* each of which has several recognized varieties, are worthy of passing notice. Both are hardy in the Arnold Arboretum and will some day play a part in nut culture in this country. The first has leaves variable in shape, as its name indicates, and an equally variable husk which is laciniated and often crested but open at the summit exposing the roundish, thick-shelled nut. It is a low bush, seldom more than 6 feet high and usually less, which suckers freely and is a feature of open mountain slopes in Korea, Japan, the Amur region and Manchuria. In China it is represented by the varieties *sutchuenensis* and *yunnanensis* which are large bushes often 20 feet tall and differ in technical characters. The other species *(C. Sieboldii)* resembles the American *C. rostrata* in that the husk completely encloses the nut and, moreover, is contracted above the apex of the nut into a narrow tube which is often twice as long as the nut itself. Several varieties, based largely on the length and shape of the husks, have been distinguished. On Quelpaert, a volcanic island off the south coast of Korea, grows a small-fruited form in which the husk is contracted into a very short beak. This has been named *C. hallaisanensis*. Siebold's Hazel is a large bush, similar in habit and foliage to the European *C. avellana* and is widely distributed in Japan and on the mainland of eastern Asia westward to the Chino-Thibetan borderland.

Finally, mention may be made of the Almond *(Prunus Amygdalus)*, a tree closely related to the Peach and Apricot, native of Persia and Asia Minor. In Syria and in southern Europe, especially in Spain, and also in California, it is much cultivated for the kernels of its fruits which constitute the almonds of commerce. There are many varieties distinguished mainly by the thickness of the shell enclosing the kernel.

TREES OF UPRIGHT HABIT

REES of upright habit have a decided value in garden landscape. They relieve low monotonous lines of vegetation and enhance by contrast the beauty and characteristics of other and different types of growth. They add grace and lightness when sparsely associated with round-topped trees and they may be associated to advantage with buildings. Some, like the Lombardy Poplar, are well adapted for planting in narrow streets or by bridges, or walls where they tower to excellent advantage. There may be an air of austerity or even rigid sternness about them but one upright branched tree stirs the emotions much in the same manner as does a fine church spire. Rightly placed and rightly used they are most useful trees in garden art.

These upright branched forms of tree-life are known as fastigiate trees and the best known example is the Lombardy Poplar, so widely planted and so familiar as to need no further comment. But although it is the oldest authentically known deciduous-leaved tree of this class, the Lombardy Popular is by no means unique. Even among the Poplars there are two others which have erect branches. One of these is *Populus alba pyramidalis,* better known as *P. Bolleana,* a form of the White Poplar, native of central Asia and introduced into Europe and this country some fifty years ago. In habit it is as fastigiate as the Lombardy Poplar, and it exhibits much variation in shape of leaves which are white on the underside. The second Poplar is known as *P. thevestina* which in habit and foliage is similar to the Lombardy but its bark is nearly white. This tree grows in Serbia in the Crimea, and in Algiers. In the

CYPRESS OAK, QUERCUS ROBUR FASTIGIATA, 50 FEET TALL, OAKDALE, LONG ISLAND, NEW YORK

ORIGINAL DAWYCK BEECH, FAGUS SYLVATICA FASTIGIATA, 42 FEET TALL,
TRUNK 4 FEET GIRTH, DAWYCK, SCOTLAND

Arnold Arboretum it has made rapid growth and has proved quite hardy; it ought to be a most useful tree throughout the Middle West.

In all there are quite a number of fastigiate trees that are hardy in the colder parts of this country. They belong to widely separated families and their number is constantly being added to. Probably all known are seminal variations of spontaneous origin, and owe their preservation to man who has propagated them vegetatively by cuttings or graftings. It is in countries where raising trees from seeds has long been practised that most of these fastigiate trees have been detected. Among American species five only (Silver, Sugar, and Red Maples, Tulip-tree and White Pine) have given rise to fastigiate trees. Of these that of the Tulip-tree and of the Silver Maple originated in Europe and probably that of the Red Maple also. The other two owe their preservation to the Arnold Arboretum, and they rank among the best of their class. The fastigiate Sugar Maple *(Acer saccharum monumentale)* is one of the narrowest of all trees and is strikingly distinct in appearance. The branches are comparatively few and quite erect, and the tree is well adapted for planting by the side of narrow roads. The parent tree was discovered in 1885 growing in an old cemetery in Newton, Massachusetts. The specimen in the Arboretum collection is 50 feet tall and is a graft from the original tree. The upright form of the Red Maple *(A. rubrum columnare)* was found growing in 1889 in the old Parsons Nursery, Flushing, New York, but nothing is known of its history. It is rather broader in outline than the fastigiate Sugar Maple and is most decidedly a valuable tree. The form of the Silver Maple *(A. saccharinum pyramidale)* originated in Spaeth's Nursery in Germany. As its name suggests it is pyramidal in outline, but it is not so striking in appearance as the two trees already described. Of the many species of Maple native of the Old World only the Norway Maple has sported into an upright form.

It is known as *A. platanoides columnare* but it is really pyramidal in habit.

A very distinct tree is *Liriodendron Tulipifera pyramidale,* the fastigiate Tulip-tree, which has been growing in the Arnold Arboretum since 1888. It has the familiar, large leaves of the type but the branches are quite upright. Like the parent it is not attacked by pests of any sort and it deserves to be widely known.

One of the narrowest of trees is *Ulmus glabra fastigiata,* the Exeter Elm, a form of the Scotch Elm which originated in a nursery in Exeter, Devonshire, nearly a century ago. Truth to tell it is a rather ugly tree of little merit save that it is curious. On the other hand, the Cornish Elm *(U. nitens stricta)* is beautiful. This is the common Elm in Cornwall and parts of Devonshire, and at its best is a tree 80 feet tall and 15 feet in girth of trunk. The lower branches curve outward and upward while the upper ones are short and ascending, and the symmetry of the tree is graceful and pleasing. Very similar in habit is the Guernsey Elm *(U. nitens Wheatleyi)* which appears in some nurserymen's catalogues under the name of *Ulmus campestris monumentalis.*

Fairly well known is *Quercus pedunculata fastigiata,* the Cypress Oak, a variety of the English Oak, and very variable in foliage. In western Europe it grows to a large tree but in this country, though it is quite hardy, it is short-lived. It grows rapidly here but rarely lives more than thirty or forty years. The same is true of the fastigiate Birch *(Betula pendula fastigiata),* which has a narrow crown of erect branches. It is strange that among such a large tribe as the Birches the common White Birch of Europe alone has sported distinct forms.

Among that summer-flowering group of trees, the Lindens, there is but one with upright branches. This is *Tilia platyphyllos pyramidalis,* a European tree whose branches taper from a broad base to a pointed apex, and is pyramidal rather than erect in habit. The European Hornbeam *(Carpinus betulus)* has given rise to two forms of upright habit. One *(globosa),* in spite of its name, is a dwarf, very compact, fastigiate plant, the other *(pyramidalis)* is well described by its varietal name.

One of the most interesting of all fastigiate trees is the Dawyck Beech *(Fagus sylvatica fastigiata).* This remarkable form of the European Beech originated on an estate in Dawyck, Peebleshire, Scotland, and is now 50 feet tall. It is an odd tree with dense, quite upright branches in striking contrast to those of the type. The propagation of this fastigiate Beech has recently been taken up by European nurserymen, and young plants in the Arnold Arboretum are doing well.

The European Hawthorn *(Crataegus monogyna)* has produced two varieties with upright branches. One *(stricta)* is a tree with a broad crown and bears dull red fruit; the other *(monumentalis)* is a narrow and strictly pyramidal plant, and is a recent acquisition.

Among Conifers such as Juniperus, Libocedrus, Thuja, Chamaecyparis and Cypress many species are columnar in outline. In some, especially the Thujas and Libocedrus, the branches are actually ascending, but in most the habit is produced by the branches being very numerous, short and of equal length and radiating at a right angle. In every case these trees assume a different form as they grow into adults, the character being essentially a youthful condition even though it obtains for very many years. Some of the more distinct forms are perpetuated by vegetative propagation, and wherever these and the parent forms are hardy they have great garden value. In fact, the oldest cultivated tree of upright habit, the Italian Cypress *(Cupressus sempervirens)* belongs to this class. In some trees both erect and pendulous forms are known in the same species. This is the case in the English Yew, European Beech and Birch.

Among hardy Conifers of the type of growth under consideration *Pinus strobus fastigiata* is destined to be of great importance.
The original tree was discovered about 1895 in a garden at Lenox,
Massachusetts and the trees now growing in the Arnold Arboretum
are grafts from it. This handsome tree has compact, ascending
branches forming a conical crown; it ought to be widely propagated by nurserymen. The Scots Pine *(P. sylvestris)* has many
seminal and geographical forms and among them at least three *(fastigiata, engadinensis,* and *Watereri)* with erect branches. The parents
of the first two are said to be wild in the European forests.

One of the loveliest of hardy pyramidal Conifers is Douglas'
Arborvitae *(Thuja occidentalis Douglasii)*, sold by many American nurserymen under the name of *Thuja occidentalis pyramidalis Douglasii*. It is a tall, narrow tree of a rich green hue, and
was raised some time before 1855 by Robert Douglas in his nursery
at Waukegan, Illinois. The Incense Cedar *(Libocedrus decurrens)*
has ascending branches forming a columnar crown, and is of a rich,
dark shining green hue. This is one of the most distinct of all hardy
or nearly hardy Conifers. Unfortunately, in the Arnold Arboretum
it is hardy only in a sheltered nook near the top of Hemlock Hill.

One of the most famous and best known of erect-growing trees
is the Irish or Florence Court Yew *(Taxus baccata fastigiata)*.
This most distinct Yew was discovered on the mountains of Fer-
managh, Ireland, near Florence Court, the seat of the Earl of
Enniskillen about 1780, by a tenant-farmer named Willis. He
found two plants, one he planted in his own garden where it died,
the other he gave to Florence Court where it is growing to this day.
From this tree, which is female, cuttings have been distributed and
all the true Irish Yews in existence have been so derived. Many
fine specimens of this Yew are known, some more than 30 feet
tall. The habit is columnar and compact with all the branches and

branchlets directed vertically upward. The leaves are dark green and shining and spread radially in all directions from the branchlets. It is very effective as a garden tree but requires pruning and tying at intervals to keep it in good shape. There are forms with golden *(aurea)* and silver *(argentea)* tips to the branchlets. Pollinated by the Common Yew, seeds have developed and have given rise to less fastigiate forms, such as *erecta* and *cheshuntensis*, which have found their place in gardens. Another form *(elegantissima)*, raised from seeds the result of pollination by the Golden Yew *(Taxus baccata aurea)*, has the young leaves yellow and the old ones with white margins.

Valuable for gardens in the colder parts of this country should prove the upright hybrid Yew *(Taxus media Hicksii)* which quite recently appeared among some thousands of seedlings of the *T. cuspidata* in the nursery of I. Hicks & Son, Westbury, Long Island.

A Japanese plant analogous to the Irish Yew is *Cephalotaxus drupacea fastigiata,* which is cultivated in the warmer parts of this country but is not hardy in eastern Massachusetts. The branches are strictly erect and the leaves, which spread on all sides of the shoot, are leathery and blackish green.

There are other trees of fastigiate and pyramidal habit but finality is not attempted, and this essay may conclude with reference to a remarkably distinct and valuable variety of *Ginkgo biloba.* This form *(fastigiata),* with dense ascending branches has a bright future before it as a street and avenue tree. The oldest and finest trees known are the specimens in Fairmount Park, Philadelphia. One measures 3 feet 2½ inches in circumference and is 36 feet high; the other four measure from 4 feet 5 inches to 4 feet 9½ inches in circumference and are from 45 to 55 feet high.

TREES OF PENDENT HABIT

N THE preceding essay we discoursed on trees of upright habit of growth. These naturally suggest trees of the opposite character, for the two types are complementary and help to create harmonious landscapes. It seems fitting then to give some account of trees of pendulous or weeping habit. Such trees are largely the product of cultivation and must be used sparingly in our gardens or the effect is monotony rather than grace and elegance. Weeping Willows are the trees of pendent habit with which the public are mostly familiar and these are ever seen to best advantage when associated with water. Viewed across a large pond or lake the effect of long, streaming, pendent branches, either in summer when clothed with foliage or in winter with their glistening bark and buds, is beautiful. Placid waters with lawn or bare ground behind enhance the effect. As a matter of fact, pendent trees must be associated with a smooth surface—a well-kept lawn for preference, failing this, bare rock or earth. In a meadow or park, where the grass is allowed to grow long, weeping trees lose not a little of their charm. They need the velvet pile of close-cropped green to show their beauty to best advantage.

Willows we have mentioned as best by water. On the lawn itself a Weeping Beech, Linden or Cherry standing sentinel-like is ever an arresting feature. Indeed, for the lawn there are no finer trees than these. Weeping trees also have peculiar value in association with buildings whose contours are angular and severe in the same manner as flat-crowned, rigid branched trees enhance the effect of dome-shaped or rounded architectural buildings. The weeping

Camperdown Elm makes a delightful shady arbor, where tea may be served on a summer afternoon or where one may retire with a book. If planted for this purpose it should, of course, be not far removed from the house and on one side or corner of the lawn.

Weeping trees are an eccentric product of Mother Nature—freaks, if you will—but useful in garden planning when properly used. Some trees, like certain Willows, the Weeping Cherry *(Prunus subhirtella pendula)* and the Weeping Linden *(Tilia petiolaris)* are naturally pendulous and although they form no distinct leading shoot they increase sufficiently in height without assistance. Another type, to which belong the Weeping Beech and Ash, form an erect leading shoot and stem but the branches themselves are pendulous. A modification of this is seen among certain Conifers which have an erect trunk, more or less horizontally spreading branches and weeping branchlets. Here belong such lovely subjects as the Sargent Hemlock *(Tsuga canadensis pendula)*, the Weeping Douglas Fir *(Pseudotsuga taxifolia pendula)* and many Cupressus. These three types are natural weeping trees. A fourth type is really prostrate in habit, the Camperdown Elm and Tea's Weeping Mulberry are well-known examples. Unless these are grafted high up on standards or artificially trained to form an upright stem they remain sprawling shrubs. If the trunk is not tall enough they are dumpy in appearance and devoid of grace and elegance, which is the real charm of all weeping trees. How often one sees on suburban lots low, squat, ugly specimens of Weeping Mulberry and Camperdown Elm, the former especially being a great favorite. Really such monstrosities ought not to be perpetrated on a long suffering world, and the fact that it is the tyro in the game of gardening that is imposed upon makes the offence of those who plant these ugly ducklings all the greater. As a matter of fact, unless the lawn is spacious weeping trees should be avoided. They need space, ample space, and a smooth lawn, then their effect is a perfect combination of elegance, grace and beauty.

In various parts of the world different trees with pendent branches are to be found, some of which are well suited for growing in California, Florida and other parts of this country. In India one of the most magnificent of all trees with a wide-spread umbrageous crown, streamer-like, hanging branches is *Ficus Benjamina*. This is a member of the Fig family with small, polished evergreen foliage which should be widely grown as a shade tree in the warmer parts of Florida. In India and Malaya grows *Casuariana equisetifolia*, which resembles a gigantic Horsetail with whip-like, dark green branches. Its effect is sombre but since it will grow in pure sea-sand it has a decided value in the tropics and sub-tropics. Very beautiful is *Agonis flexuosa*, a common tree in parts of Western Australia where it often forms an undergrowth in the park-like Eucalyptus forests. It has narrow, oblong, Willow-like leaves, axillary clusters of pure white, Myrtle-like flowers strung along pendent branchlets. Its principal branches are ascending and spreading and make a round-topped, umbrageous tree. For California it should make not only a fine ornament in parks but an excellent street tree.

In the north when weeping trees are thought of, Willows at once suggest themselves to the mind. Possibly the oldest of such cultivated trees is the Willow of Babylon, under which name, as a matter of fact, quite a number of weeping Willows pass. The story of the Willow of Babylon is old, very old. A Chinese tree, it is doubtful if it was ever known by the waters of Babylon for which it is named and endeared to the minds of most people. Truth often shatters fond delusions and robs us of many pleasant myths to which we fain would cling. So much has the name Willow of Babylon captivated the popular mind that weeping Willows generally are considered to be this tree. In spite of the shock to popular belief truth necessitates the record that the trees in the Psalmist's wail (Psalms CXXXVII, verse 1, 2: "By the rivers of Babylon, there we sat down, yea, we wept, when we remembered Zion. We hanged our harps upon the Willows in the midst thereof.") are not Willows at all but a Poplar *(Populus euphratica)*. The Willow of Babylon is common on alluvial areas in China, especially those of the Lower Yangtsze. It has been much planted and it is often difficult to tell the wild from the cultivated trees. Near Shanghai it is abundant but it does not grow so far north as Peking, where the winters are too cold for it. In central China it is common, but the largest wild trees I have seen were in western Szechuan, near the Chino-Thibetan borderland. In its typical form it is a broad-topped, spreading tree often from 60 to 80 feet tall, from 6 to 10 feet in girth of trunk, and from 50 to 60 feet from the crown. The pendent form is really an extreme condition but it is common. In relation to this it is worthy of note, for the fact has not been properly appreciated, that many Tree-willows have these forms of habit. The typical form has a broad crown, and one extreme inclines to be more or less conical and the other pendent. This range of variation—this diversification into three forms—obtains not alone in *Salix babylonica* but also in *S. Matsudana*, common around Peking and westward; *S. koreensis*, abundant in Korea, and in *S. Warburgii* of Liukiu and Formosa. It also occurs in other Tree-willows, whose names are less familiar.

An old Chinese book says, "the Emperor Yang Ti of the Sung dynasty built a great canal a thousand li (Chinese miles) in length, and encouraged the people to plant Willows along its banks. For each tree planted a roll of silk was given and the trees were named after the Emperor and called Yang-liu." In Japan the highest type of feminine beauty is symbolized by the Willow for gracefulness, the cherry-blossom for youthful charm, and the plum-blossom for virtue and sweetness. A celebrated Japanese beauty is known as Yanagi-no-oriu, or Willow-woman, and is said to have a Yanagi-koshi, *i.e.*, Willow-waist, because she is slender and graceful like the hanging branches of that tree. Dancers, too, are said "to sway like the branches of the Willow when wafted by the summer's breeze." On the willow-pattern crockery and porcelain is perpetuated the legend of the Chinese maiden Koong Shee who loved her father's secretary, Chang, and eloped with him. A similar legend is current in old Korean literature. In our own folk-lore and songs the Willow is associated with love, unrequited or forbidden. Someone has asserted that the beautiful always awakens sadness, and perhaps this explains why the Willow and grief are inseparably linked in the poetry and prose of many lands.

In China the Babylon Willow is a favorite garden tree and is also planted by graves and in temple grounds. In northern China and Korea its native confreres are used in the same manner. To Japan the male form of *S. babylonica* was taken long ago and in many cities—Tokyo for example—it is a favorite street tree, being kept severely pruned; in Japanese gardens, temples, and palace grounds, it is also common. This male tree has been introduced from Japan to California where around San Francisco it is commonly planted.

How, when, and by what means it reached Europe is not known, but in all probability by the old caravan routes across central Asia. On St. Helena, Babylon Willows were planted by General Beatson, governor of the island, about 1810. One of these trees became a favorite with Napoleon during his exile there, and, at his own request, a seat was placed beneath it and there he often sat.

All the Babylon Willows known in Europe are female and in all probability originated from a single tree. It is rather tender, not long-lived and large specimens are rare in northern Europe. When

WEEPING CHERRY, PRUNUS SUBHIRTELLA PENDULA. 80 FEET TALL, TRUNK 11 FEET GIRTH, KYOTO, JAPAN

it was brought to this country we know not, but probably toward the end of the Eighteenth Century. It has also been carried to South America, and travelers tell us that in Chile, especially by sides of irrigation canals, magnificent specimens occur. Near Boston, Massachusetts, it is scarcely hardy, but in the Arnold Arboretum some trees raised from cuttings I sent from central China are promising.

A hybrid supposed to be between *S. babylonica* and *S. alba,* named *S. sepulcralis* but better known as *S. Salamonii,* and of which only the female is known, is a much more hardy tree. It is a great asset. Handsome is the Wisconsin weeping Willow, a supposed hybrid between *S. babylonica* and *S. fragilis,* named *Salix blanda,* a much more hardy tree than the Babylon Willow. It is very fast-growing with long, pendent branchlets which almost reach to the ground. There are two weeping forms of the White Willow *(Salix alba)*, one with yellow shoots called *vitellina pendula,* and one with reddish shoots known as *chermesina.* Then there are *Salix purpurea pendula* and *Salix elegantissima,* both weeping Willows. In the northern parts of this country these different forms pass for the Willow Babylon but, as a matter of fact, the real tree is unknown there since the cold is too great for it to live.

The most beautiful flowering tree with pendulous branches is *Prunus subhirtella pendula* also a native of the Orient and cultivated from immemorial time around the temples and palaces of Japan. This is a natural variety of a Cherry widely distributed in northeastern Asia. A small percentage comes true from seeds and this is the best way to propagate this plant but it requires careful training to develop a tall upright stem. A quicker method is by grafting the weeping form on its own seedlings. The Weeping Cherry was sent from Japan to this country so long ago as 1861 but one rarely sees a decent specimen. In Japan, trees 70 to 80 feet tall with widespreading crowns and enormous boles are found up and down the country. The long pendent branches are slender and in spring when strung with pink blossoms are transformed into waving masses of pink. The Japanese name translated signifies Hanging Thread Cherry which has reference to a slender character of its branchlets. Truly there is no more beautiful tree in spring than the Weeping Cherry and some nurseryman ought to make a specialty of growing these plants for the garden-loving American public.

For the centre of a large lawn in full view of the house the grandest of weeping trees is the pendent Beech *(Fagus sylvatica pendula)*. Visitors to Newport, Rhode Island, must have admired the many fine specimens to be seen in the grounds of the older houses. At Flushing, Long Island, is a magnificent specimen which one is glad to learn the town has undertaken to preserve. The Weeping Beech has its main branches very irregularly disposed, forming, especially in youth, rugged lines. Later it fills out and becomes a handsome tumbling mass of foliage through the summer and an irregular tangled thicket of gray branches throughout the winter. A tree of this Beech may be tall and slender or low, broad and irregular according to the direction of the larger branches which may grow upward or outward or almost any direction. The smaller branches are uniformly pendulous. It is a natural variety, which was found wild in a forest in France many years ago. There are several other forms with more or less pendulous branches as well as a very curious variety known as the Parasol Beech *(tortuosa)*, which has a short, twisted trunk, a hemispherical crown with all the branches directed downward and often touching the ground. It is seldom more than 10 feet high and truth to tell is more curious than beautiful.

Rivaling the Weeping Beech as a noble subject for large lawns, is *Tilia petiolaris*, a European tree, at maturity 80 feet and more tall, irregular, dome-shaped in outline with pendent branches and branchlets and large, handsome foliage showing white on the underside when stirred by the gentlest breeze.

Tea's Weeping Mulberry *(Morus alba pendula)* has been mentioned and the abuse it has suffered in the hands of garden planners commented upon. It is, if properly grown, and by properly grown I mean grafted high up on a stout standard, a very useful, quick-growing, weeping tree with handsome, lustrous foliage and long slender, perfectly pendent branches. Unless grown right it is, however, more like a mop than a tree. Light and graceful, and best suited for the comparatively small lawn, are the weeping forms of the common European Birch *(Betula pendula)* of which the best is *Youngii*, which has the principal branches spreading and recurving from an irregular pyramidal head and very slender hanging branchlets. Unfortunately, these Birches are short-lived.

In parts of this country, where the English Holly can be successfully grown, *Ilex Aquifolium pendula* should find a place on every lawn. It is a shapely tree of moderate size with stiffly, arching and pendulous branches, dark, lustrous green leaves. Lovely at all seasons of the year it is especially so in winter. There is also a weeping form with the margins of the leaf edged with white *(argenteo-marginata)*, which is well worth growing. It is known in the trade as Perry's Weeping Holly. Both are essentially lawn trees and may be accommodated on one of moderate size.

A form of the Scotch or Wych Elm, known as the Camperdown Elm, from an estate near Dundee, Scotland, where it originated a century and more ago, is an excellent arbor tree. If grafted high up on a standard it makes a rigid, wide-spreading, umbrella-like crown beneath which a tea table and lounge chair can be accommodated easily. It is best planted not far from the house and to one side of the lawn. It is stiff in appearance but is a noteworthy and exceedingly useful weeping tree. Of many of the older known trees more or less pendulous forms are known, but many of them are more curious than beautiful and more fit for museums, such as the average botanic garden, than for the lawn, large or small, of the garden lover.

There are, however, several Conifers of pendent habit and beautiful at all seasons of the year. The most familiar perhaps is the Weeping or Sargent Hemlock, whose history is interesting. It was discovered many years ago on the mountains behind Fishkill Landing on the Hudson River by the late General Howland and named by him Sargent's Hemlock for his friend and neighbor, Henry Winthrop Sargent. General Howland found four or five of these Hemlocks, and one of his original discoveries is still living at Holm Lea, Brookline, Massachusetts, the estate of the late Professor C. S. Sargent. The variety has been extensively propagated by grafting but such plants grow more rapidly, are of more open, less compact habit, and not so beautiful as the original seedlings.

The Weeping Douglas Fir, which was picked out among seedlings of the type, is handsome for broad lawns with its long, pendent branchlets. In western North America grows *Picea Breweriana*, a naturally weeping Spruce, with long, hanging, rope-like stems clad with dark green leaves, silvery on one side. Unfortunately this tree is not quite hardy in Massachusetts but farther south it can and should be grown. Similar in habit is the Himalayan *Picea morinda*, a splendid subject for California and other warm states. Much cultivated in China and long ago introduced into Europe, is the Weeping Cypress *(Cupressus funebris)*, a cheery mass of green at any season of the year. This Cypress is not hardy in New England but thrives splendidly in California. Nearly all the different Cupressus and the related genus, Chamaecyparis, have weeping forms; so, too, have many Junipers. The most beautiful Juniper that is hardy in Massachusetts is *Juniperus rigida,* native of Korea and Japan. This has the main stems erect and secondary stems ascending and spreading. From these hang a tufted mass of branchlets clothed with dark green, needle-like leaves.

TREES FOR STREET AND HIGHWAY

HROUGH the good sense and foresight of the forefathers, the villages, towns and cities of the older settled parts of this country, and of New England in particular, possess fine shade-giving trees. Nowadays between those who wish to cut them down or lop their branches and those who want them left alone, these old trees are a continual bone of contention. Always there is much to be considered on both sides and usually both have merit. Only those with a full knowledge of local conditions and necessities are qualified to decide such questions. Citizens are to be commended for a zealous affection for the tree legacy they enjoy but sentiment must not be a stumbling block in the path of genuine progress.

Our cities and towns have greatly increased in size and the character of many has changed completely since their founding. Manufactories have increased enormously affording employment to hundreds of thousands of people. This has caused a congestion of buildings and a vitiation of living conditions. From the chimneys of these myriad houses and factories are vomited forth smoke and gases deleterious to the health of man and trees and, indeed, to life in all its forms.

City conditions have brought into being modern sanitation and its scientific methods with the result that many diseases have been conquered. The value of trees as purifiers of the atmosphere, however, has not yet received full and proper appreciation. Trees absorb the gas carbon-dioxide, poisonous to man, and set free pure oxygen, the very life of man's lungs. They do more than this. Trees deaden noises, the curse of the age we live in; they give welcome shade in summer and tend to keep everything within their shadow cool; in winter they break the wind's force and conserve warmth. These are strictly utilitarian reasons for planting trees in towns. Their esthetic value I will not stress since it is apparent to all who think, yet I would emphasize that good roads, lined with fine trees, have commercial value in that a fair approach adds not a little dignity to any town or city, and this can be capitalized.

Thanks to the automobile, this is an era of roadmaking unapproached in magnitude in the world's history. Many millions of dollars annually are being spent on road-making in this country. It is greatly to be wished that a few hundreds of these millions were ear-marked for use in lining these new roads with suitable trees. Last August on a hot cloudless day I motored over the so-called million dollar highway toward Buffalo, and how I longed for the shade of a tree! Yes, tree-planting ought to be an essential part of modern road-making and should figure in the estimates of road costs and maintenance. But it is no use planting trees under a line of telegraph and telephone wires and, just when they are attaining shade-giving size and beauty, cutting the tops partly or wholly off because they interfere with the wires. It is always phrased, "the trees interfere with the wires," never "the wires interfere with the trees," which is actually the correct order. The wires belong underground not above, marring the beauty of the landscape as they do. The plea expense is too much heeded but some day a generation will arise that on no such plea will suffer the present hideous arrangement. We cannot have both real trees and wires paralleling our highways and it's high time the choice was decided. This would be economy. At present much of our street and road-planting is sheer waste of money.

The ideal street tree for town or city is one that will grow anywhere and under any condition flourish; one that never needs any attention in the way of food, water, air or light, never needs pruning and never resents being mutilated for the convenience of overhead wires or underground cables and if it could contrive to sweep up its own leaves, or, better still, maintain them fresh and green through all seasons and all years so much the better. It does not exist, never did and never will. Trees, no more than humans, relish the foul air and the harsh living conditions of cities and factory towns. I have mentioned the changed conditions of towns; its effect on the tree is apparent. The tree legacy we have inherited is mainly of magnificent American Elms and Sugar Maples, neither of which can adapt themselves to smoke and gas-laden atmosphere. Others of a tougher fibre will have to be found.

Now a word or two on planting, so rarely done properly. Too many people seem to think that having favored a tree by paying a dollar or so for it the same tree should be so overwhelmed with gratitude that it will grow and flourish in any old soil or place. A puny hole in the ground is made, the roots thrust in, a few spadefuls of earth thrown over them and trodden down. What more can the thing need; man has honored it by purchase, now flourish tree and beam your thanks!

Let us consider the matter. Trees are living not dead things like telegraph poles. They really should not be cemented in the ground nor just thrust in anyhow. The work should be done with thought and care and with due regard to the fact that being living things they need food and air—the roots as well as the leaves and branches. Proper pits should be made, pits 8 feet wide and 3 feet deep, the sub-soil properly broken and the pit filled with good loam enriched with fertilizer. In building new highways these pits may be blasted by dynamite which is cheaper and better than digging. The dynamite method loosens the ground outward and downward allowing the roots to ramify easily.

In this prepared pit and soil the tree should be planted and in this operation spreading out the roots is a most important thing. The ground should be firmed and the newly planted tree made fast to a stout stake for the first few years. In towns and cities it should be encased in a circular cage of iron, 18 inches at base tapering to about a foot at the top as protection from hoodlums of all kinds. In the country the pits need no covering but, for the first few years they should be forked over occasionally. In towns the pits should be covered completely with an iron grating. This admits air and water, allows pedestrians free moving space and does not obstruct the sidewalk. From time to time this grating should be raised, the surface of the pit forked over to keep the earth sweet. From 75 to 100 feet apart in the line is the distance to plant street trees.

Such is the correct method to plant. Too expensive you say? Paris and many other European cities practise this method, surely the richest country in all the world cannot seriously advance such a puerile excuse. And, remember, so planted and cared for these trees will pay dividends in the form of shade, beauty and air purification for one, two or three centuries.

Another item in the care of street trees remains to be discussed, namely pruning. As now generally practised in towns no subject gives rise to more acrimony or leads to more squabbling which not infrequently the law is invoked to settle. There is no necessity for anything of the sort and it is generally the outcome of a policy of neglect. To begin with, the trees planted should be nursery grown, each from 8 to 12 feet tall with a clean single stem and a straight leading shoot. Each year for the first twenty, attention should be directed to keeping the leading shoot free of strong-growing side shoots; the lower branches should be removed one by one until the trunk is from 12 to 20 feet tall, all strong-growing lateral branches should be shortened and weak interior or cross branches removed entirely. Such amputation should be done cleanly with sharp tools close to the parent stem and the wound coated over with pruning compound which acts as a styptic and antiseptic. In a few years the wound will be healed completely over with new tissues and quite invisible. On paper this may seem a formidable undertaking but it is not so really. If done every year the material removed will be little in quantity and small in size. If pruning be neglected, in the course of time the tree becomes round-headed, unshapely or too broad necessitating a heavy expenditure of time and money in the removal of large branches and the tree is left unsightly often for years, sometimes ruined forever, and the ire of many a citizen is raised. It is when through neglect street trees have reached such conditions that trouble of all sorts breaks out. In every town or city there should be a competent man in charge and labor provided for the work of street tree management.

Trees need a protective league just as much as do birds and children. And such a league needs be lynx-eyed. The town and city beautiful with streets and highways lined with pleasant trees is a slogan worthy of the best citizens. The need is great, for the towns and cities of this broad land are fast reproducing the worst features of those of the crowded parts of Europe and Asia.

It has been stated that the ideal street tree does not exist, also that the trees quite suitable when the towns were young are no longer so. What are the requirements necessary and desirable in trees for street planting? These depend considerably on the width of the streets but, above everything else, a type of tree that will grow freely and live long under city conditions is demanded. The highways are easily accommodated but streets are difficult and those of cities very much so. Books do not help much for the subject has

AMERICAN ELMS AT SANDWICH, MASSACHUSETTS

received scant study. Neither can the experience of other lands solve our problem which is one that each country must solve for itself. Moreover, in a land so large as the United States and with such extremes of climate, what is good for one region is worthless in another. Resort to our forests does not aid for, strange to say, the native trees resent most strongly city conditions. We have to look farther afield. Of a truth there is little enough to choose from yet there are trees suitable for nearly every city condition, but in no branch of gardening is more care necessary than in selecting trees for streets and highways.

Admitting that they will grow freely, the fitness of trees for street planting depends upon their possessing several other qualities. They must not have wide-spreading crowns, they must stand pruning well, they must not have objectionable fruits, they must hold their foliage late into the fall, they must not be prone to pests or disease. Rich in virtues, they must be veritable angels among trees. Now for New England cities and large towns, for those of adjacent Canada, those of New York and Pennsylvania, the street tree best approximating these qualifications is the common Hedge-row Elm of rural England commonly known here as *Ulmus campestris*, though experts say its correct name is *U. procera*. This is a vigorous, tall, long-lived tree with a massive trunk, erect and spreading branches, and it holds its leaves late into the fall, seldom produces fertile seeds but increases readily by suckers. For nearly two centuries this tree is known to have been planted in this country, and, in the city of Boston, Massachusetts, there are fine specimens of varying ages. The best, I think, are those near the reservoir at Chestnut Hill, Massachusetts. City conditions seem to the liking of this tree and, all in all, it is rich in virtues and the best we have. In its homeland it has a sinister reputation for dropping its branches without warning and for no known reason, but I am unable to find an instance of it happening here. The Jersey and Cornish Elms, both European, have more narrow crowns and are probably equally amenable and should be given a trial.

A tree which seems to prefer bricks and mortar or ash-heaps to good soil is the so-called Tree of Heaven (*Ailanthus glandulosa*) which is quick-growing and with proper attention to pruning a good tree for city streets. It is a tall, good-natured tree with large pinnate leaves and unisexual flowers borne on different individuals. This is fortunate since the male flowers have an objectionable odor and for street work the female tree only should be planted. It is easily propagated by root-cuttings and this method should be employed.

In narrow streets, recourse must be made to trees with upright branches such as the Lombardy and Bolle's Poplars. Given good soil both grow well under city conditions but they are not long-lived.

The most famous and most widely planted street tree in the world is, of course, the so-called London Plane (*Platanus acerifolia*). This pre-eminence is due to its indifference to city conditions and ability to withstand severe pruning. For the central aisle of broad thoroughfares and for the embankments of river fronts it is splendid and its rapid growth is a fine asset, but, it has a wide-spreading crown which demands continual pruning to keep in bounds and the tree is really unsuited for the streets of ordinary cities. For town squares and small parks it is ideal.

Good-natured and in consequence much planted are the European Lindens (*Tilia vulgaris* and *T. tomentosa*), but these are really about the worst possible trees for street planting. They are very partial to aphids whose sticky exudations, added to the honey which falls from the flowers, cause dust and soot to adhere to the leaves choking the pores and the foliage turns yellow and brown before August is here. In Europe there is another Linden, known as *T. euchlora,* which is said to be immune from these disabilities and this should be given a trial as a street tree in this country.

The Horsechestnut has been much planted but this again is a bad street tree. Under town and city conditions the leaves lose their freshness and become spotted with yellow and brown soon after mid-summer, and, later the falling fruits are too attractive to boys, and their husks are a nuisance on the sidewalks. The Ash tree is no good in the city and neither is any one of the Maples. And not one of the Pine and Fir tribe can for one moment be considered as street trees for town or country villages.

For boulevards and main thoroughfares on the outskirts of towns and cities a greater variety of trees are available. Among the best trees for the colder parts of eastern North America must be placed the Red Oak *(Quercus borealis).* There is a mistaken notion current that Oak trees grow slowly. Actually they grow as rapidly as other trees and more so than many. The rows of Red Oaks which line the Parkway through Jamaica Plain, Boston, Massachusetts, bear witness of the tree's quick growth and are one of the most pleasing and impressive tree avenues in this country. The Scarlet Oak *(Q. coccinea)* is another magnificent oak for road-planting, though difficult to obtain. For moist situations the Pin Oak *(Q. palustris)* is to be commended though it does not grow old gracefully.

The Norway Maple *(Acer platanoides)* is a first-rate tree for town approaches, growing freely with a fine bell-shaped crown. The gray-barked Sycamore *(A. pseudoplatanus)* is also good. The Sargent and Avium Cherries with narrow pyramidal crowns should be used for their wealth of flowers and would add a cheerfulness in the spring. Many other trees could and should be so used, the Cucumber-tree *(Magnolia acuminata),* Keaki *(Zelkova serrata),* Asiatic

Cork-tree *(Phellodendron Lavallei)* and the Sen-tree *(Acantho-panax ricinifolius)* are examples.

For the country highways there are no better trees than the common White Elm *(Ulmus americana)* and Sugar Maple *(Acer saccharum)* of eastern North America. As an avenue tree there is no more beautiful tree in all the world than the American Elm with its wide-spreading, feathery umbrageous crown. Less graceful, but very attractive, is the Sugar Maple with its more or less ascending or spreading branches and multi-colored autumn-tinted foliage. These two trees are an impressive feature of New England roadways and lesser towns, but, unfortunately, they cannot withstand modern city conditions. But for its highways at large, the colder parts of eastern North America need not look beyond these two splendid native trees.

Poplars in general should not be used in eastern North America but in the Middle West they are of great value and it will be a long time before they can be dispensed with. Some of the European sorts such as Norway, Volga, and Berlin Poplars are very hardy. The handsome oriental *Populus Maximowiczii* is worthy of more attention. For the same regions the east Asiatic *Ulmus pumila* is showing great promise. This is a tall and shapely tree with small foliage, remarkably hardy and fast-growing. Likely enough it will withstand city conditions.

In California Eucalyptus trees, chiefly *E. globulus,* have been much planted along highways. This is by no means a good tree for the purpose since it grows too rapidly and sheds its bark too freely. The wondrous red-flowered *E. ficifolia* would be much more serviceable and infinitely more beautiful. Another excellent species is *E. sideroxylon* with smaller, pink to crimson flowers and tenacious dark bark.

In southern California and in Florida the curious *Casuarina equisetifolia* is much planted but the west Australian *C. glauca* and *C. Fraseri* would be found better subjects than the Malayan species. And better still I think would some of the Australian Cypress Pines like *Callitris robusta, C. rhomboidea* and *C. arenosa.* These are medium-sized, round-topped trees that grow well in warm, sandy soils.

The practical among us will say that it is all very well to talk about trees for streets and highways, but where are they to be obtained? We used to draw them ready grown from Europe but where are they now? The problem of supplies is up to the nurserymen. The wise among that class would find a good investment in raising in quantity a selection of the best and most desirable kinds. Here in New England for street purposes in quantity almost unlimited should be raised that peer among trees for our cities, the English Elm—the *Ulmus campestris* of our elders, nowadays styled *Ulmus procera.*

DWARF TREES

REVIOUS essays have dealt with the patriarchs, the giants, and the eccentric types of tree-growth; also with trees of strictly utilitarian interest, and it now remains to treat of the pygmy forms which also have their niche in Nature's scheme. A number of these plants, the dwarf Conifers in particular, have considerable garden value. Most people are familiar with the dwarfed trees of Japan which in recent years have been much in demand in this country and in Europe. I shall have something to say about these later, but first let us consider the diminutive forms of tree-growth produced by Nature to suit the exactions of exposed situations and severity of climate. In the rich valleys and on the lower, sheltered slopes of mountains grow the giants of the tree world. On the higher parts of mountain ranges the wind exercises a strong influence on vegetation, diminishing the height of trees and on the topmost regions reduces them to a low, scrubby growth. On seacoasts the wind has full play and the same effects are seen; also on broad plains and plateaux. In short, the effect of strong winds everywhere is to retard tree-growth, and so it comes about that on the coasts, open plains, plateaux, and on the summits of mountains dwarf, stunted forms of tree-growth are common. These adaptations to environment, or ecological forms, as they are technically called, are often very distinct from the parent types, but if raised from seeds and cultivated under normal conditions they usually revert to their ancestral forms. For example, the upper slopes of Mt. Fuji in Japan are clothed almost exclusively with a dwarf Larch which is merely an ecological form of the species

252

(Larix Kaempferi) that in the forests which cover the base and
lower slopes of the mountains grows fully 80 feet tall. Near its altitudinal limits the gnarled stems of this dwarf Larch fairly hug the
lava and cinders. Some thirty-eight years ago seeds from this prostrate form were sown in the Arnold Arboretum but the plants raised
from them have rapidly grown into tall trees, and are now quite
indistinguishable from others raised at the same time from the
typical Larch-tree of the lower forest zone. Of course, there are
genuine dwarf Larches which cannot be persuaded to grow into
anything else, no matter how they are propagated; but in general
the stunted forms of tree types have to be increased by cuttings
or by grafting or they lose their diminutive character.

Besides the wild pygmies of tree-growth which are the product
of the eternal war waged between the vegetable kingdom and the
elemental physical forces of Nature represented by temperature,
wind, and precipitation, there are others of similar appearance which
from time to time have appeared among trees long associated with
our gardens and pleasure grounds. In fact, many of the dwarf
trees best known are of this origin. The Japanese are passionately
fond of small trees and their skill in developing them by starvation, clipping, and grafting exceeds that of any other nation. Among
the familiar types of deciduous-leaved trees of our northern forests—the Oaks, Beeches, Birches, Alders, Chestnuts, Elms, and
others—there are scrubby forms. Some of the dwarf evergreen Oaks
of western North America, eastern Asia, and the Mediterranean
are worthy plants where climate admits of their out-door culture;
so, too, are certain Maples, but in general the dwarfs of the broad-
leaved trees of the North have very little garden value. Among the
Conifers and Yews the story is different and in passing it may be
mentioned that these frequent alpine regions more generally than
do their broad-leaved kin. And so it comes to pass that the Arbor-

vitaes, Junipers, Pines, Spruces, Firs, Hemlocks and Yews supply nearly all the decorative dwarf forms of tree-growth our gardens possess.

One of the best known and most widely used of these dwarf evergreens is the Mugho Pine *(Pinus mugo,* often known as *P. montana, P. mughus,* or *P. pumilio).* This is a native of the mountains of central and southern Europe. On the Pyrenees it occurs both as a shrub and as a tree of moderate size; on the Tyrolese alps it is everywhere a low, densely-branched bush. In cultivation it is a broad shrub with many erect stems, occasionally reaching the height of 15 feet, and covered with dark green leaves.

On the higher mountains of eastern Asia and northern Japan, and reaching sea-level in Saghalien, grows *Pinus pumila,* in many ways the counterpart of the Mugho Pine but belonging to the 5-needled section of the genus. This oriental dwarf Pine is creeping in habit and forms an impenetrable tangle from less than a yard to fully 10 feet in height. Unfortunately, it has not taken kindly to cultivation—yet why it should be intractable is inexplicable.

Of the noble White Pine of eastern North America *(P. strobus)* there are several dwarf forms of pleasing appearance. The best is the variety *nana,* a compact, bushy shrub with short, slender branches and numerous branchlets clothed with short leaves that are densely clustered at the extremities of the branchlets. Others are *compacta* and *pumila,* sufficiently described by their names and rare in cultivation. The Scots Pine *(P. sylvestris),* widely distributed in northern Europe and northern Asia, has given rise to many varieties, among them two or three pygmies. The best are *nana* and *Watereri* which are pyramidal in outline and, with their gray-green, stiff foliage, quite attractive little shrubs. A stunted form of the Japanese White Pine *(P. parviflora)* is common in the gardens of this country and Europe often under the name of *P. pentaphylla.* This

Sargent Hemlock, Tsuga canadensis pendula, circumference 75 feet, Holm Lea, Brookline, Massachusetts

form is produced by grafting on the Black Pine *(P. Thunbergii)*, which is an uncongenial stock that causes very slow growth and stunted development.

Of the Japanese Red Pine *(P. densiflora)* there are many forms, of which the Tanyosho *(umbraculifera)* and Bandaisho *(globosa)* are among the most useful of all dwarf Pines. The Tanyosho or Table Pine grows from 5 to 12 feet tall and has a dense, rounded umbrella-like crown and gray-green leaves. The Bandaisho is more diminutive, being seldom 6 feet high, and has grass-green foliage.

The Norway Spruce *(Picea Abies* or *P. excelsa)* has been extraordinary prolific in abnormal forms of many kinds and among them half a dozen dwarfs. The variety *Clanbrasiliana* is seldom seen taller than from 5 to 6 feet; it is globose or rounded in habit and has much-shortened and close-set branches, branchlets, and leaves. It originated on the Moira Estate near Belfast about the end of the eighteenth century and was introduced into England by Lord Clanbrassil, hence its name. A diminutive variety is *Gregoryana* which seldom grows higher than 2 feet; its branches and branchlets are very numerous, short, and spreading and are thickly clothed with short, stiff leaves spreading obliquely from all sides. The variety *pygmaea* is equally small and its branches and branchlets are excessively shortened; the leaves are very small, prickly, and close-set. Of dense conical habit is the variety *pumila,* and its leaves, spreading from all sides of the branchlets, are dark green and glaucescent. Lastly, mention may be made of the variety *dumosa* in which the branches are quite prostrate and furnished with many slender branchlets clothed with rather distant, short leaves. For general purposes *Clanbrasiliana* and *Gregoryana* are the best and they rank among the most useful of dwarf Conifers.

Of the native Black Spruce *(P. mariana)* there is a variety

(Doumetii) which is compact and pyramidal in habit, seldom more than 10 feet high and of bluish color. There is also an interesting dwarf form of the Blue Spruce *(P. pungens)*. This originated several years ago in the nurseries of the Arnold Arboretum and promises to be of value as a decorative plant; also, of the White Spruce *(P. glauca)* there is a diminutive form *(nana)* which has been known for nearly a hundred years. The most delightful of dwarf Spruces and a most charmingly attractive plant is that being distributed under the erroneous name of *Picea Albertiana*. It is of narrow, pyramidal growth with short, close-set, twiggy branches which are densely clothed with almost pellucid grass-green leaves of singular delicacy. It much resembles the Summer Cypress *(Kochia scoparia)*, and for its successful cultivation requires a moist soil and a shady situation with protection from strong winds. It is essentially an alpine plant and is really a dwarf form of the western variety of the White Spruce *(P. glauca Albertiana)* and has recently been named *conica* by Rehder. Its history is simple. In 1904 Mr. J. G. Jack of the Arnold Arboretum collected near Laggan, Alberta, some seedling plants of what he thought was *Albertiana*. These he sent home where they developed into the lovely plant above described.

The Firs have produced but few dwarf forms. The oldest known is *Abies balsamea hudsonica*, a form of the common Balsam Fir, but it has very little horticultural value. Of the common European Fir *(Abies alba*, better known as *A. pectinata,)* there is a reputed dwarf form but after a few years this is apt to lose its character and to grow into a tall tree. The best pygmy Fir is *A. lasiocarpa compacta* which originated in the Arnold Arboretum from seeds sent by Dr. C. C. Parry from Colorado in 1873. It is a genuine dwarf of compact habit. Both interesting and useful are the diminutive forms of the Douglas Fir *(Pseudotsuga taxifolia)*, known as *compacta* and *globosa*.

The common Hemlock *(Tsuga canadensis)* has given rise to several abnormal forms the most distinct of which are *pendula* and *compacta*. The first-named is a compact form with closely over-lapping pendulous branches forming a broad, low, round-topped mass. It was discovered many years ago on the mountains back of Fishkill Landing, on the Hudson River, by the late General Howland of Mattapan, New York, and named by him Sargent's Hemlock. General Howland found four or five of these Hemlocks, and one of his original discoveries is still living at Holm Lea, Brook-line, Massachusetts, the estate of the late Professor C. S. Sargent. The variety has been extensively propagated by grafting but such plants grow more rapidly, are of more open, less compact habit, and less beautiful than the original seedlings. The variety *compacta* is of upright, broadly pyramidal habit, very dense, and of rather stiff appearance. Both these Hemlocks are exceptionally useful gar-den plants.

The White Cedars (Chamaecyparis) and Arborvitaes (Thuja) supply our gardens with a majority of the dwarf Conifers they enjoy. These and the Junipers seem extraordinarily unstable in character and when seedlings are raised all sorts of abnormal forms develop. Some have round, compact heads only a foot or two high, others grow into large globular masses and some into narrow pyra-mids. They are of much value for the rockery, lawn, and for making hedges. Many dozens of such forms have received names, and specialists are often at fault in determining their identity. Their number is legion, and did I attempt to enumerate a tithe of them the rest of this essay would be a catalogue. The Arborvitae of the eastern United States *(Thuja occidentalis)* has been amazingly prolific in these seminal variants, a number of which are valuable dwarfs. Among them the forms *umbraculifera, recurva nana, Tom Thumb, Woodwardii, Reedii,* and *Little Gem,* are of the best. The Chinese Arborvitae *(T. orientalis),* which has been in cultivation in Europe since 1752, has given rise to many abnormal forms parallel in character with those of the native species but less hardy in New England. Of the common White Cedar *(Chamaecyparis thyoides)* there are two pygmy varieties *(ericoides* and *leptoclada)* which are very hardy. The Japanese species *(C. obtusa* and *C. pisifera)* have vied with the Arborvitae in the production of a multiplicity of curious forms, and such as *obtusa nana* and *pisifera filifera* are now indispensable to our gardens. Their American relative *C. Lawsoniana* of the Pacific slope has been equally prolific though it and its progeny are more tender. In England and parts of this country favored with a moderate climate the dwarf forms of the Lawson Cypress are delightful garden plants.

The inherent peculiarity of the above Arborvitaes and White Cedars to produce when raised from seeds great variety in form, height, and appearance is likewise shared by some Junipers. The Red Cedar *(Juniperus virginiana),* its Chinese relative *(J. chinensis),* the Common *(J. communis),* the Savin *(J. Sabina),* and the scaly Juniper *(J. squamata)* are well-known illustrations. In fact, the probability is that all Tree-Junipers develop dwarf forms, but the genus is difficult to classify and its nomenclature is in a sorry state. Such dwarf Junipers as *J. virginiana tripartita, J. chinensis Pfitzeriana, J. communis montana, J. communis adpressa, J. Sabina tamariscifolia* and *J. Sabina humilis* are too well known to need comment. The typical *J. squamata* is a favorite groundcover, and its tree-form is represented by the variety *Fargesii.* The low-spreading *J. virginiana reptans* is a comparatively recent discovery in

Maine where it grows on the seacoast at Bald Head Cliff, near York Harbor; the variety *globosa*, well described by its name, is a lovely plant worth a place in every garden. The prostrate *J. chinensis Sargentii*, common on the mountains of Korea, and in eastern Siberia, and less so in northern Japan, is perhaps the best of all prostrate Junipers that are ecological forms of arborescent species. Dwarf Yews have been mentioned previously so there is no need to discuss them here.

There are a few flowering trees that must not be forgotten. Foremost among these is the Fuji Cherry *(Prunus incisa)* native, as its name suggests, of the region around the famed Mount Fuji. At its best this is a small tree, occasionally 30 feet tall but as usually seen it is less than 10 feet, with twiggy, ascending-spreading branches from near the ground up. The petals are pure white and the sepals are reddish and long persistent. It commences to blossom when young and not more than a yard high and is exceedingly floriferous. I saw it first in the spring of 1914 when traveling in Japan and then and there became its willing captive. It is a quite recent addition to gardens, having been introduced into Germany by seeds sent from Japan under the erroneous name of *Prunus pseudocerasus*. It is appreciated by the Japanese gardeners as the only Cherry they can dwarf and cause to flower in pots. Another dwarf Japanese Cherry is *P. subhirtella autumnalis* which has semi-double pink flowers, and blossoms in spring or autumn, or both seasons. It is a twiggy, often vase-shaped tree from 6 to 12 feet tall, and about as free-blooming as its most charming parent, the lovely Spring Cherry, *P. subhirtella*.

The low-growing *Malus Sieboldii* is less beautiful in flower and fruit than other Japanese Crabapples but a close relative, *M. Sargentii*, is especially valuable. This species is native of the salt marshes around Muroran, Hokkaido, northern Japan, where it was discovered in 1892 by the late Professor C. S. Sargent, and introduced into the Arnold Arboretum. It has rigid, spreading branches, the lower ones flat on the ground, and is particularly well suited for covering slopes and banks. The flowers, abundantly produced in umbel-like clusters, are saucer-shaped, round, and of the purest white; they are followed by a wealth of wine-colored fruits which are covered by a slight bloom and remain long on the plants.

PLEACHED ALLEYS

LEACHED Alleys revive memories of Elizabethan days
when the Virgin Queen ruled and her sailors scoured
the seas in quest of treasures, settled new lands and at
odd moments returned to their ancestral homes, a time
when Haddon Hall was in its hey-day and Dorothy Vernon led
the Duke, her father, a merry dance. They revive memories of lav-
ender and old lace, of knights with their squires jousting before
their ladies, days when no one questioned woman's place being
home while her knightly master roamed the world to do her honor.
Within the castle grounds the verdant alley provided for Milady
cool, fragrant walks in summer and in winter she could take her
constitutional protected from the wind's biting blast. This tunnelway through verdure, the Pleached Alley, gave peace and quietude
to the scene. The monk could stroll and say his rosary or study
his breviary; the mistress with her attendants could walk rapt in
thoughts of her knight in distant lands, and the daughters with
their squires could, then as now, speak sweet nothings, for lovers
in those days were not different from lovers of today, and where
better could they plight their troth than 'neath a sanctuary of
interlacing branches, a web of verdure.

In the Elizabethan era youth was up and doing; America was
young and virile men and women pushed their way across the
ocean to found homes in the newly discovered land. As the returned
knight and his lady, arm in arm, strolled down the Pleached Alley,
building, perhaps, castles in the air, never a castle did they build

so vast as the outcome of their labors in planting new colonies in the New World across the seas. Little did Smith or Raleigh dream of the development a few centuries would bring to the land in which they gave so much effort to found.

The Pleached Alley is rare in this country, much too rare, perhaps, because the country is young. In the old manors of England it is still a feature, and one cannot walk beneath its shade without reviving memories of the days when love and war ranked ahead of commerce and diplomacy.

Someone has said that gardens are too much affected by the fashions of the day, a saying in which there is much truth, yet I do not think this is any serious disadvantage, although some rather ugly fashions are preserved. However, on the whole the contrary is true, and the gardens of the world faithfully depict the culture of the era in which they were created. Some of these features of bygone days are of museum value to the age we live in. Others could be revived to the advantage of the garden art of today. Among them the Pleached Alley.

The modern arbor or pergola now in vogue has greater architectural value, can accommodate a greater variety of plants, particularly vines, but it cannot give the old world air of an archway of interlacing twigs, a tunnelway of verdure, which marks the Pleached Alley. Not far from where I write there is, in the town of Brookline, Massachusetts, a very excellent old Pleached Alley of Hornbeam which dates back a century. This garden is walled and secluded and many fine old bushes of Boxwood scent the air. Within the enclosure one can forget the hustle and bustle of business and the hurly-burly of modern life, for so peaceful is this garden that it might well be four hundred miles instead of four from the State House of Massachusetts. Age, dignified age, enshrouds old gardens and at will one can summon forth scenes of childhood,

PLEACHED ALLEY OF CARPINUS BETULUS, BROOKLINE, MASSACHUSETTS

of laughing, romping children and of merry maid and youth who played their part in hallowing the scenes.

Pleached Alleys belong not to the small garden, for they must have length to be effective, although they themselves lend enchantment to distance. The suburban land owner and others with small lots must be content with the Pleached Alley's poor sister, the arbor or pergola, but for the large garden, the country estate, or even the small garden that abuts on a farm, the Pleached Alley should find a place. However, no matter how large a place may be, the Pleached Alley cannot be set out anywhere and everywhere. It must have a definite axis, must lead from some given point to another, if it be only the beyond. It may be entered by a gate and stretch from 50 to 100 yards or more. It must always be planted in a straight line on level land; it should never wind or lead uphill. In the distance there should be some architectural feature, a sculptured monument, small temple or fountain, a distant spire or dome, or if there be a dip in the distant land a clump of Pine or Oak trees will serve the purpose. There must, however, be some objective to tie the Pleached Alley to the landscape. Such a sheltered pathway then becomes a most intimate and enchanting spot, bringing unrelated features into pleasant proximity. It should be enclosed from the house by a wall or a tall hedge. If its length be considerable, there may be lateral openings from which paths could lead to other parts of the garden and also help the play of light and shadow. Dependent on its length, the alley should not be less than 12 feet and up to 18 feet in width and if 100 yards can be given to its length the vista looking down will seem half a mile or more. The arch should not be less than 8 or more than 12 feet high in the centre.

It is necessary that much thought be given to the material used in planting. In Italy, where Pleached Alleys probably originated, the Holm Oak *(Quercus Ilex)* and the Olive *(Olea europaea)* are used and as evergreens in countries where they are hardy have never been superseded. In this country, in the South, the Live Oak *(Quercus virginiana)* and in California, from Santa Barbara northward, the Golden Oak *(Quercus chrysophylla)* would make fitting subjects. In France, and here and there in England, fruit trees, especially Pear and Apple, have been trained to serve this purpose and combine beauty of blossom and foliage with the lure of tempting fruit. In America these, together with the Peach and Almond, where climate permits, can be used. The trees most generally used, however, are those which have a natural tendency to inosculate, that is to say, those trees whose branches readily unite when the outer tissue is broken by friction or otherwise. Of these the Beech *(Fagus sylvatica)* and the Hornbeam *(Carpinus betulus)* are most eminent. The American Beech and Hornbeam have just the same peculiar properties and are just as useful except that the American Beech transplants badly. The Lindens are excellent for making Pleached Alleys and, so, too, are the Hazelnuts, of which there are a number of species. Where climate admits the Crepe Myrtle *(Lagerstroemia indica)* with its pink and white fringed blossoms would be a charming subject. In eastern North America the Flowering Dogwood *(Cornus florida)* would make an ideal plant for this purpose. I wonder that no one has tried this lovely tree with a few of the pink variety interspersed. What a glorious picture it would be in spring with its flowers, and in the fall with brilliant fruit and colored foliage! I know of one Pleached Alley in this country made of the Golden Willow *(Salix vitellina)* and, indeed, it is very effective, especially throughout the winter months, but a good deal of care is entailed in clipping, tying and bending the branches.

In the Pleached Alley proper no frame work is used; the structure is formed entirely by interlacing stems and branches of the plants. However, a few wires are permissible and if these be used Wistaria and even the Grapevine can be fashioned into a lovely archway. I am told of a place where the common Privet *(Ligustrum vulgare)* is used to form a green alley. It does not recommend itself very much to me, but in a warm climate the broad-leaved Shining Privet *(Ligustrum lucidum)* would make an ideal subject. There are other plants that might be used but those mentioned above are sufficient proof that there is no dearth of suitable material.

Now, as to planting, first of all a proper trench should be made and filled with good garden soil enriched with fertilizer; the plants, trimmed to a single stem and the lateral branches shortened to mere spurs, should be planted about 18 inches apart. If Hornbeam, Beech or Hazelnut are used, the plants should not be placed perpendicularly but at an angle and in opposite directions in such a manner that they cross above the middle at which point the bark should be broken or sliced with a knife and the plants tied. In a few months a natural union will have taken place. Pruning to a single shoot should be continued until the plants meet in the centre of the archway, then the lateral branches may be allowed to intercross and interlace and so the Pleached Alley becomes an accomplished fact. Trimming and feeding are the only other cultural details necessary. A century is not the compass of its life's span. Properly planted and tended the Pleached Alley is as permanent a garden ornament as any living bush or tree can be.

INDEX

INDEX

A CATALOGUE OF SELECTED DOVER BOOKS
IN ALL FIELDS OF INTEREST

A CATALOGUE OF SELECTED DOVER BOOKS
IN ALL FIELDS OF INTEREST

AMERICA'S OLD MASTERS, James T. Flexner. Four men emerged unexpectedly from provincial 18th century America to leadership in European art: Benjamin West, J. S. Copley, C. R. Peale, Gilbert Stuart. Brilliant coverage of lives and contributions. Revised, 1967 edition. 69 plates. 365pp. of text.

21806-6 Paperbound $3.00

FIRST FLOWERS OF OUR WILDERNESS: AMERICAN PAINTING, THE COLONIAL PERIOD, James T. Flexner. Painters, and regional painting traditions from earliest Colonial times up to the emergence of Copley, West and Peale Sr., Foster, Gustavus Hesselius, Feke, John Smibert and many anonymous painters in the primitive manner. Engaging presentation, with 162 illustrations. xxii + 368pp.

22180-6 Paperbound $3.50

THE LIGHT OF DISTANT SKIES: AMERICAN PAINTING, 1760-1835, James T. Flexner. The great generation of early American painters goes to Europe to learn and to teach: West, Copley, Gilbert Stuart and others. Allston, Trumbull, Morse; also contemporary American painters—primitives, derivatives, academics—who remained in America. 102 illustrations. xiii + 306pp. 22179-2 Paperbound $3.50

A HISTORY OF THE RISE AND PROGRESS OF THE ARTS OF DESIGN IN THE UNITED STATES, William Dunlap. Much the richest mine of information on early American painters, sculptors, architects, engravers, miniaturists, etc. The only source of information for scores of artists, the major primary source for many others. Unabridged reprint of rare original 1834 edition, with new introduction by James T. Flexner, and 394 new illustrations. Edited by Rita Weiss. 6⅝ x 9⅝.

21695-0, 21696-9, 21697-7 Three volumes, Paperbound $13.50

EPOCHS OF CHINESE AND JAPANESE ART, Ernest F. Fenollosa. From primitive Chinese art to the 20th century, thorough history, explanation of every important art period and form, including Japanese woodcuts; main stress on China and Japan, but Tibet, Korea also included. Still unexcelled for its detailed, rich coverage of cultural background, aesthetic elements, diffusion studies, particularly of the historical period. 2nd, 1913 edition. 242 illustrations. lii + 439pp. of text.

20364-6, 20365-4 Two volumes, Paperbound $6.00

THE GENTLE ART OF MAKING ENEMIES, James A. M. Whistler. Greatest wit of his day deflates Oscar Wilde, Ruskin, Swinburne; strikes back at inane critics, exhibitions, art journalism; aesthetics of impressionist revolution in most striking form. Highly readable classic by great painter. Reproduction of edition designed by Whistler. Introduction by Alfred Werner. xxxvi + 334pp.

21875-9 Paperbound $3.00

VISUAL ILLUSIONS: THEIR CAUSES, CHARACTERISTICS, AND APPLICATIONS, Matthew Luckiesh. Thorough description and discussion of optical illusion, geometric and perspective, particularly; size and shape distortions, illusions of color, of motion; natural illusions; use of illusion in art and magic, industry, etc. Most useful today with op art, also for classical art. Scores of effects illustrated. Introduction by William H. Ittleson. 100 illustrations. xxi + 252pp.

21530-X Paperbound $2.00

A HANDBOOK OF ANATOMY FOR ART STUDENTS, Arthur Thomson. Thorough, virtually exhaustive coverage of skeletal structure, musculature, etc. Full text, supplemented by anatomical diagrams and drawings and by photographs of undraped figures. Unique in its comparison of male and female forms, pointing out differences of contour, texture, form. 211 figures, 40 drawings, 86 photographs. xx + 459pp. 5⅜ x 8⅜.

21163-0 Paperbound $3.50

150 MASTERPIECES OF DRAWING, Selected by Anthony Toney. Full page reproductions of drawings from the early 16th to the end of the 18th century, all beautifully reproduced: Rembrandt, Michelangelo, Dürer, Fragonard, Urs, Graf, Wouwerman, many others. First-rate browsing book, model book for artists. xviii + 150pp. 8⅜ x 11¼.

21032-4 Paperbound $2.50

THE LATER WORK OF AUBREY BEARDSLEY, Aubrey Beardsley. Exotic, erotic, ironic masterpieces in full maturity: Comedy Ballet, Venus and Tannhauser, Pierrot, Lysistrata, Rape of the Lock, Savoy material, Ali Baba, Volpone, etc. This material revolutionized the art world, and is still powerful, fresh, brilliant. With *The Early Work*, all Beardsley's finest work. 174 plates, 2 in color. xiv + 176pp. 8⅛ x 11.

21817-1 Paperbound $3.00

DRAWINGS OF REMBRANDT, Rembrandt van Rijn. Complete reproduction of fabulously rare edition by Lippmann and Hofstede de Groot, completely reedited, updated, improved by Prof. Seymour Slive, Fogg Museum. Portraits, Biblical sketches, landscapes, Oriental types, nudes, episodes from classical mythology—All Rembrandt's fertile genius. Also selection of drawings by his pupils and followers. "Stunning volumes," *Saturday Review.* 550 illustrations. lxxviii + 552pp. 9⅛ x 12¼.

21485-0, 21486-9 Two volumes, Paperbound $10.00

THE DISASTERS OF WAR, Francisco Goya. One of the masterpieces of Western civilization—83 etchings that record Goya's shattering, bitter reaction to the Napoleonic war that swept through Spain after the insurrection of 1808 and to war in general. Reprint of the first edition, with three additional plates from Boston's Museum of Fine Arts. All plates facsimile size. Introduction by Philip Hofer, Fogg Museum. v + 97pp. 9⅜ x 8¼.

21872-4 Paperbound $2.00

GRAPHIC WORKS OF ODILON REDON. Largest collection of Redon's graphic works ever assembled: 172 lithographs, 28 etchings and engravings, 9 drawings. These include some of his most famous works. All the plates from *Odilon Redon: oeuvre graphique complet,* plus additional plates. New introduction and caption translations by Alfred Werner. 209 illustrations. xxvii + 209pp. 9⅛ x 12¼.

21966-8 Paperbound $4.00

DESIGN BY ACCIDENT; A BOOK OF "ACCIDENTAL EFFECTS" FOR ARTISTS AND DESIGNERS, James F. O'Brien. Create your own unique, striking, imaginative effects by "controlled accident" interaction of materials: paints and lacquers, oil and water based paints, splatter, crackling materials, shatter, similar items. Everything you do will be different; first book on this limitless art, so useful to both fine artist and commercial artist. Full instructions. 192 plates showing "accidents," 8 in color. viii + 215pp. 8⅜ x 11¼.   21942-9 Paperbound $3.50

THE BOOK OF SIGNS, Rudolf Koch. Famed German type designer draws 493 beautiful symbols: religious, mystical, alchemical, imperial, property marks, runes, etc. Remarkable fusion of traditional and modern. Good for suggestions of timelessness, smartness, modernity. Text. vi + 104pp. 6⅛ x 9¼.
20162-7 Paperbound $1.25

HISTORY OF INDIAN AND INDONESIAN ART, Ananda K. Coomaraswamy. An unabridged republication of one of the finest books by a great scholar in Eastern art. Rich in descriptive material, history, social backgrounds; Sunga reliefs, Rajput paintings, Gupta temples, Burmese frescoes, textiles, jewelry, sculpture, etc. 400 photos. viii + 423pp. 6⅜ x 9¾.   21436-2 Paperbound $5.00

PRIMITIVE ART, Franz Boas. America's foremost anthropologist surveys textiles, ceramics, woodcarving, basketry, metalwork, etc.; patterns, technology, creation of symbols, style origins. All areas of world, but very full on Northwest Coast Indians. More than 350 illustrations of baskets, boxes, totem poles, weapons, etc. 378 pp.
20025-6 Paperbound $3.00

THE GENTLEMAN AND CABINET MAKER'S DIRECTOR, Thomas Chippendale. Full reprint (third edition, 1762) of most influential furniture book of all time, by master cabinetmaker. 200 plates, illustrating chairs, sofas, mirrors, tables, cabinets, plus 24 photographs of surviving pieces. Biographical introduction by N. Bienenstock. vi + 249pp. 9⅞ x 12¾.   21601-2 Paperbound $4.00

AMERICAN ANTIQUE FURNITURE, Edgar G. Miller, Jr. The basic coverage of all American furniture before 1840. Individual chapters cover type of furniture— clocks, tables, sideboards, etc.—chronologically, with inexhaustible wealth of data. More than 2100 photographs, all identified, commented on. Essential to all early American collectors. Introduction by H. E. Keyes. vi + 1106pp. 7⅞ x 10¾.
21599-7, 21600-4 Two volumes, Paperbound $11.00

PENNSYLVANIA DUTCH AMERICAN FOLK ART, Henry J. Kauffman. 279 photos, 28 drawings of tulipware, Fraktur script, painted tinware, toys, flowered furniture, quilts, samplers, hex signs, house interiors, etc. Full descriptive text. Excellent for tourist, rewarding for designer, collector. Map. 146pp. 7⅞ x 10¾.
21205-X Paperbound $2.50

EARLY NEW ENGLAND GRAVESTONE RUBBINGS, Edmund V. Gillon, Jr. 43 photographs, 226 carefully reproduced rubbings show heavily symbolic, sometimes macabre early gravestones, up to early 19th century. Remarkable early American primitive art, occasionally strikingly beautiful; always powerful. Text. xxvi + 207pp. 8⅜ x 11¼.   21380-3 Paperbound $3.50

ALPHABETS AND ORNAMENTS, Ernst Lehner. Well-known pictorial source for decorative alphabets, script examples, cartouches, frames, decorative title pages, calligraphic initials, borders, similar material. 14th to 19th century, mostly European. Useful in almost any graphic arts designing, varied styles. 750 illustrations. 256pp. 7 x 10. 21905-4 Paperbound $4.00

PAINTING: A CREATIVE APPROACH, Norman Colquhoun. For the beginner simple guide provides an instructive approach to painting: major stumbling blocks for beginner; overcoming them, technical points; paints and pigments; oil painting; watercolor and other media and color. New section on "plastic" paints. Glossary. Formerly *Paint Your Own Pictures*. 221pp. 22000-1 Paperbound $1.75

THE ENJOYMENT AND USE OF COLOR, Walter Sargent. Explanation of the relations between colors themselves and between colors in nature and art, including hundreds of little-known facts about color values, intensities, effects of high and low illumination, complementary colors. Many practical hints for painters, references to great masters. 7 color plates, 29 illustrations. x + 274pp.
20944-X Paperbound $2.75

THE NOTEBOOKS OF LEONARDO DA VINCI, compiled and edited by Jean Paul Richter. 1566 extracts from original manuscripts reveal the full range of Leonardo's versatile genius: all his writings on painting, sculpture, architecture, anatomy, astronomy, geography, topography, physiology, mining, music, etc., in both Italian and English, with 186 plates of manuscript pages and more than 500 additional drawings. Includes studies for the Last Supper, the lost Sforza monument, and other works. Total of xlvii + 866pp. 7⅞ x 10¾.
22572-0, 22573-9 Two volumes, Paperbound $10.00

MONTGOMERY WARD CATALOGUE OF 1895. Tea gowns, yards of flannel and pillow-case lace, stereoscopes, books of gospel hymns, the New Improved Singer Sewing Machine, side saddles, milk skimmers, straight-edged razors, high-button shoes, spittoons, and on and on . . . listing some 25,000 items, practically all illustrated. Essential to the shoppers of the 1890's, it is our truest record of the spirit of the period. Unaltered reprint of Issue No. 57, Spring and Summer 1895. Introduction by Boris Emmet. Innumerable illustrations. xiii + 624pp. 8½ x 11⅝.
22377-9 Paperbound $6.95

THE CRYSTAL PALACE EXHIBITION ILLUSTRATED CATALOGUE (LONDON, 1851). One of the wonders of the modern world—the Crystal Palace Exhibition in which all the nations of the civilized world exhibited their achievements in the arts and sciences—presented in an equally important illustrated catalogue. More than 1700 items pictured with accompanying text—ceramics, textiles, cast-iron work, carpets, pianos, sleds, razors, wall-papers, billiard tables, beehives, silverware and hundreds of other artifacts—represent the focal point of Victorian culture in the Western World. Probably the largest collection of Victorian decorative art ever assembled—indispensable for antiquarians and designers. Unabridged republication of the Art-Journal Catalogue of the Great Exhibition of 1851, with all terminal essays. New introduction by John Gloag, F.S.A. xxxiv + 426pp. 9 x 12.
22503-8 Paperbound $5.00

A HISTORY OF COSTUME, Carl Köhler. Definitive history, based on surviving pieces of clothing primarily, and paintings, statues, etc. secondarily. Highly readable text, supplemented by 594 illustrations of costumes of the ancient Mediterranean peoples, Greece and Rome, the Teutonic prehistoric period; costumes of the Middle Ages, Renaissance, Baroque, 18th and 19th centuries. Clear, measured patterns are provided for many clothing articles. Approach is practical throughout. Enlarged by Emma von Sichart. 464pp.   21030-8 Paperbound $3.50.

ORIENTAL RUGS, ANTIQUE AND MODERN, Walter A. Hawley. A complete and authoritative treatise on the Oriental rug—where they are made, by whom and how, designs and symbols, characteristics in detail of the six major groups, how to distinguish them and how to buy them. Detailed technical data is provided on periods, weaves, warps, wefts, textures, sides, ends and knots, although no technical background is required for an understanding. 11 color plates, 80 halftones, 4 maps. vi + 320pp. 6⅛ x 9⅛.   22366-3 Paperbound $5.00

TEN BOOKS ON ARCHITECTURE, Vitruvius. By any standards the most important book on architecture ever written. Early Roman discussion of aesthetics of building, construction methods, orders, sites, and every other aspect of architecture has inspired, instructed architecture for about 2,000 years. Stands behind Palladio, Michelangelo, Bramante, Wren, countless others. Definitive Morris H. Morgan translation. 68 illustrations. xii + 331pp.   20645-9 Paperbound $3.00

THE FOUR BOOKS OF ARCHITECTURE, Andrea Palladio. Translated into every major Western European language in the two centuries following its publication in 1570, this has been one of the most influential books in the history of architecture. Complete reprint of the 1738 Isaac Ware edition. New introduction by Adolf Placzek, Columbia Univ. 216 plates. xxii + 110pp. of text. 9½ x 12¾.
                                                            21308-0 Clothbound $10.00

STICKS AND STONES: A STUDY OF AMERICAN ARCHITECTURE AND CIVILIZATION, Lewis Mumford.One of the great classics of American cultural history. American architecture from the medieval-inspired earliest forms to the early 20th century; evolution of structure and style, and reciprocal influences on environment. 21 photographic illustrations. 238pp.   20202-X Paperbound $2.00

THE AMERICAN BUILDER'S COMPANION, Asher Benjamin. The most widely used early 19th century architectural style and source book, for colonial up into Greek Revival periods. Extensive development of geometry of carpentering, construction of sashes, frames, doors, stairs; plans and elevations of domestic and other buildings. Hundreds of thousands of houses were built according to this book, now invaluable to historians, architects, restorers, etc. 1827 edition. 59 plates. 114pp. 7⅞ x 10¾.
                                                            22236-5 Paperbound $3.50

DUTCH HOUSES IN THE HUDSON VALLEY BEFORE 1776, Helen Wilkinson Reynolds. The standard survey of the Dutch colonial house and outbuildings, with constructional features, decoration, and local history associated with individual homesteads. Introduction by Franklin D. Roosevelt. Map. 150 illustrations. 469pp. 6⅝ x 9¼.   21469-9 Paperbound

THE ARCHITECTURE OF COUNTRY HOUSES, Andrew J. Downing. Together with Vaux's *Villas and Cottages* this is the basic book for Hudson River Gothic architecture of the middle Victorian period. Full, sound discussions of general aspects of housing, architecture, style, decoration, furnishing, together with scores of detailed house plans, illustrations of specific buildings, accompanied by full text. Perhaps the most influential single American architectural book. 1850 edition. Introduction by J. Stewart Johnson. 321 figures, 34 architectural designs. xvi + 560pp.
22003-6 Paperbound $4.00

LOST EXAMPLES OF COLONIAL ARCHITECTURE, John Mead Howells. Full-page photographs of buildings that have disappeared or been so altered as to be denatured, including many designed by major early American architects. 245 plates. xvii + 248pp. 7⅞ x 10¾. 21143-6 Paperbound $3.50

DOMESTIC ARCHITECTURE OF THE AMERICAN COLONIES AND OF THE EARLY REPUBLIC, Fiske Kimball. Foremost architect and restorer of Williamsburg and Monticello covers nearly 200 homes between 1620-1825. Architectural details, construction, style features, special fixtures, floor plans, etc. Generally considered finest work in its area. 219 illustrations of houses, doorways, windows, capital mantels. xx + 314pp. 7⅞ x 10¾. 21743-4 Paperbound $4.00

EARLY AMERICAN ROOMS: 1650-1858, edited by Russell Hawes Kettell. Tour of 12 rooms, each representative of a different era in American history and each furnished, decorated, designed and occupied in the style of the era. 72 plans and elevations, 8-page color section, etc., show fabrics, wall papers, arrangements, etc. Full descriptive text. xvii + 200pp. of text. 8⅜ x 11¼.
21633-0 Paperbound $5.00

THE FITZWILLIAM VIRGINAL BOOK, edited by J. Fuller Maitland and W. B. Squire. Full modern printing of famous early 17th-century ms. volume of 300 works by Morley, Byrd, Bull, Gibbons, etc. For piano or other modern keyboard instrument; easy to read format. xxxvi + 938pp. 8⅜ x 11.
21068-5, 21069-3 Two volumes, Paperbound $10.00

KEYBOARD MUSIC, Johann Sebastian Bach. Bach Gesellschaft edition. A rich selection of Bach's masterpieces for the harpsichord: the six English Suites, six French Suites, the six Partitas (Clavierübung part I), the Goldberg Variations (Clavierübung part IV), the fifteen Two-Part Inventions and the fifteen Three-Part Sinfonias. Clearly reproduced on large sheets with ample margins; eminently playable. vi + 312pp. 8⅛ x 11. 22360-4 Paperbound $5.00

THE MUSIC OF BACH: AN INTRODUCTION, Charles Sanford Terry. A fine, nontechnical introduction to Bach's music, both instrumental and vocal. Covers organ music, chamber music, passion music, other types. Analyzes themes, developments, innovations. x + 114pp. 21075-8 Paperbound $1.50

BEETHOVEN AND HIS NINE SYMPHONIES, Sir George Grove. Noted British musicologist provides best history, analysis, commentary on symphonies. Very thorough, rigorously accurate; necessary to both advanced student and amateur music lover. 436 musical passages. vii + 407 pp. 20334-4 Paperbound $2.75

JOHANN SEBASTIAN BACH, Philipp Spitta. One of the great classics of musicology, this definitive analysis of Bach's music (and life) has never been surpassed. Lucid, nontechnical analyses of hundreds of pieces (30 pages devoted to St. Matthew Passion, 26 to B Minor Mass). Also includes major analysis of 18th-century music. 450 musical examples. 40-page musical supplement. Total of xx + 1799pp.

(EUK) 22278-0, 22279-9 Two volumes, Clothbound $17.50

MOZART AND HIS PIANO CONCERTOS, Cuthbert Girdlestone. The only full-length study of an important area of Mozart's creativity. Provides detailed analyses of all 23 concertos, traces inspirational sources. 417 musical examples. Second edition. 509pp.

21271-8 Paperbound $3.50

THE PERFECT WAGNERITE: A COMMENTARY ON THE NIBLUNG'S RING, George Bernard Shaw. Brilliant and still relevant criticism in remarkable essays on Wagner's Ring cycle, Shaw's ideas on political and social ideology behind the plots, role of Leitmotifs, vocal requisites, etc. Prefaces. xxi + 136pp.

(USO) 21707-8 Paperbound $1.50

DON GIOVANNI, W. A. Mozart. Complete libretto, modern English translation; biographies of composer and librettist; accounts of early performances and critical reaction. Lavishly illustrated. All the material you need to understand and appreciate this great work. Dover Opera Guide and Libretto Series; translated and introduced by Ellen Bleiler. 92 illustrations. 209pp.

21134-7 Paperbound $2.00

BASIC ELECTRICITY, U. S. Bureau of Naval Personel. Originally a training course, best non-technical coverage of basic theory of electricity and its applications. Fundamental concepts, batteries, circuits, conductors and wiring techniques, AC and DC, inductance and capacitance, generators, motors, transformers, magnetic amplifiers, synchros, servomechanisms, etc. Also covers blue-prints, electrical diagrams, etc. Many questions, with answers. 349 illustrations. x + 448pp. 6½ x 9¼.

20973-3 Paperbound $3.50

REPRODUCTION OF SOUND, Edgar Villchur. Thorough coverage for laymen of high fidelity systems, reproducing systems in general, needles, amplifiers, preamps, loudspeakers, feedback, explaining physical background. "A rare talent for making technicalities vividly comprehensible," R. Darrell, *High Fidelity*. 69 figures. iv + 92pp.

21515-6 Paperbound $1.25

HEAR ME TALKIN' TO YA: THE STORY OF JAZZ AS TOLD BY THE MEN WHO MADE IT, Nat Shapiro and Nat Hentoff. Louis Armstrong, Fats Waller, Jo Jones, Clarence Williams, Billy Holiday, Duke Ellington, Jelly Roll Morton and dozens of other jazz greats tell how it was in Chicago's South Side, New Orleans, depression Harlem and the modern West Coast as jazz was born and grew. xvi + 429pp.

21726-4 Paperbound $3.00

FABLES OF AESOP, translated by Sir Roger L'Estrange. A reproduction of the very rare 1931 Paris edition; a selection of the most interesting fables, together with 50 imaginative drawings by Alexander Calder. v + 128pp. 6½x9¼.

21780-9 Paperbound $1.50

AGAINST THE GRAIN (A REBOURS), Joris K. Huysmans. Filled with weird images, evidences of a bizarre imagination, exotic experiments with hallucinatory drugs, rich tastes and smells and the diversions of its sybarite hero Duc Jean des Esseintes, this classic novel pushed 19th-century literary decadence to its limits. Full unabridged edition. Do not confuse this with abridged editions generally sold. Introduction by Havelock Ellis. xlix + 206pp. 22190-3 Paperbound $2.00

VARIORUM SHAKESPEARE: HAMLET. Edited by Horace H. Furness; a landmark of American scholarship. Exhaustive footnotes and appendices treat all doubtful words and phrases, as well as suggested critical emendations throughout the play's history. First volume contains editor's own text, collated with all Quartos and Folios. Second volume contains full first Quarto, translations of Shakespeare's sources (Belleforest, and Saxo Grammaticus), Der Bestrafte Brudermord, and many essays on critical and historical points of interest by major authorities of past and present. Includes details of staging and costuming over the years. By far the best edition available for serious students of Shakespeare. Total of xx + 905pp. 21004-9, 21005-7, 2 volumes, Paperbound $7.00

A LIFE OF WILLIAM SHAKESPEARE, Sir Sidney Lee. This is the standard life of Shakespeare, summarizing everything known about Shakespeare and his plays. Incredibly rich in material, broad in coverage, clear and judicious, it has served thousands as the best introduction to Shakespeare. 1931 edition. 9 plates. xxix + 792pp. (USO) 21967-4 Paperbound $3.75

MASTERS OF THE DRAMA, John Gassner. Most comprehensive history of the drama in print, covering every tradition from Greeks to modern Europe and America, including India, Far East, etc. Covers more than 800 dramatists, 2000 plays, with biographical material, plot summaries, theatre history, criticism, etc. "Best of its kind in English," *New Republic*. 77 illustrations. xxii + 890pp. 20100-7 Clothbound $8.50

THE EVOLUTION OF THE ENGLISH LANGUAGE, George McKnight. The growth of English, from the 14th century to the present. Unusual, non-technical account presents basic information in very interesting form: sound shifts, change in grammar and syntax, vocabulary growth, similar topics. Abundantly illustrated with quotations. Formerly *Modern English in the Making*. xii + 590pp. 21932-1 Paperbound $3.50

AN ETYMOLOGICAL DICTIONARY OF MODERN ENGLISH, Ernest Weekley. Fullest, richest work of its sort, by foremost British lexicographer. Detailed word histories, including many colloquial and archaic words; extensive quotations. Do not confuse this with the Concise Etymological Dictionary, which is much abridged. Total of xxvii + 830pp. 6½ x 9¼. 21873-2, 21874-0 Two volumes, Paperbound $7.90

FLATLAND: A ROMANCE OF MANY DIMENSIONS, E. A. Abbott. Classic of science-fiction explores ramifications of life in a two-dimensional world, and what happens when a three-dimensional being intrudes. Amusing reading, but also useful as introduction to thought about hyperspace. Introduction by Banesh Hoffmann. 16 illustrations. xx + 103pp. 20001-9 Paperbound $1.00

POEMS OF ANNE BRADSTREET, edited with an introduction by Robert Hutchinson. A new selection of poems by America's first poet and perhaps the first significant woman poet in the English language. 48 poems display her development in works of considerable variety—love poems, domestic poems, religious meditations, formal elegies, "quaternions," etc. Notes, bibliography. viii + 222pp.

22160-1 Paperbound $2.50

THREE GOTHIC NOVELS: THE CASTLE OF OTRANTO BY HORACE WALPOLE; VATHEK BY WILLIAM BECKFORD; THE VAMPYRE BY JOHN POLIDORI, WITH FRAGMENT OF A NOVEL BY LORD BYRON, edited by E. F. Bleiler. The first Gothic novel, by Walpole; the finest Oriental tale in English, by Beckford; powerful Romantic supernatural story in versions by Polidori and Byron. All extremely important in history of literature; all still exciting, packed with supernatural thrills, ghosts, haunted castles, magic, etc. xl + 291pp.

21232-7 Paperbound· $2.50

THE BEST TALES OF HOFFMANN, E. T. A. Hoffmann. 10 of Hoffmann's most important stories, in modern re-editings of standard translations: Nutcracker and the King of Mice, Signor Formica, Automata, The Sandman, Rath Krespel, The Golden Flowerpot, Master Martin the Cooper, The Mines of Falun, The King's Betrothed, A New Year's Eve Adventure. 7 illustrations by Hoffmann. Edited by E. F. Bleiler. xxxix + 419pp.

21793-0 Paperbound $3.00

GHOST AND HORROR STORIES OF AMBROSE BIERCE, Ambrose Bierce. 23 strikingly modern stories of the horrors latent in the human mind: The Eyes of the Panther, The Damned Thing, An Occurrence at Owl Creek Bridge, An Inhabitant of Carcosa, etc., plus the dream-essay, Visions of the Night. Edited by E. F. Bleiler. xxii + 199pp.

20767-6 Paperbound $1.50

BEST GHOST STORIES OF J. S. LEFANU, J. Sheridan LeFanu. Finest stories by Victorian master often considered greatest supernatural writer of all. Carmilla, Green Tea, The Haunted Baronet, The Familiar, and 12 others. Most never before available in the U. S. A. Edited by E. F. Bleiler. 8 illustrations from Victorian publications. xvii + 467pp.

20415-4 Paperbound $3.00

MATHEMATICAL FOUNDATIONS OF INFORMATION THEORY, A. I. Khinchin. Comprehensive introduction to work of Shannon, McMillan, Feinstein and Khinchin, placing those investigations on a rigorous mathematical basis. Covers entropy concept in probability theory, uniqueness theorem, Shannon's inequality, ergodic sources, the E property, martingale concept, noise, Feinstein's fundamental lemma, Shanon's first and second theorems. Translated by R. A. Silverman and M. D. Friedman. iii + 120pp.

60434-9 Paperbound $1.75

SEVEN SCIENCE FICTION NOVELS, H. G. Wells. The standard collection of the great novels. Complete, unabridged. *First Men in the Moon, Island of Dr. Moreau, War of the Worlds, Food of the Gods, Invisible Man, Time Machine, In the Days of the Comet.* Not only science fiction fans, but every educated person owes it to himself to read these novels. 1015pp.

(USO) 20264-X Clothbound $6.00

LAST AND FIRST MEN AND STAR MAKER, TWO SCIENCE FICTION NOVELS, Olaf Stapledon. Greatest future histories in science fiction. In the first, human intelligence is the "hero," through strange paths of evolution, interplanetary invasions, incredible technologies, near extinctions and reemergences. Star Maker describes the quest of a band of star rovers for intelligence itself, through time and space: weird inhuman civilizations, crustacean minds, symbiotic worlds, etc. Complete, unabridged. v + 438pp. (USO) 21962-3 Paperbound $2.50

THREE PROPHETIC NOVELS, H. G. WELLS. Stages of a consistently planned future for mankind. *When the Sleeper Wakes*, and *A Story of the Days to Come*, anticipate *Brave New World* and *1984*, in the 21st Century; *The Time Machine*, only complete version in print, shows farther future and the end of mankind. All show Wells's greatest gifts as storyteller and novelist. Edited by E. F. Bleiler. x + 335pp. (USO) 20605-X Paperbound $2.50

THE DEVIL'S DICTIONARY, Ambrose Bierce. America's own Oscar Wilde— Ambrose Bierce—offers his barbed iconoclastic wisdom in over 1,000 definitions hailed by H. L. Mencken as "some of the most gorgeous witticisms in the English language." 145pp. 20487-1 Paperbound $1.25

MAX AND MORITZ, Wilhelm Busch. Great children's classic, father of comic strip, of two bad boys, Max and Moritz. Also Ker and Plunk (Plisch und Plumm), Cat and Mouse, Deceitful Henry, Ice-Peter, The Boy and the Pipe, and five other pieces. Original German, with English translation. Edited by H. Arthur Klein; translations by various hands and H. Arthur Klein. vi + 216pp.
20181-3 Paperbound $2.00

PIGS IS PIGS AND OTHER FAVORITES, Ellis Parker Butler. The title story is one of the best humor short stories, as Mike Flannery obfuscates biology and English. Also included, That Pup of Murchison's, The Great American Pie Company, and Perkins of Portland. 14 illustrations. v + 109pp. 21532-6 Paperbound $1.25

THE PETERKIN PAPERS, Lucretia P. Hale. It takes genius to be as stupidly mad as the Peterkins, as they decide to become wise, celebrate the "Fourth," keep a cow, and otherwise strain the resources of the Lady from Philadelphia. Basic book of American humor. 153 illustrations. 219pp. 20794-3 Paperbound $1.50

PERRAULT'S FAIRY TALES, translated by A. E. Johnson and S. R. Littlewood, with 34 full-page illustrations by Gustave Doré. All the original Perrault stories— Cinderella, Sleeping Beauty, Bluebeard, Little Red Riding Hood, Puss in Boots, Tom Thumb, etc.—with their witty verse morals and the magnificent illustrations of Doré. One of the five or six great books of European fairy tales. viii + 117pp. 8⅛ x 11. 22311-6 Paperbound $2.00

OLD HUNGARIAN FAIRY TALES, Baroness Orczy. Favorites translated and adapted by author of the *Scarlet Pimpernel*. Eight fairy tales include "The Suitors of Princess Fire-Fly," "The Twin Hunchbacks," "Mr. Cuttlefish's Love Story," and "The Enchanted Cat." This little volume of magic and adventure will captivate children as it has for generations. 90 drawings by Montagu Barstow. 96pp.
22293-4 Paperbound $1.95

THE RED FAIRY BOOK, Andrew Lang. Lang's color fairy books have long been children's favorites. This volume includes Rapunzel, Jack and the Bean-stalk and 35 other stories, familiar and unfamiliar. 4 plates, 93 illustrations x + 367pp.

21673-X Paperbound $2.50

THE BLUE FAIRY BOOK, Andrew Lang. Lang's tales come from all countries and all times. Here are 37 tales from Grimm, the Arabian Nights, Greek Mythology, and other fascinating sources. 8 plates, 130 illustrations. xi + 390pp.

21437-0 Paperbound $2.50

HOUSEHOLD STORIES BY THE BROTHERS GRIMM. Classic English-language edition of the well-known tales — Rumpelstiltskin, Snow White, Hansel and Gretel, The Twelve Brothers, Faithful John, Rapunzel, Tom Thumb (52 stories in all). Translated into simple, straightforward English by Lucy Crane. Ornamented with headpieces, vignettes, elaborate decorative initials and a dozen full-page illustrations by Walter Crane. x + 269pp.

21080-4 Paperbound $2.00

THE MERRY ADVENTURES OF ROBIN HOOD, Howard Pyle. The finest modern versions of the traditional ballads and tales about the great English outlaw. Howard Pyle's complete prose version, with every word, every illustration of the first edition. Do not confuse this facsimile of the original (1883) with modern editions that change text or illustrations. 23 plates plus many page decorations. xxii + 296pp.

22043-5 Paperbound $2.50

THE STORY OF KING ARTHUR AND HIS KNIGHTS, Howard Pyle. The finest children's version of the life of King Arthur; brilliantly retold by Pyle, with 48 of his most imaginative illustrations. xviii + 313pp. 6⅛ x 9¼.

21445-1 Paperbound $2.50

THE WONDERFUL WIZARD OF OZ, L. Frank Baum. America's finest children's book in facsimile of first edition with all Denslow illustrations in full color. The edition a child should have. Introduction by Martin Gardner. 23 color plates, scores of drawings. iv + 267pp.

20691-2 Paperbound $2.50

THE MARVELOUS LAND OF OZ, L. Frank Baum. The second Oz book, every bit as imaginative as the Wizard. The hero is a boy named Tip, but the Scarecrow and the Tin Woodman are back, as is the Oz magic. 16 color plates, 120 drawings by John R. Neill. 287pp.

20692-0 Paperbound $2.50

THE MAGICAL MONARCH OF MO, L. Frank Baum. Remarkable adventures in a land even stranger than Oz. The best of Baum's books not in the Oz series. 15 color plates and dozens of drawings by Frank Verbeck. xviii + 237pp.

21892-9 Paperbound $2.25

THE BAD CHILD'S BOOK OF BEASTS, MORE BEASTS FOR WORSE CHILDREN, A MORAL ALPHABET, Hilaire Belloc. Three complete humor classics in one volume. Be kind to the frog, and do not call him names . . . and 28 other whimsical animals. Familiar favorites and some not so well known. Illustrated by Basil Blackwell. 156pp.

(USO) 20749-8 Paperbound $1.50

EAST O' THE SUN AND WEST O' THE MOON, George W. Dasent. Considered the best of all translations of these Norwegian folk tales, this collection has been enjoyed by generations of children (and folklorists too). Includes True and Untrue, Why the Sea is Salt, East O' the Sun and West O' the Moon, Why the Bear is Stumpy-Tailed, Boots and the Troll, The Cock and the Hen, Rich Peter the Pedlar, and 52 more. The only edition with all 59 tales. 77 illustrations by Erik Werenskiold and Theodor Kittelsen. xv + 418pp. 22521-6 Paperbound $3.50

GOOPS AND HOW TO BE THEM, Gelett Burgess. Classic of tongue-in-cheek humor, masquerading as etiquette book. 87 verses, twice as many cartoons, show mischievous Goops as they demonstrate to children virtues of table manners, neatness, courtesy, etc. Favorite for generations. viii + 88pp. 6½ x 9¼. 22233-0 Paperbound $1.25

ALICE'S ADVENTURES UNDER GROUND, Lewis Carroll. The first version, quite different from the final Alice in Wonderland, printed out by Carroll himself with his own illustrations. Complete facsimile of the "million dollar" manuscript Carroll gave to Alice Liddell in 1864. Introduction by Martin Gardner. viii + 96pp. Title and dedication pages in color. 21482-6 Paperbound $1.25

THE BROWNIES, THEIR BOOK, Palmer Cox. Small as mice, cunning as foxes, exuberant and full of mischief, the Brownies go to the zoo, toy shop, seashore, circus, etc., in 24 verse adventures and 266 illustrations. Long a favorite, since their first appearance in St. Nicholas Magazine. xi + 144pp. 6⅝ x 9¼. 21265-3 Paperbound $1.75

SONGS OF CHILDHOOD, Walter De La Mare. Published (under the pseudonym Walter Ramal) when De La Mare was only 29, this charming collection has long been a favorite children's book. A facsimile of the first edition in paper, the 47 poems capture the simplicity of the nursery rhyme and the ballad, including such lyrics as I Met Eve, Tartary, The Silver Penny. vii + 106pp. (USO) 21972-0 Paperbound $1.25

THE COMPLETE NONSENSE OF EDWARD LEAR, Edward Lear. The finest 19th-century humorist-cartoonist in full: all nonsense limericks, zany alphabets, Owl and Pussycat, songs, nonsense botany, and more than 500 illustrations by Lear himself. Edited by Holbrook Jackson. xxix + 287pp. (USO) 20167-8 Paperbound $2.00

BILLY WHISKERS: THE AUTOBIOGRAPHY OF A GOAT, Frances Trego Montgomery. A favorite of children since the early 20th century, here are the escapades of that rambunctious, irresistible and mischievous goat—Billy Whiskers. Much in the spirit of Peck's Bad Boy, this is a book that children never tire of reading or hearing. All the original familiar illustrations by W. H. Fry are included: 6 color plates, 18 black and white drawings. 159pp. 22345-0 Paperbound $2.00

MOTHER GOOSE MELODIES. Faithful republication of the fabulously rare Munroe and Francis "copyright 1833" Boston edition—the most important Mother Goose collection, usually referred to as the "original." Familiar rhymes plus many rare ones, with wonderful old woodcut illustrations. Edited by E. F. Bleiler. 128pp. 4½ x 6⅜. 22577-1 Paperbound $1.00

TWO LITTLE SAVAGES; BEING THE ADVENTURES OF TWO BOYS WHO LIVED AS INDIANS AND WHAT THEY LEARNED, Ernest Thompson Seton. Great classic of nature and boyhood provides a vast range of woodlore in most palatable form, a genuinely entertaining story. Two farm boys build a teepee in woods and live in it for a month, working out Indian solutions to living problems, star lore, birds and animals, plants, etc. 293 illustrations. vii + 286pp.

20985-7 Paperbound $2.50

PETER PIPER'S PRACTICAL PRINCIPLES OF PLAIN & PERFECT PRONUNCIATION. Alliterative jingles and tongue-twisters of surprising charm, that made their first appearance in America about 1830. Republished in full with the spirited woodcut illustrations from this earliest American edition. 32pp. 4½ x 6⅜.

22560-7 Paperbound $1.00

SCIENCE EXPERIMENTS AND AMUSEMENTS FOR CHILDREN, Charles Vivian. 73 easy experiments, requiring only materials found at home or easily available, such as candles, coins, steel wool, etc.; illustrate basic phenomena like vacuum, simple chemical reaction, etc. All safe. Modern, well-planned. Formerly *Science Games for Children*. 102 photos, numerous drawings. 96pp. 6⅛ x 9¼.

21856-2 Paperbound $1.25

AN INTRODUCTION TO CHESS MOVES AND TACTICS SIMPLY EXPLAINED, Leonard Barden. Informal intermediate introduction, quite strong in explaining reasons for moves. Covers basic material, tactics, important openings, traps, positional play in middle game, end game. Attempts to isolate patterns and recurrent configurations. Formerly *Chess*. 58 figures. 102pp.   (USO) 21210-6 Paperbound $1.25

LASKER'S MANUAL OF CHESS, Dr. Emanuel Lasker. Lasker was not only one of the five great World Champions, he was also one of the ablest expositors, theorists, and analysts. In many ways, his Manual, permeated with his philosophy of battle, filled with keen insights, is one of the greatest works ever written on chess. Filled with analyzed games by the great players. A single-volume library that will profit almost any chess player, beginner or master. 308 diagrams. xli x 349pp.

20640-8 Paperbound $2.75

THE MASTER BOOK OF MATHEMATICAL RECREATIONS, Fred Schuh. In opinion of many the finest work ever prepared on mathematical puzzles, stunts, recreations; exhaustively thorough explanations of mathematics involved, analysis of effects, citation of puzzles and games. Mathematics involved is elementary. Translated bv F. Göbel. 194 figures. xxiv + 430pp.   22134-2 Paperbound $3.50

MATHEMATICS, MAGIC AND MYSTERY, Martin Gardner. Puzzle editor for Scientific American explains mathematics behind various mystifying tricks: card tricks, stage "mind reading," coin and match tricks, counting out games, geometric dissections, etc. Probability sets, theory of numbers clearly explained. Also provides more than 400 tricks, guaranteed to work, that you can do. 135 illustrations. xii + 176pp.

20335-2 Paperbound $1.75

MATHEMATICAL PUZZLES FOR BEGINNERS AND ENTHUSIASTS, Geoffrey Mott-Smith. 189 puzzles from easy to difficult—involving arithmetic, logic, algebra, properties of digits, probability, etc.—for enjoyment and mental stimulus. Explanation of mathematical principles behind the puzzles. 135 illustrations. viii + 248pp.
20198-8 Paperbound $1.75

PAPER FOLDING FOR BEGINNERS, William D. Murray and Francis J. Rigney. Easiest book on the market, clearest instructions on making interesting, beautiful origami. Sail boats, cups, roosters, frogs that move legs, bonbon boxes, standing birds, etc. 40 projects; more than 275 diagrams and photographs. 94pp.
20713-7 Paperbound $1.00

TRICKS AND GAMES ON THE POOL TABLE, Fred Herrmann. 79 tricks and games—some solitaires, some for two or more players, some competitive games—to entertain you between formal games. Mystifying shots and throws, unusual caroms, tricks involving such props as cork, coins, a hat, etc. Formerly *Fun on the Pool Table*. 77 figures. 95pp.
21814-7 Paperbound $1.00

HAND SHADOWS TO BE THROWN UPON THE WALL: A SERIES OF NOVEL AND AMUSING FIGURES FORMED BY THE HAND, Henry Bursill. Delightful picturebook from great-grandfather's day shows how to make 18 different hand shadows: a bird that flies, duck that quacks, dog that wags his tail, camel, goose, deer, boy, turtle, etc. Only book of its sort. vi + 33pp. 6½ x 9¼. 21779-5 Paperbound $1.00

WHITTLING AND WOODCARVING, E. J. Tangerman. 18th printing of best book on market. "If you can cut a potato you can carve" toys and puzzles, chains, chessmen, caricatures, masks, frames, woodcut blocks, surface patterns, much more. Information on tools, woods, techniques. Also goes into serious wood sculpture from Middle Ages to present, East and West. 464 photos, figures. x + 293pp.
20965-2 Paperbound $2.00

HISTORY OF PHILOSOPHY, Julián Marias. Possibly the clearest, most easily followed, best planned, most useful one-volume history of philosophy on the market; neither skimpy nor overfull. Full details on system of every major philosopher and dozens of less important thinkers from pre-Socratics up to Existentialism and later. Strong on many European figures usually omitted. Has gone through dozens of editions in Europe. 1966 edition, translated by Stanley Appelbaum and Clarence Strowbridge. xviii + 505pp. 21739-6 Paperbound $3.50

YOGA: A SCIENTIFIC EVALUATION, Kovoor T. Behanan. Scientific but non-technical study of physiological results of yoga exercises; done under auspices of Yale U. Relations to Indian thought, to psychoanalysis, etc. 16 photos. xxiii + 270pp.
20505-3 Paperbound $2.50